10th Anniversary Edition!

Is There *Life* After Housework?

Is There *Life* After Housework?

Don Aslett

Illustrated by Craig LaGory

WRITER'S DIGEST BOOKS

Cincinnati, Ohio

First revised edition, 1981.
Second revised and expanded edition, 1985.
Third revised and expanded edition, 1992.

Other fine Writer's Digest Books are available from your local bookstore or direct from the publisher.

99   98   8

Library of Congress Cataloging-in-Publication Data

Aslett, Don
    Is there life after housework? / by Don Aslett. —
3rd rev. and expanded ed.
          p.   cm.
    Includes index.
    ISBN 0-89879-461-7 (pbk.)
    1. House cleaning.   I. Title
TX324.A75825   1992
648'.5—dc20   91-39483
                                                         CIP

Life After Housework . . .
Ten Years Later

Not too long ago our great country celebrated its 200th anniversary . . .

. . . my home state of Idaho reached its 100th . . .

. . . and my parents celebrated their 50th.

Now, thanks to all of the above, there's one more anniversary. Ten years ago, for the first time ever, the secrets of the professional cleaner were revealed to the homemaker, bound up in a yellow book called *Is There Life After Housework?* That book, which has terrorized dirt and germs for a decade now, has not only gone on to become *the* cleaning classic, it's been offered by major book clubs, featured in major national newspapers, and translated into five languages. It was my first book on cleaning, and

though I've done many since, it's still the best known and most basic of them all. I've been called the Porcelain Preacher, and I guess you could call it my cleaning bible.

Though I revised this volume back in 1985, it needed to be done again: to catch up on what's new and different since then (not only the changes in cleaning tools and equipment, but in our lives as we head into the '90s); to make it better looking and easier to use than ever before; and to give you what I'm *always* being asked for: *more* secrets of the pros and *more* ways to reduce and eliminate housework.

Good Cleaning,

Don A. Aslett

Table of Contents

*You are entitled to a life of love,
fulfillment and accomplishment, but
these rewards are almost impossible
to obtain when you spend your life
thrashing and wallowing in a muddle
of housework. Time—the time to love,
to be, to grow—is the most precious
commodity on earth. No one's time
should be wasted cleaning needlessly
or inefficiently.*

1. A clean house

How does everyone else do it?

- Some lie. . . .
- Some have mighty lumpy rugs. . . .
- Some have no children. . . .
- Some have a maid. . . .
- Some convince their husbands to do a little of it. . . .
- Some use only one room in the house. . . .
- Some never let anyone in. . . .

Most of us don't use any of these methods to clean our houses. We represent the 95 percent of homemakers who, often in a state of cobweb confusion at the end of the day, wonder, "Just how does everyone else do it?"

Every time we see another clean-and-organized success story, we end up depressed and frustrated. We try the miracle formulas, quick tips and super systems, but when we find ourselves still not progressing in the war against grime, grit and grubbies, we again wonder why it works so well for others. "Something is surely wrong with me!" we conclude.

Newspaper columns, slick magazines and bestselling authors have tried to provide all the answers for a "perfect home"—and have convinced too many homemakers they don't have a chance. This constant bombardment of get-clean-and-organized propaganda leaves millions of women wondering, "What's wrong with my system? Why am I the only one failing?"

Well, I don't think there's anything wrong with you or with any other woman struggling to run a home (and/or raise kids, hold down a job, go back to school, do volunteer work). Housework is, for a fact, never ending and little appreciated. There are no superwoman homemakers. Most women are barely managing, meeting daily crises and demands, just like you are, wondering too what's wrong with them. It's amazing that no real training is provided for the most complicated, life-affecting job on earth: homemaking.

The superwoman articles, books and commercials are a failure if their intent is to inspire the homemaker to rise to maximum efficiency. Gimmicks, hints, formulas, and magic schedules for living happily ever after aren't the answer. Overestimating or underestimating your abilities in any situation feeds the monster of discouragement. When you're doing your best but see yourself falling short of your goals, it's hard to have a bright outlook or a sense of accomplishment.

Yet I assure you there are proven ways to have a clean house, and they don't hinge on magic, good luck, or genies in a cleaner jug. By learning how to *prevent* housework, and by using *professional* cleaning methods, you can reduce your household chore time by as much as 75 percent. You'll simply learn to clean more efficiently and effectively. My confidence in you and in this statement is anchored in more than thirty-five years as a professional housecleaner—and teaching and listening to thousands of women around the world talk about cleaning.

A housecleaner is born

Fresh off the farm and unappreciative of my mother's labors to provide me with hearty meals, ironed shirts and a clean bed, I found college life a far cry from a comfortable home. My appreciation for that home and mother became keener when I discovered how much of my time and money it took to support myself. For survival, I landed a job bottling pop for seventy-five cents an hour, my first nonfarm job. The funds left after deductions were definitely not enough to get me through college. So I looked for a better paying part-time pastime.

Cleaning yards and houses seemed to be a likely prospect, and so my

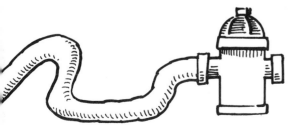

career as a world-renowned house-cleaner was launched. Following afternoon classes, I'd suit up in a white uniform and knock on doors, asking if I could assume some of the household drudgery. I received only a few sneers before I was snatched from the street and given a furnace-cleaning job, followed later by some floors, then some windows. On every job, the homemaker would watch and direct as I'd scrub, shovel and polish. Next came wallpaper-cleaning, wall-washing and cupboard-cleaning. Word got out that an eager housecleaner was loose in the neighborhood, and soon I had more work than I needed. I hired help, taught them what the homemakers had taught me—and the business grew. Carpet- and upholstery-cleaning were added to my list of skills. Soon my business was a large one, in demand in towns outside the college city of Pocatello, Idaho.

Over the next ten years my unique housecleaning business received much public recognition—"College Boy Makes Good." Between newspaper headlines I acquired a vast amount of experience in housecleaning. I ruined grand piano tops, toppled china cabinets, broke windows, streaked walls, suffocated pet birds with ammonia, ruined murals, shrank wall-to-wall carpets into throw rugs, and pulled hundreds of other goofs. But with each job I got better, faster and more efficient (at cleaning, not breaking). I cleaned log cabins with dirt floors and the plushest mansions in the country. Some days, with five housecleaning crews in operation, I'd clean several three-story homes from top to bottom.

But cleaning skill wasn't the only talent needed to run the company; organization was important. All of us working in the business were full-time students, active in church and civic affairs, and the heads of large families.

My wife Barbara and I had six children in seven years. While operating the business, going to school, and getting a degree, I lettered three years in college athletics and was on the debating team. Because my co-workers and I had no alternative, we *had* to develop efficient methods to clean houses. Fortunately we also received much opinionated coaching and direction from every homemaker we worked for.

In these years of "field experience" is based my confidence that I can show you how to attain greater housecleaning efficiency. Although I now serve as a consultant on building efficiency and maintenance for some of the world's largest companies, I know that the homemaker faces some of the most difficult cleaning problems of all. And to make the matter tougher, housework is something women are expected to do in addition to *homemaking.*

This is why I prefer to use the word "homemaker" rather than "housewife." "Housewife," like "janitor," has come to mean someone who slaves away at menial, boring work. The "home" in "homemaker" is important because home is the most personal, important place for us all. "Making" is a hint that the job can be creative and fun. Making a home a happy, welcoming place means more to life than any high-powered industrial or office job.

The root of housework evil

Do you want to know what the biggest, ugliest housework problem is? It's that 90 percent of all housework is caused by men and children—and 90 percent of all housework is done by women. Like most men, I once viewed, with a certain critical eye, my wife and other women struggling feverishly to get the housework finished. I ached to jump in and show those "disorganized gals" how an expert could square things away.

Soon the opportunity, along with a great lesson, came to me. Fresh out of college, I worked hard washing walls late at night to buy my wife a surprise plane ticket to Alaska. She was delighted to have her first flight ever and a chance to see her mother again. I bade her goodbye and told her to stay as many weeks as she wished, that I would care well for our six small children. (She wasted no time leaving, I assure you.) But my true thoughts were, "Now that I have her out of town, I'm going to shape up this disorganized house and make it as efficient as my business!"

I woke up at 4:00 the first morning and confidently mapped out the campaign of great household efficiency about to be enacted in our home. By 6:30 the kids were up, and they saluted before they went to the bathroom! By 7:30, the beds were made, the dishes were done, and I was rolling to victory. We were putting the finishing touches on a new home, and my project for the day was constructing a vanity cabinet in the master bathroom—an easy half-day's work. I had just started to glue the first board when "Waaa!" One of the kids had biffed another. I ran out and made peace, passed out the storybooks, and again picked up the hammer and board. "Waaa!"—someone cut a finger.

Three bandages and ten minutes of comforting and mercurochrome-dabbing later, I again picked up the hammer (after scraping off the now-dry glue) and had one nail started when "Waaa!"—a diaper to change (a cry that was repeated all day; I'd have sworn we had four in diapers at the same time).

Again I returned to work, and had started the second nail, when *ding-dong* (the milkman; I slammed the cottage cheese into the fridge), then *ding-dong* (the mailman; I ran down and signed for the package), then *ring-a-ling* (the school telephoning—Laura forgot her lunch money). Then *knock-knock*—"Can I borrow. . . ." Then *buzz*—time for lunch . . . *ding-dong* . . . time for bottles. "Waaa!"—diapers again, etc., etc., etc. You would not believe how my morning went. (Or *would* you?) My building project looked like a chimpanzee special—dried glue and badly cut boards all over, and no real work accomplished. I discovered that dressing a kid once is just a warm-up—one of those kids went through four outfits by 11:15. Noon came and another surprise—those little dudes don't appreciate what you do for them, all that work cooking and they threw food, slobbered, and not one of them thanked me. . . .

Nap time came, and would you believe little kids don't all go to sleep at the same time? I've bedded down 600 head of cattle easier and faster than those six kids. When I finally got them all down, no way was I going to hammer, play the stereo, or even turn a page loudly and risk waking one of them! Fortunately, the day ended just before I did. I had two boards up on the cabinet by the time the last baby was read to sleep at midnight. The most famous housecleaner and best organizer in the West . . . had accomplished nothing! I was *so* tired and discouraged. The day before I'd bought five trucks, four people had asked me to lunch—I'd expanded my company into a new area—but that day, nothing!

The next morning, I again woke at 4:00 and again decided I was going to run things like my business. I'd change all the diapers ahead for the whole day! But it didn't work. Leaving out all the gory details of the next few days, my half-day cabinet job, only half-complete, bit the dust.

A week later my wife called to check on things. I pinched all the kids to get them howling in the background so I wouldn't have to beg her to come and save me. She did return at once, and I suddenly got efficient again.

Since this experience, my compassion, respect and appreciation for the homemaker have grown considerably. I realized then for the first time how frustrating, time-consuming, and just plain hard the job of making a home is, and how much patience and ingenuity it takes.

In preparing this book I've tried to keep in mind the hundreds of other jobs the homemaker must perform simultaneously with housecleaning. Laundry, shopping, cooking, mending and errands *ad infinitum* will always be required. Though housework can be shortened, and there *is* life after housework, life *during* housework must also go on.

This is why rigid cleaning methods and plans seldom work. Schedules and demands are different in every household, big houses are proportionately easier to clean than small ones, new houses are easier than old; so homemakers trying to pattern their lives after others are eventually disillusioned—like the determined woman who tried a simple "foolproof" formula for keeping children from getting their dirty fingerprints all over the walls. She had read a "how to run a perfect home" article that advised, "Take Junior, sit him down and say, 'Junior, if you wash your hands three times a day, Mommy will give you a twenty-five-cent raise in your allowance.'" Immediately the woman called her dirty-fingered son in and presented the proposal to him. "I promise," said

the son. But the spots were still on the wall. The mother observed her son one morning, and indeed, he was keeping the bargain. He went to the sink, washed his hands and dried them, and repeated the procedure twice more. Then he left to play in the dirt.

It's frustrating to see commercial exaggerations of how well cleaning methods and materials work, especially when they're applied to a house in which everything is already perfect. You're not alone in being offended by the gorgeous TV homemaker in expensive evening clothes who flips her pearls out of the way to mop the floor with Magic Glow. Occasionally an immaculate kid or two tiptoes past or a well-groomed dog ambles through the place, after which the "super-smelling clean-all," applied effortlessly, takes over. But don't be discouraged — there's something wrong with them, not you!

Miracle formulas, tricks, gimmicks and solutions aren't the answer; and if they haven't worked for you, don't let it get you down, because they aren't the key to freedom from housework. The first principle of effective housework is not to have to do it! Being able to do it well is great, but it's greater not to have to do it at all. Your real goal is to *eliminate* all of it you can. In this book you'll learn how to get rid of a lot of it, and the rest I'll show you how to take care of quickly and efficiently.

Just remember that, while getting finished with any housework chore is a worthwhile goal, doing it in teeth-gritting agony is self-defeating. There are "have-to" jobs, no matter how good we are (like bathtub rings, fingerprints, etc.). You'll never escape them. But when you learn to minimize the time you spend on the have-to jobs, you'll finally be able to get to the "get-to" jobs, and they'll both become more pleasant, I promise! There *is* life after housework — and if you do it right,

there can even be life *during* housework.

Once you start finding the extra time that once was all spent on housework, nothing in your home will be mediocre or dull. You'll rip down anything that's faded or ugly and replace it with the prettiest, most colorful, most refreshing things you can find or make. You'll throw out or trade things that don't fit in. If something is torn or worn or forlorn, you'll look forward to taking care of it, not as a chore, but as a chance to better yourself and your home. You'll want to mend it, because it will be mending *you*. Once you have time, you'll be inspired to repair and refinish. The real struggle before wasn't the chore or item you had to service — it was the hopeless feeling that there was never any time for it. A lot of little things that need to be done really aren't work once you can get to them — and once you really believe that you can, you'll start looking forward to them! That's life *during* housework!

At the housecleaning seminars I've taught across the country, I've passed out thousands and thousands of registration cards with a space left for comments, special requests or housecleaning wisdom. This was written on one: "I must tell you, I love to clean. I have a clean house and I've been using the same techniques you use for years now. Everything in my house looks good, but my husband accuses me of being lazy because I don't exhaust myself every day like his mother did. I make lots of handicrafts and things, and he can't get over the fact that everything is clean and yet I still have time to goof off. He is honestly upset. He thinks I have too much fun and don't work enough."

You can't win 'em all. You'll discover in your worrying about how other people do it that 90 percent of the time you're overestimating their results. Even in the cartoon world, Wonder Woman in all her glory never raised children, stabilized a husband, or cleaned and managed a house. Wonder Woman faced only criminals, not housework horrors.

You can be as much a Wonder Woman as anyone you'll meet or read about, if you'll only learn to harness your own resources. Not many others are more efficient or have a neater house than you.

By following the simple secrets in this book, you'll become even more efficient, and will have more time to enjoy life after housework.

WILMA SEEMS TO BE HAVING A LOT MORE FUN EVER SINCE SHE GOT THAT YELLOW BOOK.

The professional cleaning approach won't take cleaning away entirely, but it will give you a lot of extra hours. The time rewards of efficient cleaning are real, and the busier you are, the more you'll appreciate them.

2.

Is it organization . . . or your energy level?

"I get the feeling at the end of every day that I haven't gotten anywhere and I'm never going to get anywhere. . . ." This is how a lovely young mother with a brand-new house and four small children rather concisely summed up a basic problem of homemaking: understanding what needs to be done but feeling that you lack the skill or direction to accomplish it. Even if you know what the rewards will be, constantly thinking you aren't getting there will discourage you and begin to prevent you from *wanting* to get there.

The big magic word

The big magic word to homemakers, business managers—in fact, all of us—is "organization." If we could just get ourselves properly organized, we could do anything (so we think). We spend a great deal of time trying to organize ourselves like the superwoman and superman formulas say we should, but still we seem to get little accomplished. We subconsciously figure the "organizing" is going to do it for us.

This is wrong. No organization plan can supply the whole answer or do the work. Is there hope? Yes, and this bit of good news will start this chapter off right: Women are much better organizers than men. I say so, and if you ask any boss, school principal or minister who organizes best, they'll agree with me: Women do! (If you want to prove it, send a man and woman to town, each with a list of things to do and get. The woman will be home in two hours with everything. Six hours later, the man will lumber in, only partly successful and mean as a bear.)

There is no one best way to organize

Organization is an ever-changing process; it's a journey, not a destination. Every minute of every day a new approach is being thought up. Everyone is different in temperament, attitude, build, energy and ambition; every situation requires a different style of organization to get the job done. The secret isn't in how you get organized—it's in *wanting* to be organized and committing yourself to it. Once that's achieved, everything will fall into place. You can organize as well as anyone if you want to or have to. There isn't any "set" way to do anything. You don't have to eat the soup first or second in a meal—you can eat it last!

Your system of organization should fit you personally. It should be tailored to your style, your schedule and your motivation. Some of us are day people; some, night. You run your own life—the clock doesn't run it.

Some organizational myths

I'm convinced that everyone can be organized if they have to be and if they quit trying to follow "know-it-all" methods and formulas. For example, some efficiency experts give this "foolproof" method of accomplishment: They say, in essence, "Sit yourself down and make a list of the things you want to get done. Put the most important ones first. When you get up in the morning, start on the first one and don't leave it or go to the next one until the first is finished. Then go on to the second one and so on until you've finished with the list."

I can't imagine anyone being able to exist (let alone succeed) following that kind of organizational concept. It's grossly inefficient, noncreative, inflexible—not to mention no fun. For years I've worked closely with top executives from some of the world's largest corporations, and I've never met one who worked this way. Yet I know many homemakers who've been trying desperately to organize their lives to fit this ridiculous concept, and they are paying dearly for it, suffering endless frustration because they can't make it work. If I followed that style of organization in my business or personal activities, I'd be twenty years behind!

Look where trying to follow the one-two-three style of getting things done can lead you. Let's say you make a list of the following things to do this week (in addition to your regular chores):

1. Make the kids a birdhouse.
2. Water the garden.
3. Memorize my part of the poem for PTA play.
4. Send Grandmother a birthday card.
5. Get the new lawn in.

Enthusiastically, you tackle the five projects in the down-the-list style outlined by the efficiency experts. While in town, you pick up the birdhouse materials, and soon you get started on the house with full gusto; however, you forgot to get an adjustable bit to make the hole in the front of the birdhouse. So, at a critical point, you're stopped. The one-two-three track compels you to leave the task and take time out to secure the needed tool, which you do at a cost of twenty-three miles of driving and two hours of searching. You then paint an undercoat on the birdhouse, wait a day for it to dry, and then put on the second coat. After two days, task number one is at last finished, so out to the garden next. You turn on the water. Four hours later the water is finally down the rows and task number two is finished. Next you go into the house for a few hours to memorize the PTA poem, number three on the list. Grandmother's card, item number four, you then pick up at the store, bring home, sign and address, and take to the post office. To put a hero's touch on number five, you pick up a book on lawns, work on the lawn for the last three days, and are finished with all your projects in one week!

Efficiency experts might have a week to spend to do all this, but you don't, and neither do I. The tasks could easily be done in a day or more, of course, with a little margin for daydreaming on the side. How? By relying on your creativity and a more flexible system. While in town, before anything is started, pick up the card for Grandmother. While driving on to get the birdhouse materials, mentally build the house so you'll be aware of each thing that has to be picked up. While waiting for the lumberyard clerk to round up the materials, chat with one of the staff about lawn season and grass and at this time get the fertilizer, mulch and seed for the anticipated lawn.

On the way home, turn off the car radio and start to memorize the PTA poem. Once you get home, lay out the materials for the birdhouse and build it. (Oops, we forgot the adjustable bit, too.) Let's stop the birdhouse immediately and go turn on the water for the garden, taking the poem with us to memorize while waiting for the water to get down the rows. Once the water is going, planting the lawn gets attention. Next, phone your brother-in-law, asking him to send his adjustable bit for the birdhouse home with your child who'll be coming by in a while from school. Continue to work on the lawn until you're too tired to hustle. After washing for supper, write out Grandmother's card so the children can take it to the mailbox on their way to school next morning. When your child arrives with the adjustable bit, drill the hole and paint the birdhouse. By this time, you're rested, so you tackle the lawn again. When tired—but finished with the lawn—you come in and give the birdhouse a second coat (you were smart enough to buy a fast-drying primer). By then it's late, but just time for another shot at the poem, and you've memorized it. Now all five things are completed in *one day* instead of a week, and look at the time you have left for yourself.

Impossible to do all that in one day? No. And you can apply this same principle to housework if you rely on your own skills and really want to get it done. Your freedom and ingenuity will produce creative energy. It's simply a matter of "multiple-track" organization. In housework, if you wait until one thing is completed before you start another—the single-track system—you'll take forever to finish and never get around to any freedom to enjoy life. Once you train yourself to the multiple-track method, thinking will be effortless. You'll just roll along, accomplishing things. You won't have to drain your think tank or worry or sweat to organize. It will come naturally.

Here's the secret: The start and finish of a job are the difficult parts. So start the first project at once! As it gets rolling, begin the second. As the second gets in gear, attack the third.

By then the second one is done,

so pounce on the fourth, fifth and sixth; and if the third isn't done, start on the seventh. Don't start and finish any two tasks at the same time. Don't start one thing when you're finishing another. Start another project while you're in the middle of three or four, but don't start one at the end of another project. The multiple-track system is the right way to run many projects at the same time—and it's easy if you alternate starting and finishing times.

The way some people cook is a prime example of doing things the most efficient way. I've watched my grandmother, who had fifteen children, prepare eight different dishes for twelve people in just minutes—a miracle. But it wasn't a miracle—just good organization and the multiple-track system. She simply got eight things going at alternate times, nothing starting or ending at once. You've done that, haven't you, when you had to? No sense waiting for water to boil, biscuits to rise, salads to cool, butter to melt. She simply used the waiting time productively.

I've watched a one-track-system mother with one small child crumple in total frustration trying to manage her baby. Five years, a couple of sets of twins and two singles later, she's doing a marvelous job. How? She learned the four- or five-track organization system and applied it! Your mind is capable of it and your body is, too. The success of this system is amazing, and once you get it down, you'll benefit from it in every area of your life.

A large percentage of our housecleaning time is spent "putting out brush fires," as it's called in business—such as spending three days hunting for your dog, because you didn't take three seconds to close the gate behind you. Many a homemaker fails because all her efforts are spent taking care of problems that a little timely action would have prevented. They spend twenty hours a year (and a lot of mental anguish) trying to remove felt-tip marker writing from walls, instead of a minute putting the pens out of reach of the kids; ten hours a year cleaning ovens or stovetops instead of fifteen minutes choosing a pot or pan that won't boil or slop over!

Simplicity vs. procrastination

A great deal of effort is expended as a result of failure to put out a simple timely effort. Here's a common every-day example: doing the dishes later instead of right after the meal. Notice how a simple chore multiplies itself into an insurmountable obstacle of negative feeling and freedom-robbing discouragement. Do you take the time, over and over, to cope with an unsatisfactory situation instead of correcting the underlying problem? For example, do you have to adjust the faucet handle just right when you turn it off so the drip is minimized? Or angle and massage that sticky drawer for thirty seconds every time you use it to get it to slide back in? Or wonder and experiment every time a fuse blows— which breaker switch is the lights, which is the heater, which is the outlet, which is the. . . . I think you know what I mean. (See the checklist at the end of chapter eight.)

The best "organization" is simply deciding to do things before they get out of hand and dictate to *you* how and when they'll be done. Are you the slave or the master? Simplicity seldom goes hand in hand with procrastination. Do you clean up and put away things as soon as you're through (simplicity), or do you throw them in a pile to be rummaged through as they're needed (procrastination)? It only takes a few minutes to iron a blouse. Do you do it well ahead of the appointment, or five tense minutes before you have to dash out the door? (And of course then you have to take out and set up the ironing board for just one piece of clothing—and you risk scorching the blouse in your haste and having to find and iron another.) Do you make your bed when you jump out (simplicity) or just before you go to bed again at night (procrastination)?

Do you fill out that committee report when it's still fresh in your mind and will take only a few minutes, or do you do it when it's overdue? You've been strongly reminded to get it in, and now you'll spend hours doing so, be-

Clean in the daytime whenever you can. Cleaning at night shortchanges you on helpers, energy, light and safety.

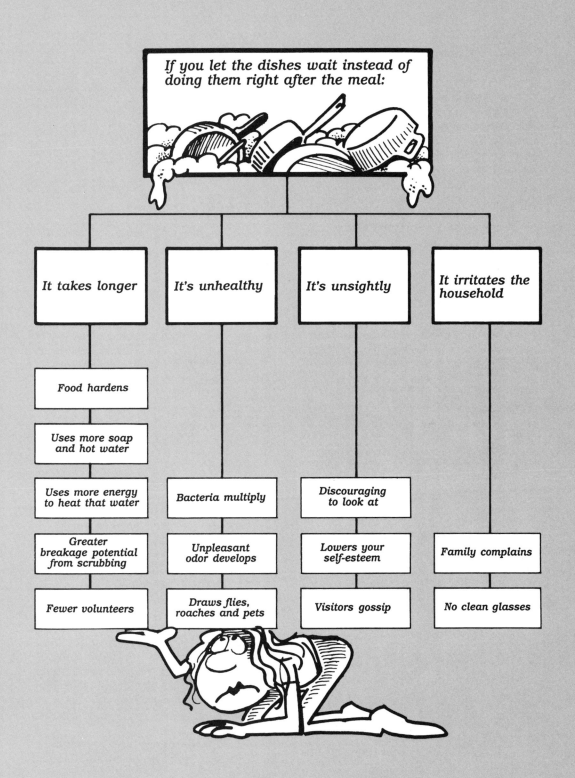

If you let the dishes wait instead of doing them right after the meal:

It takes longer
- Food hardens
- Uses more soap and hot water
- Uses more energy to heat that water
- Greater breakage potential from scrubbing
- Fewer volunteers

It's unhealthy
- Bacteria multiply
- Unpleasant odor develops
- Draws flies, roaches and pets

It's unsightly
- Discouraging to look at
- Lowers your self-esteem
- Visitors gossip

It irritates the household
- Family complains
- No clean glasses

cause by now you've forgotten facts, mislaid evidence, and had to write an excuse letter.

The time gap between doing most things promptly and doing them late compounds and multiplies problems. You end up spending time not simply getting the job done, but fighting and recovering from the problems created because you waited. Doing things when they take less time is not only good scheduling, it makes good sense: It will save energy and motivation to apply to more personally satisfying efforts than housework.

Back to the ever-growing list

Lists are great—as long as they don't run our lives. We all have our lists of things to do. I'd be lost without mine! We don't always *do* the things on the list, but they're always jotted down. At one time, my list grew to seventy-six "immediate" things to be done. It took all my time just to transfer the list to a new piece of paper when the old one wore out. If your list follows the typical pattern, at the bottom are the hard, unpleasant tasks, such as:

19. Clean the oven
20. Clean the 3-section storm windows
21. Volunteer to tend Dennis the Menace
22. Kick cousin Jack out of the front room
23. Go thru 700 old issues of Good Housekeeping

_____

or

_____

38. Tell Jack he's to be terminated.
39. Pour concrete for the back steps.
40. Go face the banker and get the loan.
41. Get my wisdom teeth pulled
42. Speak to George about taking a few more baths

We have to be careful with that villain list. We're often so proud of ourselves for even writing something down on our list that we immediately relax. We say to ourselves, "Boy, I'm glad I got that one started." After a few days we suddenly realize that nothing has been done, and we sneak a look at the list to see if that item has disappeared. It hasn't. We're so relieved to know that it wasn't forgotten, we leave it for a few more days. The day before the deadline, we've no choice but to face it, and we generally get the item done in half the time we feared it would take!

A list has one big value, and that's getting things recorded before you forget them. That's all! As for using a list to discipline yourself, forget it. *You* have to do the things—the list won't do them for you.

A schedule won't do them for you either. I dislike the regimentation of set schedules; they're only for inefficient people afraid they're going to run out of things to do. Some scheduling and budgeting of time is needed, but not to the extent that it dictates your every move and mood. You should run a schedule for your benefit, not the reverse.

It can't be illustrated better than by this skit sent to me by homemaker Gladys Allen:

[Aslett arrives at the highly polished door of Ms. Polly Programmed.]

Polly: [Wearing a huge watch on her arm, feather duster in hand. She's immaculately groomed and dressed.] Hi, Mr. Aslett, won't you please take off your shoes and come in? [Dusts him off lightly as he removes his shoes.] How nice to have a visitor drop by. I have [checking her watch] 6¼ minutes' relaxation time before I have to knead the bread and water the alfalfa sprouts.

Aslett: Ms. Programmed, I see that you're busy. . . . I just stopped by to invite you to a little efficiency seminar.

Polly: Nonsense! Now you come right here and sit down. I still have five minutes and thirty-three seconds of leisure time.

Aslett: [Sits down.] As you know, Ms. P. . . .

Polly: [Interrupting.] Oh, Mr. Aslett, would you mind sitting on this cushion? That one has already been sat on this morning. I like to alternate. The fabric wears much longer that way.

Aslett: [Moving to another cushion.] Really? Now, I never would have thought of that.

Polly: My, yes! My last divan lasted seventy-eight days longer just by using that one little trick.

Aslett: What I've come to tell you, Ms. Programmed, is that I've come up with a great new idea for a seminar, and I'd like to invite you to come preview it tomorrow morning at 10:00.

Polly: Ten o'clock Thursday? [Rushes to a big box labeled "Daily Schedules."] I've just typed up my schedules for the month. I'll have to check. [Pulls out a long folded sheet.]

Aslett: Is that your schedule for just one month?

Polly: One month? Oh, my no! This is my schedule for Thursday. [Studies it carefully, consults watch, makes a few changes with a pencil.] Now, what time did you say that would start tomorrow?

Aslett: Ten a.m.

Polly: [Making a few more changes.] Yes, yes, I think I'll be able to work it in after all. If I get up at 5:00 a.m. instead of 6:00, I can have my laundry sorted and my Scripture studies done by 7:00. I can get my drapes vacuumed and my children fed by 7:47. While they practice their violins, I can shine the furniture and wash the dishes. They leave for school at 8:19, which gives me just enough time to stir up a casserole for supper and get myself ready. Umm, yes. I should be able to leave here by 9:37 at the latest. By the way, Mr. Aslett, what did you say your seminar will be about?

Aslett: [Stands up with a sigh, shrugs weakly, unable to speak.]

Highs and lows

The old up-and-down pattern is entrenched in our style of living—but how devastating it is to human feelings and efficient housekeeping! Most housecleaners unthinkingly roll along in this style. Once a week (or once a month) we clean the house, water the plants, and do everything just so, then we're "up." But immediately the spotlessness and satisfaction attained begin to erode as dust, spiders, children, animals, spouse and guests mount their attack. It's frustrating because we've expended so much dedication and energy getting the house to its peak.

One elderly gentleman, recalling his mother's approach to housework, said, "She organized herself and the family so that all the housework (washing, ironing, baking, sewing, etc.) was done on Monday (one day, mind you). What an accomplishment! But she spent the other six days recovering to prepare for the big Monday cleanup again."

This kind of housecleaning approach gets old fast, and it gets you nowhere except an early grave. Even if your house is clean as often as it's dirty, 50 percent of the time, or 50-50, you'll not be rewarded 50-50, because it's human nature to notice and respond to the negative, not the positive. Little is heard about the house if it's clean—but if it's dirty, everybody squawks, gossips and complains. It's demoralizing, but you can't give up the battle. So you buckle down and restore your domain to order and cleanliness.

Hold it. Now that you've got your house in top shape again, try something different.

A little consistency saves a lot of time, energy and discouragement. Avoid the "up-and-down" style of housekeeping. Establish an *acceptable* cleanliness level and maintain it daily. If you really want to be freed from housework drudgery, this one change in style will work wonders for you. When you learn to keep house on a straight line, you'll not only find extra hours appearing, but some of the other up-and-down styles you've been struggling with for years (exercising, cooking, letter writing, reading, gardening, etc.) will follow your housecleaning system and suddenly begin to be manageable. Your home will never stay static. It will be in a constant state of flux, if it's used as all homes should be. Avoid extremes both ways—too much polish is just as disconcerting as too little. Gold-plating a house won't bring you anything but discouragement and worry.

To keep your home in a steady state of cleanliness and livability, you'll learn to wipe down shower walls and plumbing fixtures daily to avoid having to acid-bath hard water deposits monthly. You'll carry in a manageable armload of firewood whenever you enter the house, instead of spending a back-breaking hour lugging a week's worth in on Saturday. You'll wipe up spills immediately, when it's five times easier, faster, and much less damaging than putting it off.

You'll also discover that *eliminating* work does wonders for your efficiency. (See page 68.) And try delegating, say, 60 percent of the daily chores to your family—you'll be amazed how much the need for picking up the house will decrease.

Do your big yearly cleaning each fall instead of spring; you'll marvel at how much longer the house looks nice.

Remember to tie scheduling and organization to your own personal motivation or energy level. Add to that the conviction that what you have to do or want to do is really worth it, and organization will fall into place. You're a human being, not a machine. You don't start running at full efficiency the minute you're cranked up. If you try that, you're going to end up mighty discouraged. By tying my energy level to production, I can knock out three magazine articles in an hour; but I can't finish one in eight hours when I have the drags. When I'm rolling, I tackle my most active and demanding work. When the drags invade, I file, sort, or do something that requires no creativity or mental energy. In both situations, I'm accomplishing a lot by fitting the task to my mood and personality.

Be yourself and decide what's most important to you. Wade into it during your best hours for that particular chore, and a miracle will happen. (You might end up writing a book on organization and selling it back to the supermen and -women of the world.)

3.

Treasure sorting & storage strategy

While cleaning a large, plush home during my junior year in college, I managed to wade through and clean a luxurious, treasure-laden bedroom and embarked on cleaning the closet. In addition to the expected arsenal of pricey wearing apparel, I had to move five exquisite cigarette lighters, forty-seven pairs of women's shoes (I kid you not), a case of 1920s *National Geographic*s, several tennis racquets, fourteen boxes of Christmas cards, six poodle collars, and numerous other items. It was a neat but completely stuffed closet, in harmony with the style of the woman who lived there. She was fifty-five years old and possessed a handsome home filled with elaborate furnishings and decorations, and all kinds of other possessions that she had spent part of her life collecting and the rest of her life cleaning and keeping track of. For thirty-five years, she had managed to keep her house clean and organized and all of her things dusted. This project of shuffling treasures around had taken her more than half a lifetime.

Most of us are in the same condition. Our treasures may not be expensive, but we have as many of them crammed in as many cubbyholes, which we shuffle through, sort and re-sort, climb over, worry about, and maintain for hours on end. What does it contribute to our lives or our personal edification? Even the Salvation Army store would label most of it "junk." Junk has frustrated more women than Robert Redford. It's burned down more homes, caused more ulcers, and resulted in more arguments than can be imagined.

All for what reason? Accumulation? Sentiment? Security? Who knows?

The other 30 percent of the "stuff" that we have stored or lying around somewhere may be of some worth to us. But remember, we're talking about 30 percent of what we have. Why own a houseful of useless objects that rob you of time and energy?

The burden of junk

It's amazing how we get ourselves into the junk habit. As the Law of the Pack Rat goes, "Junk will accumulate in proportion to the storage room available for it."

Before learning the shortcuts and professional methods of cleaning a house, we must first learn the art of "treasure sorting." This means differentiating between valuable and useless things and promptly disposing of the latter. This is a job you can't palm off on anyone else, or postpone too long, because there's no escape from the toll that junk takes on your life. Everything stashed away or hidden—discreetly or indiscreetly—is also stashed in your mind and is subconsciously draining your mental energy. Once discarded, it's discarded from your mind, and you're free from keeping mental tabs on it.

Second homes often drain their owners. The owners maintain them mentally and physically for the entire year, yet only use them for a couple of weeks. If it were possible to calculate the emotions and affections, the human caring and sharing energy that's silently burned up worrying about the home, it would surely outweigh the benefits of a couple of weeks or months occupying it.

Another burden junk thrusts on us is that we feel obligated to use it whether we need it or not. If we don't or can't use it, then we worry about why we have it at all! Junk will get you—don't sit there and argue that it won't.

The most valuable "someday useful" junk will stymie your emotional freedom if not handled properly. Inasmuch as all of us feel guilty and frustrated about our piles of junk, we have to eliminate the problem. In turn, it will eliminate an unbelievable amount of housework.

The origin of junk

There's a reason we quit using something: It's outdated, broken, unsafe, unattractive or inoperable. This simply means that we don't need it anymore—except, of course, for sentimental value. As each day goes by, it becomes more outdated, more unsafe, more unattractive, and will remain broken and inoperable. So learn to follow the 70-30 law that a magazine publisher made famous. He held up an

in the pictures were meant to be bronzed, not eaten!). Instead of piles of magazines, you'll have a thin, usable file of articles you want.

Other junk can be treated the same way. The faucet leaks and the handles are corroded, so we replace them with a sleek new chrome beauty.

ordinary magazine and said, "Look, 70 percent of this magazine is advertising." So anyone who has any magazines or newspapers lying in boxes or piles around the house has up to 70 percent junk (depending on how healthy ad sales are). The first time you read a magazine, remove any article of interest to you and throw the 70 percent junk away. If you start doing this regularly, you'll rejoice for having eliminated those hernia-causing and guilt-producing boxes of magazines (and besides, all those sculptured squash and hand-carved carrots we see

But we can't bear to throw the old ones away, because some day (even though they're broken, outdated, unattractive and inoperable) we just might need a washer out of them. So we put them in the junk drawer or closet or hang them in the garage to get tangled up in the bicycle spokes. We could have removed the washers in two minutes and thrown the rest in the garbage, saving hours over a lifetime of shuffling the old faucet around and dodging it. What a mighty grip junk has on us! We'll keep that worthless worn-out faucet for fifteen years, then in our move to Denver or Boston, into a new house, guess what we take with us . . . yes, the old faucet. We never know when we might need it. The average American moves fourteen times in a lifetime. If a third of your stuff is clutter, you could save eight moving van loads if you de-junked! People spend literally millions moving junk.

No matter how we may rationalize, "Oh well, we can put it in the attic," or "There's room in the basement," that junk should go to the dump. The number one secret of proper junk disposal or dispersal is to make the decision *at the time something is to be put away.* Because once you store it, sentimental attachment and mental obligation to use it (to justify the storage) begin to mount. And you'll never have time later to go back through all that stored stuff and decide.

Another good way to come to terms with junk is to face the fact of just how much room is really available for storage. If you can't conveniently store an item, then you can't use it conveniently.

The economics of storage

Keeping costs—anything that's anywhere costs. Period! The costs are clever ones, too. Like a little bit of

It's the "maybes" that get you!

space and rent, a little bit of energy (heat and lights), a little bit of accident and fire potential, a little bit of insurance and moth and burglar-proofing money, a little bit of your emotions, a little bit of prestige and respect you lose (from those who laugh at you behind your back for saving dumb things, even if they do it too). All of these little costs of keeping add up to a big price tag. Stored junk and clutter is also prime argument fodder. You know exactly what I'm talking about—the fights, resentments, grudges and even divorces that can come from stored stuff. Out of sight is not out of mind. It might be out of the middle of the room, but it's not out of mind. Every day a little money and merit ticks away as that stored stuff rots and goes out of style. Stored stuff is subtle; it takes your life and cash brilliantly and indirectly. Like my neighbor, who, when a piece of farm machinery wore out and was worthless, would pull it out on the field to save for "parts." Year after year, as the older ones rusted, fresh clutter was lined up until he covered five acres of good farm ground. I figured out one day that the total "parts" saved might have been worth at most $600, while the total value of the crops lost, due to inactive acreage, was $11,000. Great economy, eh?

I know a woman who bought and stored 900 yards of fabric to sew up "someday"—she'd have it just in case. Today she's 94, and still has 876 yards of polyester stockpiled for . . . someday.

We all know folks who have several freezers though they live only a mile from three grocery stores. They save ten cents a pound on meat in bulk so they buy and store it and keep it forever. I know one who was very proud of the three dollars "cold cash" she saved this way, until she found out it cost $40 per month to run the freezer.

My company cleans lots of homes after floods and fires (what is called "restoration" work for insurance companies). Have I seen some sad sights in the course of it—all of that stored stuff, charred or soaking in sewer water, has to be pawed through (as every relative and friend helping gasps and expresses wonderment as to why anyone would keep all this). Talk about heartbreaks and wallet aches—storage will do it every time. One insurance man who handles losses in those self-storage complexes we see everywhere tells me that when they're robbed or burned most of the owners can't remember half of what was in there, all that stuff they were so carefully keeping and paying room and board for. Often the storage cost of an article is far higher than the cost of replacing it; it's not uncommon for people to pay $300 a year to rent a storage spot for $200 worth of stuff.

But these things are valuable, you say? What about the value of the life and time to store, to clean, to insure, to transport, to protect—what does that cost? "Afford" is not simply a question of money. What is the effect on your job, your physical being, your peace of mind? "Afford" is the capacity to absorb into your being, not your bank balance.

Think about the storage problem in your home. A lot of that stuff you're storing is useless. It's a constant source of worry. Most of it is unsafe, outdated and ugly, so why keep it? Why spend a valuable part of yourself polishing, washing, dusting, and thinking about it? *You can't afford junk.* It will rob you physically, emotionally and spiritually. Freeing yourself from junk will automatically free you from much of your housework (and it won't take any soap and water either); a cluttered house takes *much* more time and effort to clean. You double your cleaning time by having to "pick up" a sloppy house, but even a neat house

will take longer to clean than it ought to, if there's too much furniture or it's over-decorated.

Junk makes every job take longer

Clutter is one of the greatest enemies of efficiency and stealers of time—and that includes yours.

For every chore tackled, the average person spends more time getting ready—hunting for a place, the tools, a reason to do it, etc.—than actually doing it. It takes only six seconds to drive a nail, often ten minutes to find the nails and hammer.

Junk makes every job harder and makes cleaning take forever. Any project we tackle, from building to disassembling, will be slowed, dampened and diluted if we constantly have to fight our way to it in the midst of clutter.

If junk is taking up your storage space, it means you have to reach farther and dig deeper to get the tool, book, suitcase, shirt, etc., you need. "Getting something out," instead of being a few-second job, often ends up a twenty-minute search-and-rescue mission.

If you'll just de-junk your home, the time you'll have left over in the course of a year will be enough to complete and pay for three credit hours in that night class you've always wanted to take. (When I say "de-junk," I don't mean sort your four cubbyholes of worthless stuff into three cubbyholes of worthless stuff— or I'll tell on you!)

Now don't say, "Oh, I know my junk has got to go, and one of these days, I'm going to. . . ." There are more reasons than housecleaning to de-junk your house (and your life).

This might surprise you, but it's a reality: many people are buried so deep in junk that their mates can't navigate the clutter to get to them. Your spouse can't give you attention and affection until he or she can find you. I've cleaned (or tried to clean) hundreds of homes where lonely, frustrated men and women, buried in junk, can't understand why they and their families aren't closer. Junk is the barrier! Junk (and junk projects and activities) prevents you from being free, available for affection or opportunity. Too often the things we save and store—for sentiment's sake or because they might be valuable some day—end up as tombstones for us. Boxes of mummified prom corsages and piles of corroded hubcaps will bury you but good.

To start your de-junking program, begin with yourself! At an all-day seminar once I convinced the entire audience that junk is a universal problem, not the "other guy's." I gave every member of the audience two minutes to gather just the junk they were carrying with them (in pockets, purses, briefcases), offering a prize for the most unique collection of junk (they initialed it for proper identification). My son passed around a large drawer and in minutes it overflowed. What did I get, you wonder? (We all love other people's junk, don't we!) It was hilarious. It was all junk! Used flashbulbs, a ten-year-old calendar, old speeding tickets, partly eaten chocolate-covered peanuts, half a hacksaw blade, two-year-old food coupons, rocks and pebbles, expired membership cards, half a pair of pantyhose, old Christmas lists, broken compacts and empty lipstick containers, plus some censored items—and I suspect they held back plenty on me! The winner had a whole bulging hankyful . . . and she was the best-dressed person there! *Junk is a reality.*

If having piles, rooms or buildings full of junk (even labeled "antique") is worth all those hours to shuffle it and all that mental energy to keep track of it, then unfortunately you value junk more than your time and freedom. (So much for those fantasies of being a happy, carefree vagabond.) If having a closet full of gleaming silver is worth hours of polishing time a month, you enjoy impressing people more than you value your time and your freedom. The storage strategy message is simple: Nothing exists in and of itself. Everything has a cost to acquire and to maintain. The majority of the cost you pay with your time and energy. Eliminate the junk around your house. It's one of the easiest ways to free yourself from household imprisonment.

P.S. If you think you need emotional permission and physical direction to de-junk, check out my books on the subject, *Clutter's Last Stand* and *Not for Pack Rats Only.* Cured junkers rave about them and give them as gifts.

What to expect from your husband and children

On this subject I'll gladly assume the role of the learner. When you find something that works the miracle of getting husbands and children to take on their rightful share of the housework, let me know so I can tell the thousands of exasperated women I hear from every year.

This lack of cooperation from men and children is a grim reality, all right, but it doesn't have to be. While doing a consulting study for a large Eastern school district, I was introduced to a quiet grade school cafeteria. At the stroke of noon, 420 children converged enthusiastically on the polished lunchroom with trays and brown bags. Forty minutes later the room was quiet again, but not polished. It looked like a tornado had feasted instead of humans. Forks, food and wrappers decorated the floor, the tables, chairs, walls, and even the light fixtures. When we finished the building tour *two hours* later, I noticed the janitor just finishing the cleaning. *Two 30-gallon garbage cans* were required to contain the mess the janitor picked up from that lunchroom.

The next day we were touring a similar school in town: same floor plan, same area, and 412 students. This time we arrived about fifteen minutes after lunch ended—and the place was immaculate! The janitor was scooping up what appeared to be the final dustpan of debris. I was told by the guide that not only was it the last dustpan, it was the *only* dustpan! This janitor had spent fifteen minutes restoring the room and filled only a small pan of dirt, while the janitor at the other school labored two hours in the same area, after the same number of children, and accumulated two garbage cans full. What was the difference? Same number of kids, same community, same size building—but *not the same boss!*

It's not circumstance that causes you to have a messy house and spend two hours cleaning when you could spend fifteen minutes. It's you! The only difference between the schools was the principals. The first principal allowed the students freedom to eat and leave a mess; the other principal allowed the students the freedom of eating and simply added the responsibility of cleaning up their own mess. "Anything you mess up, you clean up" was the fair and simple rule. That meant crumbs, drops and dribbles on tables, chairs and floors. It took each kid seconds to perform the task and unquestionably taught and reinforced the most important ingredient of greatness: responsibility. Any woman who cleans up after a husband or a kid over two years old deserves the garbage cans she has to lug out every day!

I don't ordinarily suggest open rebellion or brute force, but I do offer these suggestions:

1. Refuse to be the janitor for the kids' and husband's messes. Picking up after them is bad for everyone involved. You teach irresponsibility when you assume someone else's responsibility (except those who don't know any better or can't help themselves). Insist that everyone clean up his or her own messes and premises: If they're old enough to mess up, they're old enough to clean up!

2. Write down and post needs. When you ask for (or demand) help, most family members will begin to assist you. Written messages eliminate short memories and the innocent phrase, "I didn't know you needed anything done."

3. Make it easy for them to help. To encourage bed-making, for instance, use one heavy blanket instead of several thinner ones (better yet, invest in European-style comforters that serve as blanket and bedspread). Teach the kids to spread the sheet and blanket and then circle the bed once, tucking as they go. Make sure everyone has plenty of bins and hangers for personal belongings, and the house will be tidier.

4. Be patient. Be persistent. Things don't change just because you say they will. You have to stick with it. The biggest threat to success here is the "If you can't beat 'em, join 'em" syndrome. Hang in there. Refuse to pick up the slack for nonperformers. Don't fall back on "It's easier to do it myself than to get them to do it." The reason is this: If you work to make others clean up after themselves, you'll eventually get them trained and you won't have to worry about it. But if you break down and do it yourself, you'll be doing it for the rest of your life.

5. Use praise lavishly when it's deserved. Appeal to their vanity (this may work especially well on a husband). Remember, you can catch more flies with honey than with vinegar.

6. Leave home or play sick, if necessary.

Sorry I can't help you more on this one! Just remember—it's as much for your husband's and kids' good as it is for yours. So stand your ground!

P.S. My apologies to the 5 percent of husbands and children who already do their share around the house.

5.

The old wives' tales

Ever hear these?

"Never shampoo carpets when they're new; they get dirty faster."

"Toothpaste and peanut butter remove black marks."

"Start washing from the bottom of the wall and work up."

"Use newspaper to polish your windows."

"Dried bread crumbs clean wallpaper."

Some of these might possibly work, but why go the long way around to get the job done? Spring isn't the best time to clean indoors—late fall is. Who wants to be cooped up with paint and ammonia fumes when springtime blossoms are fragrant? Painting isn't cheaper than cleaning; cleaning averages 60 to 70 percent less. Carpets don't get dirty faster after the first shampooing, if you do it right. Newspapers aren't good for polishing (only for training puppies and peeks at the funnies). Toothpaste and peanut butter do remove marks because they're abrasive—but they also cut the gloss of good enamel paint, and the resulting dull patch looks worse than the original mark.

For centuries, "secrets" of sure-cleaning brews have been passed on to

young housekeepers. These formulas are applied unsuccessfully, yet on deathbeds are whispered to the next generation. Hence, even in this day of modern science, well-educated home-makers living in up-to-the-minute homes are still using powdered frogs' legs to remove ink stains from their carpets and crumbled cottage cheese to polish brass doorknobs.

I have yet to find a magic cleaner or solution that will take all the work out of cleaning a house. Less than 5 percent of the hundreds of old wives' tales sent or repeated to me even *worked*. And there's no magic in the bottle, either. The "cleaning cyclone" that whips out of the container isn't interested in cleaning for you when it's getting $150,000 for a minute on TV. Even if that solution—or any solution—is as good as advertisers say it is, it will have little effect on your cleaning time.

It's not what you clean with so much as how you go about it that really matters. So forget most of the old wives' tales you've heard and commercials you've seen and follow some simple professional methods that have been used efficiently and safely for decades.

Whatever you do, don't feel it's your patriotic or economic duty to mix up your own money-saving brew. Some of the results are ridiculous. For example, it's easy to make your own glue, isn't it? Just find an old cow, kill it, and cut off as many hooves as you need for as much glue as you want. Grind them up in your trusty blender, then add. . . .

It's not worth it when you can spend $1.59 and get something better. Besides, it's cheaper than finding a cow and not nearly as messy as killing one.

Homemakers trying to make their own home brew furniture polish can spend three hours rounding up the materials and mixing up a solution that costs $5.45 for ingredients alone—instead of buying a commercial polish for $2.49 that's tested, safe, and guaranteed not to rot, explode or poison. Remember, *it's your time that's valuable*. A half-century of professional cleaners' records show that out of every dollar spent for cleaning, only 5½¢ is for supplies and equipment; almost the same ratio holds true in the home. Your time and safety are the valuable commodities, not the supplies.

Most home brews are misguided formulations. For instance, most homemade furniture polishes call for linseed oil—a penetrant that conditions raw wood but that, when smeared on *finished* wood (which most furniture is), acts as a sticky magnet to every passing speck of dust. Many homemakers pour chlorine bleach into everything from mop water to toilet bowls, to no avail—bleach is an oxidizing agent that doesn't clean a thing. And don't spend your precious hours grinding and rubbing trying to get vinegar to perform like soap. Vinegar isn't a cleaner, it's a rinsing agent. The "squeak" is what turns you on!

Figuring this from a "free me from housework" angle, using good, efficient—even expensive—supplies and equipment is a cheap way to go if it cuts your time down. For example, if you pay $15 for a gallon of wax, it's a wise buy if it means that whatever you apply it to will only need annual or biennial cleaning and waxing.

Your household tools are your power tools

A gross injustice is usually inflicted on women in this area. Over and over, I see homemakers using an old rattletrap vacuum hardly capable of running, let alone sucking up any dirt. The hose is full of holes, the cord is worn and offers instant electrocution if touched in the wrong place. Every day women wrestle with these machines to do the housework, while in basements and garages sit $400 radial-arm saws and other power tools their husbands haven't used in six months! Men need these macho tools to give their masculinity an occasional boost—while women fight unsafe, ineffective vacuums for hours, every day! Husbands' closets are full of expensive toys that they use one or two days a year, while their wives are cooking three square meals on an electric stove with worn-out switches, or bunching tricot on a twenty-year-old single-stitch sewing machine—daily! The kitchen junk drawer (you know, that drawer with all the parts, spare tools, lids, screws, handles, matches, nails, etc.) is used more by the average man than his $800 solid oak workbench.

In most cases, after an industrious project or two, men seldom use their expensive tools; as investments go, such tools are poor ones. Time is our most valuable commodity, and good housecleaning tools and equipment can save hundreds of hours a year.

My wife, the bread-mixer

A confident husband pulled up in front of a specialty shop, carefully parked his $43,000 Mercedes, and strolled into the store. He paused to examine a new bread-mixer, advertised to cut breadmaking time dramatically. The clerk eased up to him and politely suggested, "Why don't you buy a bread-mixer for your wife?" "Ha!" said the man triumphantly, "Why should I buy one? I *married* a bread-mixer."

This kind of attitude is an unimaginable infringement of one individual upon another. Men are the greatest offenders because traditionally a

man's time has been considered to be of greater value. Tradition has validity, but not here. No one's time is worth more or less than another's: for every one of us, time is to love, to feel, to be, to experience, to serve, to relax, or to edify self. Position, sex, status, age, etc., have no bearing on the matter. Too many men think that they married a bread-mixer, maid, taxi driver, gardener, nurse, laundress — forgetting that their mate is entitled to the same share of "time" that they are. The average man reacts almost violently when his wife quietly asks for a $75 pressure cooker to make meal preparation more efficient and provide better nutrition for the family. The same man will slap a $149 telescopic sight on his rifle (used once a year at hunting time) and never even bother to mention it to his wife.

On this earth, no one's time is worth any more than anyone else's. I used to send my wife to town or on errands to do "the piddly things" because my time was worth "so much" — after all, I could get $50 to $100 an hour for consulting jobs. I was way off base. Any woman's time is worth what any man's is.

Take a hard look around your home. The tools likely to be used most and those capable of saving the most time are the ones to purchase. Anything that can be purchased to save time in housework is just as important as a new computer for the business! Buy up! (And don't spend all the money on little-used and often useless "trinket" attachments to cleaning machines or appliances; concentrate on solid, basic tools and supplies.)

What's a homemaker to do?

If you can read, you can forget the witch potions and the glamorously packaged, overpriced household cleaners you've been using. The Yellow Pages in almost every phone directory in the world list janitorial-supply stores. These are (generally) wholesale outlets where commercial cleaning companies buy many of their supplies. It's here you'll find the items I refer to in this book that can't be bought at the supermarket or hardware store. Professionals buy the rest at a local supermarket, same as you do. The prices at janitorial-supply stores vary, but I've never run into one in the multistate area where I've cleaned that wouldn't sell to a homemaker.

Wholesale or retail? Well, you can get either price. And either is better than the price of comparable supplies at the supermarket. The best way to try for a wholesale price is to walk in with dignity and authority, squinting confidently at the shelves of cleaning material and equipment (few of which you'll recognize the first time), and say, "I'm Mrs. Van Snoot of Snoot, Snoot, Frisky and Melvin (you, your husband, cat and dog; the more you sound like a law firm, the better). I need one gallon of metal interlock self-polishing floor finish." This usually convinces the seller that you're official, and he or she will generally offer you the contractor's price, since most suppliers are great people and run "hungry" establishments. If the supplier asks you a question like, "Do you want polymer or carnauba base?" don't lose your nerve. Just say,

Give me the house's best-selling brand.

(Forty janitorial companies can't be wrong!) I'm sure if you don't get the contractor's price, you'll at least get a discount.

Which supplies to use: where and when?

I'll discuss these as we cover each area of cleaning. Just remember this: There's no magic in the bottle or machine. The basics of effective cleaning are extremely simple, and you need just a few professional supplies. A chart at the end of this chapter lists the basic tools you'll find useful. A home will be well prepared for efficient cleaning and maintenance if it's equipped with the items listed. (If you can't find them, write me at the address on page 44 and I'll send you a mail-order catalog.)

Proper supplies — big returns

There are more benefits from using the right equipment and supplies than merely doing a (1) faster and (2) better job. There are: (3) safety— you'll be using fewer, simpler items that will be safer to use and easier to store out of children's reach; (4) cost— in the long run you'll spend a lot less on cleaning supplies if you select and use them properly; (5) depreciation— using proper cleaning supplies and tools reduces damage to and deterioration of the surfaces and structures you're cleaning; (6) storage—fewer and more efficient concentrated supplies take up less of the storage space you probably don't have enough of anyway.

If your cleaning closet is full of fancy cans and bottles—Zippo, Rippo, Snort, Rubb Off, Scale Off, Goof Off— I promise a roomier closet when you learn the secrets of proper cleaning. Many of those chemicals and cleaners crammed into every cupboard and under every sink aren't all that effective. They use up valuable room, they're safety hazards for children, and many of them actually damage household surfaces.

Most homemakers' cleaning supply storage areas (under the sink, the pantry, the closet) look like Tom Edison's chemical cache just seconds before the explosion. Many of these things simply get wasted: We have so many, we forget to use them.

Canned expense

The aerosol can has pressured itself into the lives of all. Cosmetics, hair spray, deodorizers, medicines, lubricants, paints, even food—just about everything comes in aerosol because we've been convinced it takes too much effort to do any more than push a button. We've carried this principle

Limit your use of aerosols—they're expensive and bulky. Buy concentrates whenever possible.

supply store and buy four or five reusable commercial plastic spray bottles. Buy your chemicals, cleaners and disinfectants concentrated, in gallons. Mix them with water at the suggested dilution ratios and put the solutions in the spray bottles. Label the bottles with a waterproof marker or make sure each chemical is a different color, lest you end up cleaning windows with upholstery shampoo. These plastic spray bottles are unbreakable, durable, won't nick cupboards, and are extremely efficient and economical to use, whether for heavy-duty cleaning or smaller "keep-up" jobs.

Cleaning concentrates are also now available in little plastic packets (like those little single servings of catsup or mustard), preventing waste and wrong dilution, and making storage and handling a cinch. They're premeasured for use in a bucket or spray bottle—just snip them open and mix

over into our housecleaning systems, paying dollars for pennies' worth of cleaners and compressed gas. Yes, they are convenient, and they may use a propellant that doesn't harm the environment. But considering the small amount of cleaner you get this way, how easily the nozzle clogs, and the dangerous can you have to dispose of afterward, it's cheaper and more environmentally sound to dilute your own concentrated cleaner into good plastic spray bottles.

They last and last, you can see what's in them at any time, and you can control the spray (mist or stream). Some bug killer, paint and grooming products are hard to beat in aerosol, but when it comes to cleaning, I'd go with the spray bottles for speed, economy and safety.

To replace most of the aerosols you now use, go to the janitorial-

Cleaning concentrates are now available in "single-serving" plastic packets. Since they're premeasured for use (either in a bucket or a spray bottle), mixing is easy—and storage is even easier.

41

Concentrates are 80 percent cheaper than ordinary "household cleaning" products. They take a lot less room to store, and, because they're professional products, they do a better job.

with water as directed on the label. Being able to bring a year's worth of cleaning supplies home in a small sack and store them safely in a little lockable drawer instead of under the sink is the thing of the future. And using concentrates reduces the number of aerosols we use, and the number of empty containers to be disposed of.

When mixing up cleaners from concentrate, fill the bottle with water before you add the concentrate. You won't have four inches of foam in the bottle this way, and it prevents chemical splashes, too.

Neutral cleaner

Neutral cleaner is a cleaner that's mild and safe enough for most any surface because it's neither acid nor alkaline. A detergent doesn't have to be strictly neutral (have a pH of 7.0) to qualify—it just has to be somewhere close. Most neutral cleaners have a pH in the range of 7 to 9. Professionals use these cleaners for many light-duty cleaning jobs such as floor-mopping and wall-washing, which call for streak-free results with no detergent residue. Give yourself a big supply of neutral cleaner to handle the majority of the cleaning chores around the house safely and inexpensively by going to a janitorial-supply store and getting a jug of "neutral all-purpose cleaner concentrate." (It's even available with a pump-dispenser top.) Then just dilute with water as needed and use.

When using any kind of cleaner, commercial or household, *read the label*. Don't sniff (and for heaven's sake,

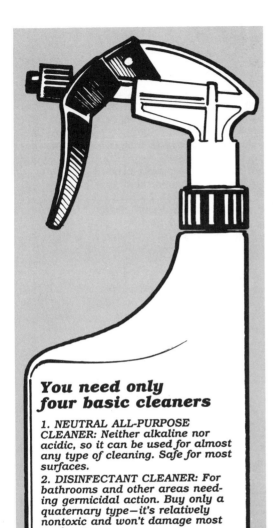

You need only four basic cleaners

1. NEUTRAL ALL-PURPOSE CLEANER: Neither alkaline nor acidic, so it can be used for almost any type of cleaning. Safe for most surfaces.

2. DISINFECTANT CLEANER: For bathrooms and other areas needing germicidal action. Buy only a quaternary type—it's relatively nontoxic and won't damage most surfaces.

3. HEAVY-DUTY CLEANER/ DEGREASER: A high-pH cleaner with good emulsifying action for tough cleaning jobs where grease is a problem.

4. GLASS CLEANER: Usually alcohol or ammonia based, so it evaporates quickly without leaving streaks or residue. For cleaning small windows, polishing mirrors, appliances, tiles, etc.

For most general cleaning purposes and "keep-up" cleaning, use a 1-quart spray bottle. Just add concentrate to water according to directions.

don't taste) to see what's in the jug; a rose will never smell the same if you get a strong whiff from a commercial ammonia bottle. And be sure to properly dilute cleaners. Our tendency is to say, "If a little does a good job, a lot will do better." This is as silly as saying, "If a teaspoon of baking powder will make the biscuits rise, then a cup should do wonders." We often gluggy-glug-glug too much soap into the water and actually destroy the chemical's dirt-suspending and grease-cutting action. Read the directions! Remember, you don't clean alone. You have two helpers, water and chemicals; they'll do most of the work.

"Miracle" solutions and "magic" tools aren't the only carry-over from old wives' tales. Newspaper and magazine household advice columns are everywhere. "Helpful hints" often only add frustration. In a recent "Forty Ways to Save Time in the Home" article, I found only one tip that was unquestionably beneficial. Be discerning, and check sources when you choose housecleaning advice.

You can do without advice like "Drop a couple of rose petals in your vacuum bag so you can deodorize as you clean," or "Color-coordinate all your bathrooms so the towels will match and you'll always be ready for unexpected company." What you need to learn most of all is how to choose and use supplies and materials so as to use fewer hours of your time to have a cleaner home than you've ever had before. Life after housework is life left over for happiness—for family, for friends, for self—and you're entitled to that. In the following chapters, I'll explain how to do this as we cover each major cleaning area in detail.

By the way—did you know that a paste of strawberries, wheat germ, ground glass and baking soda will polish the bottom of a Boy Scout's cooking kit? (But so will a 6¢ scouring pad!)

Professional Equipment & Supplies

ITEM	SIZE/TYPE	USE	SOURCE
CLEANING CLOTH *	Made from 18"x18" piece of cotton terrycloth	Replaces the "rag." Can be used for most cleaning jobs; especially effective in wall- and ceiling-cleaning. Folding and turning inside out provides 16 cleaning surfaces. (See Chapter 14 for details on how to make and use a cleaning cloth.)	Homemade; also available from the Cleaning Center
MASSLINN CLOTH*	11"x17", disposable	For dusting. The specially treated paper "cloth" collects dust instead of scattering it. Leaves soft sheen on furniture, doesn't create buildup.	Janitorial-supply store
LAMBSWOOL DUSTER *	Lambswool or synthetic puff on 24" or 30" handle	Picks up dust by static attraction. Extremely useful for high dusting, picture frames, moldings, blinds, books, cobwebs, houseplants, etc.	Janitorial-supply or housewares store
CELLULOSE SPONGE	Various sizes; 4"x6"x1½" is a handy size.	For any washing or absorbing job. You can cut a sponge to fit your hand. Always squeeze, never wring.	Discount or paint store
SCRUB SPONGE *	Two-layer nylon and cellulose	Use where gentle abrasion is needed; always wet before using. Use the type with a white nylon side on fixtures, sinks, showers, etc. Good in the bathroom and kitchen. The slightly larger scrub sponges with a harsher green nylon side should only be used on nondamageable surfaces—not on enamel, plastic, fiberglass or porcelain.	Discount store or supermarket
SPRAY BOTTLE *	22 oz. or 1 qt. plastic with professional-quality trigger sprayer	To fill with diluted concentrated cleaners for spot cleaning, bathrooms, small windows, or other general cleaning duties. Keep several around the house in convenient locations.	Janitorial-supply or discount store

The cleaning compounds described in this chart and elsewhere in this book are no more dangerous than many preparations found on supermarket shelves. But since most janitorial supplies do not come with child-proof lids, be sure to keep them out of the reach of children.

For your convenience, those items marked * are available by mail. For more information and a free catalog write to: The Cleaning Center, P.O. Box 39-H, Pocatello, ID 83204.

ITEM	SIZE/TYPE	USE	SOURCE
DRY SPONGE*	5″x7″x½″ natural open-cell rubber	(My favorite cleaning tool.) Use on flat-painted walls and ceilings, wallpaper, lampshades, oil paintings. Cleans many surfaces better, faster, and less messily than liquid cleaners. Discard when dirt-saturated.	Paint store or janitorial-supply store
WINDOW SQUEEGEE*	Brass frame, rubber blade. Ettore is a good brand. For the average home window a 10″ or 12″ blade is best; for very large panes, use a 16″ or 18″ blade.	Strictly for window cleaning. Avoid contact with rough surfaces so rubber blade will stay perfectly sharp. For high windows can be used with extension handle (see Optional Professional Equipment Chart).	Janitorial-supply store
DUSTMOP	14″ or 18″ cotton head, rotating handle	For use on all hard floors. Fast and efficient; lasts for years. Use dust treatment (see p. 98) for best results. Shake out and vacuum head regularly; launder when dirt-saturated, then re-treat.	Janitorial-supply store
SPONGE MOP*	10″ or 12″, professional-quality sponge mop with no-stoop, easy-pull wringer and changeable head	For damp-mopping in homes with a small amount of hard flooring.	Janitorial-supply store
LONG-HANDLED FLOOR SCRUBBER*	Long-handled tool with 5″x10″ nylon scrub pad	Also called a Scrubbee Doo or Doodlebug. For effortless scrubbing of hard floors, showers, baseboards, glass, concrete—almost anything. I wouldn't trade mine for a gold-plated floor machine. The holder comes prepacked with pads of three different strengths for light, medium and heavy-duty scrubbing. Dustmop and wax applicator heads also available.	Janitorial-supply store
FLOOR SQUEEGEE*	18″ push-pull. Ettore is a good brand	For floor-cleaning, picking up water, and drying sidewalks and garage floors. Use instead of a slop mop when stripping or refinishing a hard floor. See Chapter 9 for detailed instructions on using a floor squeegee when stripping a floor.	Janitorial-supply store

ITEM	SIZE/TYPE	USE	SOURCE
BOWL SWAB *	Cotton or rayon head on plastic handle	Enables you to use bowl cleaner neatly and safely. Swab is used to force water out of toilet bowl (see p. 150), soaked with bowl cleaner, then swabbed around interior of bowl.	Janitorial-supply store
MATS (indoor and outdoor) *	3′×4′, 3′×5′, or 3′×6′ —nylon or olefin fiber on vinyl or rubber backing for inside or covered exteriors. Use a synthetic grass-type or rough-textured nonperforated mat for outside.	Help keep dust, grit and other debris from being tracked in. Absorb mud and water from foot traffic.	Janitorial-supply store
UPRIGHT VACUUM *	12″ 6 amp commercial beater-brush model with 12″ head. Don't buy half a dozen attachments; get a long cord.	For carpet and rug vacuuming.	Janitorial-supply or vacuum store
WET/DRY VACUUM	10-gallon metal or plastic tank. Be sure you get one with a rust-resistant tank. And get squeegee, upholstery and edge tool attachments with it.	Can be used like a canister vacuum for all household vacuuming, as well as to pick up water when scrubbing floor, to pick up spills and overflows.	Discount, hardware or janitorial-supply store
NEUTRAL ALL-PURPOSE CLEANER *	Concentrate—gallon or packet size	Dilute as directed for mopping, spray-cleaning, cleaning painted surfaces, and all general cleaning where a disinfectant isn't needed. Won't damage household surfaces.	Janitorial-supply store
DISINFECTANT CLEANER *	Quaternary type, concentrate—gallon or packet size	Dilute as directed for use in bathroom-cleaning and wherever else sanitation is essential.	Janitorial-supply store

ITEM	SIZE/ TYPE	USE	SOURCE
*FAST-EVAPORATING GLASS CLEANER** 	Concentrate—gallon or packet size	Dilute as directed to clean mirrors, small windows, appliances, chrome, etc.	Janitorial-supply store
*HEAVY-DUTY CLEANER/ DEGREASER** 	Concentrate—gallon or packet size	For tough cleaning jobs where grease is a problem (vent fans, top of refrigerator, etc.).	Janitorial-supply store
COMMERCIAL WAX REMOVER 	Nonammoniated, 1-gallon size	For removing wax from hard floors.	Janitorial-supply store
*FLOOR FINISH ("WAX")** 	1-gallon size, metal interlock self-polishing	To protect all hard floor surfaces—wood, tile, linoleum, sealed concrete and no-wax floors.	Janitorial-supply store
*OIL SOAP** 	A mild soap often made of vegetable oil	Safely cleans and leaves a soft sheen on wood furniture, paneling, etc.	Discount store or supermarket

Optional Professional Equipment

ITEM	SIZE/ TYPE	USE	SOURCE
EXTENSION HANDLE*	4' to 8' aluminum or fiberglass, rubber handle	Lightweight, easy to use. Extends from 4' to 8' to safely reach high places. Fits squeegees, window washing wands, paint rollers, etc.	Janitorial-supply store
WINDOW WASHING WAND*	10" or 12" aluminum holder with fabric head	Use to apply cleaning solution to windows prior to squeegeeing. Great for high windows and high dusting. Fits extension handle.	Janitorial-supply store
WET MOP*	16 oz. rayon/cotton; Layflat is a good brand. Screw-type handle enables heads to be replaced easily.	For damp-mopping if you have a great deal of hard flooring.	Janitorial-supply store
MOP BUCKET*	18-quart metal or plastic with self-contained roller wringer.	If you wet-mop, the self-contained wringer saves injuries from hand-wringing. Use for mopping or as a punchbowl at a janitor's wedding.	Janitorial-supply store
PUMICE STONE*	Small bar or block of pumice	To remove accumulated hard-water ring in toilet. (Not for use on tubs, bold-colored fixtures or tile.) Always wet before using.	Janitorial-supply store
PHOSPHORIC ACID CLEANER*	Professional-strength (8% or 9%), 1 quart	To remove mineral deposits from tile and fixtures.	Janitorial-supply store

ITEM	SIZE/TYPE	USE	SOURCE
PROFESSIONAL ALL-PURPOSE SCRUB BRUSH	Nylon bristles and handle; also called utility brush	For cleaning textured or indented surfaces without getting your hand wet or scraped.	Janitorial-supply store
CLEANING CADDY	Plastic (pick a bright color so it's easy to keep track of)	The easy way to carry all your supplies with you as you clean from room to room. Use a caddy, too, to keep all you need to clean a particular area (such as the bathroom) right there in the room.	Discount store or janitorial-supply store
ANGLE BROOM ✱	Professional-quality plastic broom such as the Rubbermaid 2021, with split-tip nylon bristles.	For quick cleanups, sweeping small areas, and doing edges and corners before vacuuming or dust-mopping.	Janitorial-supply store
PUSH BROOM ✱	Professional-quality with 18″ or 24″ head, nylon bristles, handle brace	For sweeping sidewalks, driveways and unsealed concrete.	Janitorial-supply store
PET RAKE ✱	12″, crimped nylon bristles	For removing pet hair from furniture, bedding, carpets and clothing.	The Cleaning Center

49

Green clean

In the old days, "white" and "shiny" was what we were all after. Now, with ozone depletion, pollution, litter, algae overgrowth, toxic waste, and too much solid waste of any kind to worry about, keeping things "green" is the battle cry of concerned cleaners. None of us wants to ruin our home planet while cleaning, so strong solvents, acids, and other dangerous chemicals and abrasive cleaning materials are getting pretty unpopular in the social circle of the clean. I agree, the real clean is green, and here are some simple, practical things you can do to help out:

1. Buy good, solid cleaning gear and take care of it

Brooms, squeegees, vacuums, etc., can last twenty-plus years. That means less energy and fewer raw materials used manufacturing, and less worn-out tools being disposed of.

2. Simplify

You don't need fifty different cleaning preparations, scores of cleaning machines and attachments. Reread page 3.

3. Use concentrates

If you get premeasured cleaner concentrates (see page 41), you can bring a year's worth of supplies home in a small sack. Fewer bottles and containers will be left to litter and to bury. Not transporting all that water also saves on shipping and energy costs.

4. Do it right

Skillful cleaning cuts 75 percent or more of the time you spend cleaning, and that means three-quarters, too, of all the lights, heat, water, gas, and other energy consumed cleaning. And it prevents premature wear and destruction of paint, carpet, hard flooring and other household furnishings and surfaces.

5. Use no more than you need

And use the gentlest cleaner that will do the job (see page 55).

6. Take advantage of preventive measures

Use mats, maintenance-free design, sealing, etc. This will cut down the need to redo or to clean at all, saving energy, supplies, packaging, etc.

If we all took just these six steps tomorrow, it would help a lot every day. Remember, you don't have to wait until everyone else does it. Be a leader: think green, and white will take care of itself.

6.

Relax, & work less

A big event was coming to a small town and in preparation, the townspeople resolved to clean the hardwood floor in the village recreation center. They decided to scrub all the dirt and old wax buildup from the floor and apply a new coat of varnish. The committee in charge chose four of the best housecleaners and the building janitor to do the job. It took the group of seven most of a Saturday to finish it. Six hours they labored, spending a total of forty-two hours to get the floor ready for the finish application.

Four years later, after much hard use, the floor again needed attention. I had a free day, and since I enjoy cleaning floors, I volunteered to do the job at no charge. I refused the help of other volunteers and the janitor and instead used my sons, who were twelve and eight years old. We showed up at 10:30 and went home early for lunch at 11:45. The job was completed perfectly in 1¼ hours, or for the three of us 3¾ total hours, much less than the 42 hours used by the group. We used three fewer mops, half the cleaners and strippers, and one-tenth the hot water—and did a much better job.

I'm not any faster a worker than most of you, nor did I have any secret tools. Any of you could have done the same thing, using a valuable principle of cleaning: Relax, and work less. To relate this principle more directly to the domestic front, let's take a glimpse of Betty Betterhouse in action.

It's been an unbelievable morning. In addition to her own seven children, fourteen friends and relatives, caught in a snowstorm, were overnight guests in her home. They consumed dozens of whole-wheat pancakes, eggs, and other breakfast goodies. Two hours later, Betty finally saw her unexpected guests depart and the children off to school. She then turned to restoring her kitchen to livable condition. Drops of batter, jam and grease covering her stove and countertop were now hard and dry. Betty began scrubbing one end of the counter furiously. Finally loosening (or wearing away) the spattered batter in one spot, she'd move on another few inches to grind some more of the droplets away. Fifteen minutes of exhausting effort later, the counter was presentable.

Eliminate— Saturate— Dissolve— Remove

Betty could have saved more than ten minutes and been easier on the countertop surface if she had used the cleaning principle my sons and I used on the floor. You could call it the universal law of cleaning: Eliminate—saturate—dissolve—remove. You can do 75 percent of your cleaning with your head, not your hands—because 75 percent of soil removal is done chemically, not by elbow grease. Scrubbing to clean something went out with beating your clothes on a rock by the riverside.

Betty needs only to sweep all the loose food particles from the countertop (*eliminate*: 15 seconds). She should then soak her dishcloth in soapy water and generously wet the entire area (*saturate*: 15 seconds), giving the liquid a few minutes to soak and loosen the spatters (*dissolve*). Then she merely has to wipe the mushy residue off (*remove*). Just a few minutes for the entire job.

Of course, many of us have been doing this for years, not only on our countertops, but on appliances, floors, walls, sinks, tubs, shower stalls, automobiles, and four hundred other places that might have used Betty's old time-consuming system. Hard soap crust on the bathroom sink where the hand soap sits can take several minutes of scrubbing, but if it were sprayed or dampened first, it could be wiped off in seconds. Almost everything will clean *itself* with water and the right chemical. Water is practically free and with a few cents' worth of chemicals it can replace hours of your time if used according to the principle outlined above. It's incredibly easy to apply the right solution and wait.

Leave. Read. Rest!

Apply more solution in another area, or do anything you want while the solution's chemical action loosens and suspends the dirt. Unless you get your kicks out of scrubbing, there's not much reason to scrape and grind soil off.

The basic principles of cleaning

Cleaning should be done with your head, not your hands ... in *four basic steps*:

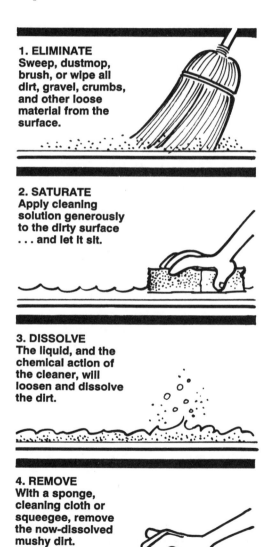

1. ELIMINATE
Sweep, dustmop, brush, or wipe all dirt, gravel, crumbs, and other loose material from the surface.

2. SATURATE
Apply cleaning solution generously to the dirty surface ... and let it sit.

3. DISSOLVE
The liquid, and the chemical action of the cleaner, will loosen and dissolve the dirt.

4. REMOVE
With a sponge, cleaning cloth or squeegee, remove the now-dissolved mushy dirt.

I've watched people try to clean the grease and dust settled on top of their fridge. They wipe the cleaning solution on—and before it has time to break the gunk down and release it from the surface, they start scrubbing furiously. Let the solution do the work! By using the simple principle of eliminate—saturate—dissolve—remove in all cleaning, you can cut time and energy expenditure as much as we cut the floor job for the town recreation center.

On your house floors, for example, remove the large, obvious objects (forks, overshoes, yoyos, dog bones), then spread the solution on as large an area as you can handle before it dries out. As you're finishing at one end of the room, the solution you first laid down is working actively on the dirt, old wax, spots, stains, and marks. When you return to the first area and begin to mop, wipe, or lightly rub it clean, the area you just left is now under heavy attack by the liquid, and most of the cleaning will have been accomplished by the time you get there with the mop.

When we cleaned the big floor in 1¼ hours we spent almost no time scrubbing. We spread the cleaning solution and I ran over the surface with a floor machine (I could also have used a hand floor scrubber—see the Equipment Chart, chapter five). I didn't try to grind or scrub the floor clean—I covered it quickly to loosen the surface dirt so the chemical solution could do the work. By the time I reached the far end of the room, the solution spread on the first part had dissolved and suspended the dirty old wax. The next pass over the same area caused every drop of dirt and wax to come off. We immediately squeegeed the floor and picked up the gunk with a plain old dustpan and put it in a bucket. (This eliminated the need for a "slop mop.") The floor squeegeed (see Equipment Chart, chapter five) clean, then only needed to be mopped with clear water. One mop bucket did the whole floor!

Abrasion evasion

Using powdered cleansers and steel wool to grind dirt off surfaces has become a ritual with too many homemakers. With the same generosity they use to apply powder to the baby's rump, they coat their sinks with cleansing powder and attack them with brisk rubbing. You can actually hear the results as the grinding abrasion quickly removes stains and spots—along with the chrome or porcelain on the unit. The cleanser then has to be flushed off. Some of it will set like concrete in the gooseneck of the sink drain, on the floor, and on the fixtures. The light scum that remains on the sink or tub has to be rubbed and polished off, again wearing away the surface. The damage is gradual but inevitable. On fiberglass or plastic sinks, tubs and other fixtures, the damage isn't even that gradual. Fiberglass isn't as tough as the old porcelain and

enameled iron. It damages easily and, once damaged, is a pain to clean.

Even more important, you lose time cleaning by the abrasion method. You should be relaxing to the cleaning principle *eliminate—saturate—dissolve—remove*. It really works. Discipline yourself to use it, and you'll reward yourself with two hours of free time out of the four hours you once wasted grinding and scrubbing away!

Beware of buildup!

In cases where all the dirt and wax won't quite come off and scrubbing seems called for, it's generally your own fault—by failing to perform good, regular cleaning, you've allowed a thick layer of wax and dirt to build up. Buildups of various kinds are the greatest obstacle to simple cleaning; they're best exemplified by the old villain hard water. Look at the brand-new sparkling tile in your shower, or your exterior windows. They're going to get hard water on them from use, accident or irrigation. Residue starts with an innocent thing called a drop. A drop doesn't seem much of a bother, because if unmolested, it will evaporate away.

At least it will *appear* to leave. A closer examination reveals that each drop has something called mineral salts, which slide to the bottom of the drop as it evaporates. Though the drop appears to have vanished, a slight deposit of mineral salts remains. Beginning so insignificantly and unseen, it's ignored. Again water is splashed on the surface, new drops form in the place occupied by previous drops, and leave their mineral marks to unite with the existing residue. Six months, sixty showers, or twenty sprinklings later, that innocent first drop has become hard-water buildup. If kept clean daily, or in many cases even weekly, it's a two-minute instead of a twenty-minute job. If done annually or "when I get around to it," it's a surface-dam-aging, chemical-squandering experience that greatly embitters one's attitude toward sanitation.

Less is best

When faced with a cleaning problem, always try to solve it with the gentlest cleaning solution or approach first. Don't call in a backhoe when a shovel will do. Aggressive cleaning methods may be necessary for very difficult situations, but they can also injure or destroy household furnishings and surfaces. As a cleaning product salesperson once put it, "Only get as tough on a stain as the stain demands." If rinsing with water will remove a stain, why start bleaching it? Don't reach for the heavy-duty cleaner till you've tried the all-purpose cleaner first. Don't scrub when you could soak. Don't scrape with a knife or razor till you've tried your fingernail first. Don't resort to a metal pot scrubber till first a white, then green nylon pad proves powerless. Less is best!

Grease removal

Removing grease is something we're especially interested in after our hands start sticking to the stovetop or the cupboard doors. Grease buildup occurs inside and out, as dirt is trapped and glued to things by airborne oils from cooking, heating, smoking, candles, auto emissions, etc. You'll have a real struggle cleaning greasy things if you don't use the right solution. Grease is acid, so a cleaner from the opposite end of the pH scale—alkaline—is what's needed to dissolve it.

This is why ammonia—which has a high pH—works. The more alkaline a cleaner, the more grease-cutting power it has. A lot of heavy-duty cleaners on the market are designed to dissolve grease, and janitorial-supply stores sell "degreasers."

I attack grease in two ways:

1. *For light degreasing*—Fill a spray bottle with a solution of heavy-duty cleaner. Spray it on and let it sit longer than usual. Give the surfactants in there time to loosen, dissolve and suspend the grease film. Then wipe dry with a cleaning cloth (see page 161).

2. *For heavy degreasing*—Fill a bucket half full of degreaser solution. Use a white-backed scrub sponge to apply a generous coat of the solution (not so much that it drips and runs) to the surface and let it sit on there as long as you can. Then scrub, rinse and wipe dry to a luster with a cleaning cloth. If necessary, repeat the process.

When you do have to scrub

The right scrubbing tool is the key. If you're cleaning something with deep crevices and textures, then a stiff nylon brush will reach in and dig out the dirt. The kind you want will have a handle to keep your knuckles unscraped and your hands out of the dirt and chemicals. See the Equipment Chart, chapter five, for the type pro cleaners use. For most other surfaces nothing beats nylon scrub pads. They have just the right degree of rub to remove rebellious residue, and they have more total contact with the surface than a brush does. The white nylon type can be used safely on most household surfaces—just don't scrub too hard or too long on soft finishes such as plastic or latex paint. Use the more aggressive green nylon pads to

remove more stubborn spots and deposits on nondelicate surfaces. The brown or black pads are too harsh for anything but wax-stripping, concrete-cleaning, etc.

Always keep any surface you scrub wet. This aids the action and reduces the chance of damage and scratching. Add more solution when you need to so the surface doesn't dry while you work. If you use a brush, remember that brushes don't hold cleaning solution—you have to pour or spray the solution on first. Rinse the surface occasionally while you work, especially if it's textured or indented, to check on your progress and remove loosened soil. (See page 65 for the right direction in which to scrub.)

Don't bear down on a brush when you use it—that actually lessens the cleaning action. You don't believe me? Go get a brush out of the cabinet, any brush, and scrub lightly, daintily, with just a wee bit of pressure. Notice the points of the bristles are really massaging the heck out of things, loosening the soil and working the soap and solution in, around and under it. Now press "eight axe handles hard" and notice how the brush flattens. Now when you go back and forth, the cleaning ends of the brush aren't doing a thing—the only part of the brush hitting the surface is the sides of the bristles, which are smooth as a bundle of eels. When you add in the slipperiness of soap, that "cleaning action" isn't even tickling the surface!

I had a bristle brush under a 150-pound floor machine once, and my cleaning instructor told me to stick my hand under the edge of the brush. I thought it would rip my finger off, but the sides of the bristles gliding over my fingers were so smooth and slippery they didn't even clean my fingernails. Likewise, notice the next time you sweep a floor how a light stroke allows the bottoms of the bristles (where all the work is done) to contact the floor so they don't miss a sesame seed. Just as light taps of a hammer are usually more effective than a full hard swing, so it is with cleaning.

Keep your working stuff near you!

I've heard claims that a homemaker walks eight to fifteen miles a day doing housework. I wouldn't doubt it. I used to walk one mile per room until I learned to keep my cleaning tools within reach. Too many peo-ple place their tools and buckets in a central "cleaning station" in the room and constantly walk three, four, even five or six steps back and forth during a project. They spend half of their time and energy traveling.

If you need the exercise, continue to use a central cleaning station. If you want to get the job done and have energy left for a tennis game or bowling or other personal sporting around, figure out how to keep your tools (sponges, buckets, cloths, screwdriver, etc.) within your reach. (For example, if you wash cupboards, set your tools on the counter instead of on the floor. Same with painting.) If you hang the bucket on the ladder or hold it in your hand, it will save the bend and dip all the way to the floor and back up. Try it—you'll be amazed at the time and effort you save!

To keep your tools rounded up and ready at all times, to pick up and use and then put back away, a little plastic cleaning caddy or "maid basket" (kind of like a miniature janitor's cart) is hard to beat. Cleaning aprons sound good on paper but they don't make much sense unless you clean steadily for several hours or so. They also make it hard to bend over, and you bump the walls as you work. I keep a caddy in every area that needs frequent cleaning, filled with whatever is needed to clean that area. Buy a bright color so you can see it easily and don't stumble over it or have to search for it.

7.

More professional secrets (for you ... at home)

Since I wrote the first edition of this book in 1981, I've constantly been asked—on radio and TV and at my seminars and in letters—for more "secrets of the pros"; more things we professionals do that make a big difference in the time cleaning takes and in the quality of the results. So here are some more ways to make your cleaning life easier.

Outsmarting interruptions

It's the same old frustrating story: you get right in the middle of something (and have a good head of steam) and someone knocks on the door, the phone rings, the kids start to shriek, you run out of supplies, something breaks, you run across something that you have to stop and deal with or handle. You might call them *interruptions*; I call them housework's number one enemy. Interruptions occur in every activity, but housework has such a humble status, people will deem you not really occupied and think nothing of asking you to stop at their convenience. Life just won't go on hold while we clean. I, too, have literally hundreds of interruptions and demands for immediate attention every day—nearly as many as the average mom—during my work time. If I yield to them all, just like you I'll suffer a mortal efficiency loss, besides being discouraged—if not driven to the rubber room. Here are three things you can do to control interruptions:

1. Wield your mop at unpopular times!

Early, late, on holidays, during lunch—the times when everyone else is sleeping, playing or eating. It's exactly like traffic time. You can go during the most popular to and from times (rush hours)

and count on losing an hour to interruptions (stops and slowdowns)—or go a bit earlier or later or by a little different route and cover the same miles in fifteen minutes. I can write or clean more from 5:00 to 8:00 a.m. than all the rest of the day put together, because there are no interruptions. Society, business, friends, relatives and even kids close down at times. Find those times, grab the bucket and run with it.

2. Clean in short bursts

Cleaning doesn't have to be one long session or giant project. Some of the most efficient cleaning is done in short bursts, which add up to a lot of things done. Fifteen-minute time fragments are much harder to interrupt than a four-hour block of time that you've set aside. Even the busiest of us have small pieces of time available every day, and what are you doing with them now? If you just take advantage of the five-, ten-, and fifteen-minute time fragments that fall your way every day, you may never have to spend all Saturday cleaning again. Take advantage of those TV

commercials, phone calls that leave your hands free, waiting time, etc.

3. Don't yield!

Simply say no. Most interruptions aren't mandatory, like so many of us think. The phone, for example: When it rings, most people run to get it as if they were possessed. Yet most of us haven't had more than one or two true emergency calls in our whole lives. One of my college professors used to say, "My life and home isn't open to any fool with a dime." (Make that a quarter now.) When I'm right in the middle of pouring cement, or up on a ladder painting, and someone comes by or calls, stopping would be a real problem, so I don't. Or if I'm on a job where stopping and then reassembling everything would double the work, I just keep on going. "But Don, it's Ms. Eclair from *Toothpaste Today*" (like God calling). Well, if she were in the middle of writing an editorial, I wouldn't expect her to break her concentration and drop everything to talk to me. So I'll call her back.

Let me share a little secret about interruptions with you: Once you refuse to lay your life and time out at will to family, friends and passing salespeople, they'll begin to adjust their timetables and curb their impositions on you. *You* are the one who sets the mood for the amount of meddling in your schedule. *You* can control it. I'm not saying to force them to make an appointment with you for everything, I'm saying demand appreciation of the value of your time—it works.

When is the best time to clean?

As we all grow more and more aware of time (and ever more short of it, it seems), this is a query I often hear.

Finding the time to clean in a world busy with "better" things to do *is* a big question, especially since cleaning doesn't usually top our morning list of "exciting things to do today." When I started looking at when I clean and at others who seemed to have the cleaning problem licked, I noticed that none of us clean in prime time. A lot of us can't, because we work outside the home during what we think of as "prime time"—but *not* cleaning during prime time is my philosophy anyway.

When we feel good and are really rolling on some other project, stopping to clean means stopping to do something someone else is just going to mess up again, anyway. It produces a certain resentment in us all. When you have momentum elsewhere, that's just not the time to stop and spit-polish a house, even if things are dirty and you've scheduled it, because you'll hate every minute of it.

I don't and won't clean during my prime time. Cleaning isn't hard, nor does it require maximum physical or mental powers—so when body and spirit are in a lull or at loose ends, when I'm not doing much anyway, that's when I jump in and clean.

It's stimulating, exercising, and best of all, I know I'm not squandering my most precious time to do it. So it's almost like getting free time.

If you clean when you're running out of energy you'll find that cleaning gives you a mental second wind and even a physical boost; it can actually be a way of recharging yourself.

And since cleaning doesn't take your full attention, you can do other things while you clean that refresh your mind and spirit, so you almost get "double duty" out of the time. For instance:

1. Note and create

I carry a pad and pencil in my pocket and jot down ideas, impressions, things I suddenly see or understand while shoveling away at clutter and dirt. Some of our best thoughts and inspirations come during half-attention times, and cleaning is certainly one of those. I've often written more creative things in half an hour of cleaning than in half a day at the typewriter with a 200,000 word thesaurus by my side.

2. Rhapsodize

You can listen to music, and then you can *listen* to music — truly hear and savor it. When most of us listen to music our minds are too occupied to pay much attention. When you clean, music can really raise the goosebumps, because cleaning doesn't take concentration and it really benefits from a rhythm backup. I wouldn't be surprised if the Lord ordained cleaning just for the purpose of allowing us a way of appreciating music to the max.

3. Teach the family

How many honest opportunities are left in the world to teach children the basic principles of cooperation and responsibility? Fifty years ago most of the world was agricultural, and parents were with their children all day, week after week, sharing chores. Today about 5 percent of us are down on the farm, and the rest of us hunt and strain to find experiences and challenges to share with our family. Cleaning is one of the few things left. You can formally sit down a fourteen-year-old and lecture about the value of self-esteem and discipline . . . or visit and converse while you clean together. You tell me which will have more impact. Busy hands always beat a moving mouth in getting a message across.

4. Daydream

I have to credit daydreaming with many of my greatest accomplishments. It's not just soothing, it's a source of endless ideas. When you're operating a machine at the construction site, typing ninety words a minute, or doing anything that takes your full attention — including driving — daydreaming is an inefficient if not dangerous thing to do. But with cleaning, you've done it all before — you know how to handle the vacuum, the squeegee, the sponge — so you can click into your "wouldn't this be a great world if" mode as you sail through the soap scum.

5. Focus on the rewards

Whenever I'm assigned to something, before I launch into it, I think first and only of the end result, the rewards after the project is finished. When I start on a room, deciding how and with what to clean it is just reflex; how neat and inviting it'll look when I'm through is what I really focus on. All during the cleaning process I concentrate on the end result. Even those stove rings that are so slow to surrender the burned-on crud, I imagine them as the shining halos they'll be when I'm done, and it makes the work something I actually *want* to do. Weird, maybe, but it works! Remember, all the rewards don't come from life's fun and play activities; most of them in fact come from the tough and responsible ones.

> **A few more rewards for us cleaners:** *Satisfaction* — that you used your skill and the result was good. *Pride* — it sits there looking great and you know *you* did it. *Relief* — it's finally done and you won't have to do it again for a while!

What can I do with the kids when I clean?

Living out West where the average family size seems to be sixteen, this is a question I hear constantly. There had to be a few cleaning problems I haven't solved, and this is one. You can't put off cleaning until the kids are in college. You learn to clean around their schedule—as long as you have to. The baby will boggle you, the teens try you, the grandkids grind down all thought of ever conquering cleaning with kids. But kids actually mold some of the world's best cleaners, giving them eternal surprises and only fragments of time to handle them in. Here are a few ways to lengthen your leash:

- Most of the principles of interruption prevention (see pages 58-60) will work with kids, especially the off-hours approach. When they're down or on nap idle, watch how quickly and cheerfully (and quietly) we clean!

- Shift the overseeing of the younger set to your mate for the occasion:

"One of us does the floors and one of us does the kids ... Which will it be, Wilbur?"

- Send the kids to the neighbors to play. (You can return the favor later in the week when they're trying to clean.)

- Hire a babysitter for a few hours a couple of days a week, or make arrangements with a nearby preschool. Or you might just decide to spend the money on a housekeeper (see page 72). Grandparents are great at watching kids while you clean (and they don't mind feeling genuinely needed either).

- When you *don't* have the kids, do as much "cleaning as you go" as you can. Clean the shower while you shower, the tub as the water goes down the drain, etc.

- A very young child, as long as he's not wet or hungry, should be happy to watch you sweep or fold laundry for a while from a portable baby seat, cradle, playpen or baby "corral" set on the floor nearby — especially if you keep up a lively dialogue or have on some peppy music. There are also nice portable battery-powered baby swings.

- Set up a play area in a basement or other room. Promise a special reward if the kids remain in the area until you're done. (Use a kitchen timer to let them see how much time remains.)

- Certain carefully chosen light chores (such as dusting with a lambswool duster or spot-cleaning) can be done with baby nestled in a carrier across your chest. Baby backpacks leave your hands freer, but they're less safe since you can't see what's going on back there.

- There's always TV, that awful time-eater that converts intelligent offspring to bug-eyed brats. To gain a little time for cleaning, it is slightly better than tranquilizing them. Go for a good, long video.

- Let them help! Even after raising six of our own and leading Scout troops and church youth groups numbering into the hundreds, I continue to be amazed at how much work a kid can do. By the age of eight — the official age of accountability — they can do almost anything as well as adults. And you tell me something better to do with kids while cleaning . . . than having them help clean!

When they're really little, you can buy them their own toy cleaning supplies: vacuum, broom, dustpan, etc., and let them pretend while you do the real thing. During the toddler years,

take some of the cleaning activities and make a game of them. Low dusting, as we call it in my business, is ideal for toddlers. Give them a dustcloth or lambswool duster and have them compete with you to reach a finish point. Three- and four-year-olds delight in vacuuming with small hand-held vacuums, and are especially handy for going after those crumbs under the kitchen table. Toddlers also like to shop. Let them use a wagon or a toy shopping cart to "police" — what we pros call picking up the clutter in the area before you vacuum.

Try to stick with sessions of no more than ten minutes so you hold their interest, and keep the games fresh so they don't get bored. Give a prize or a treat when the game is finished. Just bear in mind that cleaning with the kids is a healthy activity for them, but it can be a little aggravating for the "supervisor." When you work with kids, be sure to allow extra time for "training," and reconcile yourself to the fact that they're not going to do things the same way you would.

Yes, you could probably do a better job in half the time, but what you teach them outweighs the little extra effort you have to put into it.

As kids get older, they can help a lot more and even do major jobs themselves.

No sweat . . . and little strain

The wonderful thing about watching professionals perform is that they always make what they do seem effortless. Just remember, when you see pro window cleaners squeegeeing an acre of glass at a stretch, they do that every day and you don't. Try to imitate it, and you can quickly get sore and even injured. How can you keep cleaning casualties at a minimum?

1. Get help

Few of us get hurt doing regular housework. It's that "spring" cleaning campaign, the once-a-year effort and strain, that has the greatest possibility of leaving you with an ache or pain. It's always that giant reach or heavy lift that we justify by saying to ourselves, "It's only this once." That's all it takes. When is anything large or cumbersome moved upstairs or down, for example, without smashed fingers, chipped finishes or grazed walls? An object doesn't have to be super-heavy—"awkward" is enough to put undue strain on the spine, and back injuries are the number one cause of claims in the cleaning industry. After years of seeing even professional cleaners get hurt in such situations I have one directive that I know and live by: Get help. Even the macho man or aerobically fit woman needs help sometimes. Two people reduce the weight and risk by half, and three is even better. Help speeds things up, too.

2. Reduce bending and reaching

"Never trust a maid with clean knees," they used to say. That was probably true in Great-grandma's day, but today if you get your knees dirty cleaning, you aren't doing it right. Bending is tiring and gets old faster than we do. Minimizing bending and reaching is the secret of fast, tireless cleaning. So ask, "How can I put a handle on this?" of every cleaning operation you come across.

Use a long-handled floor scrubber (see Equipment Chart, chapter five) for all those chores you used to do on hands and knees. You can also use a long-handled floor scrubber to scrub things like shower walls, grimy outside windows and house siding.

Extension poles (see page 92) make high reaches a cinch and keep your feet on the ground. Extension poles can be used on lambswool dusters and paint rollers as well as squeegees. And they can be used to extend your reach down as well as up.

Another way to reduce reaching is to get a taller ladder or have someone hold the ladder and hand things to you.

3. Lift the right way

When lifting (light things, too) up from the floor, lift with your legs. Let yourself down to the level of the object with your leg muscles, rather than bending over it with your back. After you have a good grip, use your leg muscles to lift you and it back up.

4. Use the right-sized tools

Forget about oversized buckets, for example. You won't be able to lift them when they're full, and you'll slop, spill and strain yourself trying. If you clean with my two-bucket system (see page 165) you won't need more than two

quarts of cleaning solution, anyway.

In all your cleaning tools, get the right size. Ever try hiking in a shoe that doesn't fit? That's about where you are with a tool that's too big or too little for the job at hand. Buy not only buckets but sponges, handles, vacuums, etc., to fit you and your cleaning chores. Or adjust or whittle them to fit if you have to.

What's the best direction to clean?

- Top to bottom. When you dust, start at the top and work down, and the same when you wash walls.

- North and south, east and west. When you scrub anything, you want to go in four directions—first north and south, then east and west. That's because almost everything, even seemingly flat surfaces such as concrete or vinyl, has a grain or texture, even if you might need a magnifying glass to see it. When you scrub in circles, you really only clean and massage one side. When you scrub back and forth, you only get two sides. When you go in all four directions you agitate all the sides of the area and loosen the dirt more quickly and effectively. And you're far less likely to miss places. The carpet-cleaning people taught me this, and once I put it into practice, boy, did it make a difference in all kinds of cleaning.

- Back to front. If you clean a room from back to front (toward the door), you save steps because you walk through the room just once and then work your way back out. If you clean in the other direction, you walk through the room at least twice and probably more.

- Clockwise. Clockwise is another efficient approach, but some people may work better moving around a room toward their left, so for them counterclockwise may be best. This is a matter of taste, but the important thing is to start in one direction and keep going that way.

Switch-hitting

You probably know what this means. Most people are either right- or left-handed and do most or all of their work from that side, but some "switch-hitting" batters can swing from either side (so they can instantly adjust to either a right- or left-handed pitcher). Switch-hitting gives you an edge in cleaning, too. Once you're

really rolling on something, the longer you can keep it up, the better off you are. Once you pick up the duster, dust it all. Once the broom is in your hand, sweep it all. You get in a kind of rhythm this way, and it's a lot faster than stopping and restarting forty times in one afternoon. So when one arm gets tired, switch to the other and don't stop. It'll be awkward at first, but if you can learn to do it you can pick up hours in a day of work.

"Holidays" or misses

In six years as a high school and college athlete, there's one move I never mastered: the "squint stretch" over a newly waxed floor to see if I missed a place. After the applicator is rinsed and hung to dry, the wax bottle put away, and all the furniture back in place, finding a flat or dull spot on the floor can ruin the whole job, as well as your ego. These misses with mops, paint rollers, brushes or wax applicators are what the professionals call "holidays." How do we avoid them? Simply by crossing the area twice for total coverage and then once more for security. Whether cleaning, painting or waxing, pass over every surface a minimum of three times. Do this and your work will never go on holiday. The extra passes take half the time it takes to crane your neck enough to spot all the misses you'll make in a fast single pass.

Give yourself a janitor closet

Even the best cleaning supplies won't do much good if you can't find them when you need them. Since most homes don't have a janitor closet or any respectable space for cleaning materials, you need to engineer your own storage space. First, about 70 percent of the cleaning stuff under your sink is only used once a year, if then. De-junk this antique collection down to the things you really use. Then get a plastic cleaning caddy. Put what you need for the sink area in it, and if you don't have small children you can even leave it under the sink. When it's time to clean you can just snatch the caddy out, set it on the counter and clean from it. That way you won't set acid or corrosive cleaners on household surfaces and leave rings and burns. Keep a similar caddy of supplies anywhere else you clean frequently.

For the big stuff—brooms, mops, buckets, squeegees, the vacuum and its attachments—pre-empt a closet, perhaps near the kitchen, and even if you have to remove shelves to do it, make yourself a cleaning center. Suspend all you can off the floor; hang brooms, mops and brushes by their handles on nice, sturdy hooks (so they get enough air circulation to dry fast and won't warp out of shape). Be sure you hang a treated dustmop, too. If you lean it against the wall or leave it flat on the floor the oil will wick out and may leave a stain. Keep cleaning chemicals on an eye-level shelf (safely out of youngsters' reach) with the labels turned toward you. Keep dangerous cleaning chemicals, insect spray and even plastic bags on one or two high shelves. Use wire racks or bins if you have room to mount anything; they allow air circulation so stored cloths and sponges can dry. I generally clean my scrub pads and squeegee and drop them into the bucket I'll use them with, so they're easy to find and all ready to carry off to the cleaning site.

Don't allow any squatters here. Is your rug shampooer seldom used? Then store it neatly in the garage.

Dress for success

Shoes

You don't want any high heels or sandals when cleaning, and *never* go barefoot. You're on your feet a lot when you clean, so wear shoes or boots with good support and traction tread. (And to live to clean another day, go for rubber soles when working on wet floors.) Athletic shoes are excellent because they're light, yet sure-footed. Trying to clean in those old, tired slippers will fatigue you fast and greatly increase your chance of tripping and slipping. Besides, you'll feel lean and mean moving around the house in your Reeboks.

Clothes

I've heard of people cleaning in the altogether, but it only gives new meaning to the term "buffing." Besides, it gets drafty when you take out the trash. You don't have to clean in your aerobics outfit, but I do recommend that you wear loose, comfortable clothing such as a sweatsuit. It's tough to stretch and bend in tight jeans or a miniskirt. I always like to wear a long-sleeved shirt and leave the shirt tails out when I clean. This saves your arms from scratches and burns, and any dead spiders that fall will end up on the floor, not in your pants. (P.S. If you look neat and attractive while you clean, you'll feel better about it.)

Rubber gloves

Are a cleaner's best friend—use them when you need to. They protect your skin from harsh chemicals, protect your nails, and keep your hands out of yucky, germy messes. Long contact with even mild chemicals can dry out your hands, and some of the more toxic ones will not merely irritate or burn your skin but be absorbed right through it. (Get the good latex gloves with a comfortable flocked lining. I use one size bigger than my hand size for easy on and off.)

Safety glasses

Were invented to protect you from splashes of acids or strong alkaline chemicals, especially if you're working above your head. If in doubt, don't go without—it's not worth the chance of losing your eyesight. (And no, regular glasses aren't just as good.)

Cleaning you can ignore

Remember, as a kid, when someone did you "dirt," you snubbed them, made believe you didn't know they were there? We all did it, and it was a bad thing to do to people. But it's not at all a bad approach to some of our cleaning chores. Lots of us clean innocent things that don't really need it. Many times I've been led through a home to look at a tub, floor or fixture that won't come clean, and I've been amazed. The thing would have lasted thirty years, but it was on the way out after only ten, because. . .

"Ma'm, you've cleaned it to death, actually worn it out cleaning it up!" We all know an Annie Septic or Sam Overshine who does this. You could call it overkill, and plenty of us do it because we feel guilty if we don't clean things regularly.

Yet our outdoors is largely paved today, so we don't track in half the mud, gravel, dirt and straw they did in Grandpa's day. Modern homes with better weather stripping, carpeted floors and entryways, and fewer cracks and holes around windows and doors let in less dirt and dust. Soot and smoke from heating was a big problem thirty years ago, too, and it's almost eliminated today.

When I was in college, my cleaning crew and I often had five homes a day to clean. We had faithful clients who always called us for their annual big cleaning—washing down every wall and ceiling, shampooing all the carpet, cleaning all the windows, even painting. As their children grew up and left home, the housekeeping load was lighter, but out of habit they'd still call us to do "spring cleaning" that could have gone undone. Sometimes my cleaning water would be clear as a glass of 7-Up after cleaning three rooms! "We can't find any dirt," I'd tell the owners. And they'd say, "But Don, it's been a year. . ."

The following are a few tasks you could trim back on, and relieve yourself both of cleaning effort and a guilty conscience:

1. Windows

Glass is a nondepreciable material. No matter how dirty it gets, it doesn't rot or get ruined. If you have to let it go a little while, it won't hurt a thing—just give you a little visual pain (no pun intended). Besides, as long as you're not confronted with it close-up (it's not the top of the coffee table), even dirty glass gives the illusion of clean.

2. Vacuuming

An important procedure, to be sure, but only regularly necessary in the traffic patterns. Lint under furniture and on the edges of the carpet doesn't hurt a thing, so the rest of the carpet can be done semimonthly or even less. Meanwhile, a hand vac can catch those few dustballs or cookie crumbs.

3. Closets

Need to be *de-junked* a lot, but when it comes to actual *cleaning* (walls, floors, ceilings)—closets just don't get dirty. You might want to clean the closets once when you're moving into an older home, but then forget them for at least the next decade.

4. Ceilings

People seem to clean the ceiling every time they do the walls, which is really overkill. Ceilings just don't get the same fingerprints and bumps that walls do, so leave them till about every third or fourth time. If a heat register mars a section of a ceiling just clean the buildup around the vent—don't feel like you have to do the whole thing.

5. Pits

We all own something with a pitted or indented surface (generally a floor), and it drives us crazy trying to get it really clean. This is a flaw in the design, not in your cleaning prowess, so don't let it get you down. If the dirt doesn't lift out or dissolve away with one or two passes of a scrub brush, then leave it and call it shading. No one will know. When the dirt fills in to the top of the pits, just call it a "design correction." (You can also alleviate the problem by filling the pits with clean wax.)

6. Silverware

I've never understood this one. People polish silverware and put it up, just so they can take it out and polish it again. When they're busy feeding their faces, most people won't notice whether it's stainless steel or sterling, anyway.

7. Carpet shampooing

My wife and I went ten years in our new house without shampooing the carpet, and I own hundreds of commercial carpet shampooers, some right on the premises. The carpet continued to look good though we had seventy and eighty kids over for church socials, two hundred employees for picnics, and fifteen grandkids dragging pet goats, muddy boots and old deer hides. Commercial matting inside and out at every entrance and regular vacuuming of traffic areas will do a lot to delay the need for shampooing. You have to judge when to do it, but don't shampoo every year just because that's the schedule. Your home may only need it every two or three years.

8. Cobwebs

These aren't the ultimate index of housework neglect—they can appear overnight. You could argue that they actually aid cleaning by trapping dust and airborne grease along with the bugs. A daily cobweb safari isn't necessary, and if guests are freaked out by a fresh one, be sure to thank them for spotting it for you.

9. Absentee maid service

(For when you're gone.) Yes, there are those so clean-conscious they have a maid service come in once a week, all four weeks they're away on vacation! Why bother? A waste of money, cleaning supplies, electricity and gas.

10. Inside the cupboards

Most of us could get by honorably for ten or twenty years just wiping out the bottom of the shelves. But I see lots of people empty the entire cupboard every year to wash or paint . . . it's nonsense.

11. Towel washing

You can use a towel for a week before it's actually dirty (remember, you only *dry* yourself with towels, after you're already clean). Who needs four towels per person per week, including one so big you drag it on the floor trying to dry yourself? Why not save lots of water and washing time?

12. Bathrooms

Okay, we may go potty in there, but bathrooms are actually one of the most sanitary places in a home. Ninety percent of a bathroom is hard surfaces such as tile, porcelain and metal, which don't absorb dirt. And when we're in there, we're usually washing ourselves. If you don't clean the bathroom daily you won't disgrace yourself or endanger your family.

13. Interior chrome and stainless steel

These are usually water spotted, not dirty. It's nice to have gleaming chrome, but your guests would probably rather focus on you than the coffee table frame. As for trying to keep chrome faucets unspotted—why try to create the impression they're never used?

14. Brass and copper

Can either be left to develop a handsome natural patina, or laboriously detarnished every couple of months so that they can develop a new coat of tarnish that will have to be removed again. Which makes more sense?

15. Furniture polishing

No, you don't have to pour or blast on a puddle of polish every week—or even every month. Applying too much oil or wax to furniture may look good briefly, but it creates a sticky, gummy mess in the end.

16. Drying dishes

Guess what—letting them drip-dry in the drainer isn't just easier, it's more hygienic.

If it hasn't been used and it isn't dirty, don't clean it just because it's there. I'm not asking you to relax your cleaning standards, just to examine them. What, in the name of life and love, is of more value—germ-fighting or heart-lighting? Cleaning for the sake of cleaning is silly and unnecessary; cleaning to make things sparkle instead of just have a healthy glow is generally a waste of time and effort.

Gang-cleaning

Sounds like a street rumble, but it's the term we pro cleaners use to describe cleaning as a team instead of by one oppressed cleaner alone. For example, we had an eight-story building to clean once, and each floor took one person eight hours. So we had eight cleaners every night for eight hours, one on each floor, which also

meant the lights on each floor were on for eight hours as everyone worked alone, solely responsible for "his" or "her" area. Then we tried putting all eight people on one floor: one getting rid of the trash, one dusting, one doing desks, one doing bathrooms, two vacuuming, one straightening up, etc. Suddenly we did the whole building in six hours, and the lights were only on one floor at a time, which won us an official award of recognition for the phenomenal savings in energy this meant throughout the whole company. Plus, in the "gang" there was less piddling around and no foot-dragging—the team members motivated and disciplined each other. We humans are social animals, so naturally we enjoy performing in groups more than (pardon the pun) alone in a vacuum.

When more than one person cleans at once, it has the spirit of a team effort. It's easier to take because the total time that each person needs to spend on chores is a lot shorter. Team-cleaning is faster, more fun, less boring, and it even makes de-dirting a social experience. Like many of you, I like to work alone, but you can't really ignore the old adage that many hands make light work. They do, espe-

cially in cleaning. Once everyone knows you're all in this together, some bright spirit will set the pace and watch everyone try to match it!

If you have a gang around, you probably have a megamess. So see if you can organize them for even one hour of group-cleaning. You'll see results, not just arguments about whose turn it is to clean and whose it isn't. And best of all, the work gets done *quickly*.

To clean well as a team, you need a good coach or manager to set things up, just as in any other team sport. In your home *you* get to be the coach (even if it is a working coach). Everyone doesn't just grab a cloth or sponge and start cleaning. Assign specific duties to each person on the team. Each of you takes a different job in the same location: One does windows while another dusts and spot cleans, or one is inside the window and the other is out (you know *that* already, but I bring it up to tell you not to argue over whose side that last little spot or streak is on—it isn't worth a lost workmate ... or a marriage).

When it's time to do a really thorough vacuuming, one person can move the furniture out and back. Or when you do high cleaning, have someone at the foot of the ladder hand things up, saving the cleaner many trips up and down. When you wash walls or paint, it really speeds things up to have an extra pair of hands to help move heavy furniture, remove and replace decorations, go get the tool you forgot, and change water and towels when your hands are in the grime or paint.

After all the tasks are divvied up, the gang starts in on the target area and everyone completes assignments as swiftly as possible. Then the coach makes a quick inspection to ensure quality before everyone moves on.

The secret of successful gang-cleaning is a little bit of planning before you begin. Just as in a football play, everyone has a job to do, a time to do it, and a way to move to get it done. Here's the plan for the living room: Huddle with your two preteen kids. "Okay guys, here's the play. We're going to hit the living room. We'll start at the right of the door as we go in. Hank, you take this sack and pick up all the trash. Work to your left around the room till you get back to the door. Then place the trash bag outside the door. I'll move in after Hank and do the high dusting with this lambswool duster and work my way around the room hitting cobwebs, the top of the bookshelves, lamps, high corners, the top of the valances, and anything else above six feet. Lisa, you follow me, doing the flat surfaces with this treated dust cloth, hitting everything below six feet, including around the legs of furniture and chairs. Hank, as soon as you're done trashing, go back in and help Lisa dust, but you start on the left side of the door and work your way back until you and Lisa meet. I'll follow you guys with a vacuum and by the time you're finished, I should be close behind. I'll make sure we didn't miss anything while you go on and start the dining room. Any questions? Remember, we want to move fast but get the job done well. We've got the #1 team in town, so let's get going."

Gang-cleaning makes people feel as if they're accomplishing something. If you make it a game and even a little bit of a competition, they'll hardly notice they're cleaning. This isn't magic, of course. You still may meet resistance. But when you work right along with the team, it helps a lot to motivate them.

Remember, this doesn't have to be done on a nice, fat, valuable Saturday morning. Forty-five minutes with a gang some evening can clean any house so it'll never need to be touched on a weekend.

Call in a pro

When things get out of hand, when you're in over your head, when there's just too much on the agenda—get help. That's what the professionals do, and they're never ashamed to do it. There are more than one hundred thousand cleaning companies and maid services in the United States. Even where there isn't an official licensed cleaning firm, there are dependable individuals who clean house on a regular basis (which many people in fact prefer over "big company" service).

What kind of professional help?

Just as housework is often more than whisking up a bit of dust and adjusting an off-center lamp, so is there a difference in the types of professional people you can hire. Many maid services are essentially a sort of skim service. They often won't do any of the real housework, like cleaning outside windows, ovens or carpets, washing walls, or stripping and waxing floors. They may do these "big jobs" for a special hourly rate, but usually they just scoot in and dust, vacuum, make beds, straighten, touch up— and go.

Maid services charge by the house or by the visit. Should you use a franchised service or an independent? Independents have both more to gain and more to lose by pleasing or not pleasing you. Think about what the services offered will be worth to you, not only in terms of cost but in terms of time freed for other things. How many hours of help, how many times a week or a month, does your household need to prevent minor chores from backing up?

Hire a maid service on a trial basis to begin with. You might have to go through a few to get the maid you like and trust, but give it a while and you'll find someone reliable who works at a reasonable rate. When you find somebody good, talk to him or her about returning weekly, monthly or whatever. You need service you can count on, and if those you hire know they'll be getting regular work, they can give you a better price.

A professional cleaner (as opposed to a maid service) is the heavy-duty dude. These are the people equipped to do the big jobs calling for big, heavy equipment. Call pro cleaners when you have a big, one-time or seasonal job.

Picking a real pro

You're the only one who can decide when and if you need or want a professional to do your cleaning. But the cleaning business has a high turnover and failure rate. When you decide to go outside, how do you make sure you pick the right professional? Here are some guidelines from someone who knows the business inside out:

● *Don't just believe all the claims on the brochure*

Get and check references. Sure, they'll always give their best, but some are better than none. Remember that you'll probably use this person or outfit for years. They'll be in your house and around your children and valuables often when you're gone, so taking the time to check them out with a few phone calls or letters is well worth it—just as if you were picking a doctor for surgery. Finding out who your well-satisfied friends or neighbors use to do their cleaning can save you some detective work.

● *Ask how long they've been in business*

Anyone who's been around less than a couple of years would make me nervous. If someone lasts in this business over three years, they're generally worth a try.

● *Get a bid*

Anyone who knows the business knows what a given job involves and can give you a bid—not merely an estimate, but an actual price. Have them spell out what they will do, when, and how much it will cost. If someone says they won't, can't, or don't know, they won't get a foot in my house to experiment. Most real professionals have a form that fits all of this and a place for them, you or both to sign. Get it in writing, and hold them to it.

● *Never,* never *pay in advance*

Only 6 percent of a cleaning job is material, so paying in advance is neither necessary nor wise.

● *Get proof of insurance*

We never feel we should have to worry about such things, but an accident that happens on your premises to someone without professional insurance can easily end up your problem. This is one reason you contract work, so the pro will furnish the skill, the muscles and the tools, and assume the liabilities. The cleaners you want will not only be insured but bonded. Remember, however, that even if they do have insurance it doesn't protect the contents of your home. If they ruin a couch cleaning it, they're not insured for workmanship, generally just liability—another reason to choose wisely the people who will be within your walls.

● *Find out who will come on the job*

It's seldom the sharp, clean-cut person who gives the bid. Too often the ones who show up are surly, fresh recruits who can barely read house numbers, and you have to train them. Once a contractor knows you expect and demand the best, that's generally what you'll get.

8. Prevention: keeping the enemy out

What do we do with the dirt on the farm?

It flies from the road and comes straight from the barn.

It pours through the windows and tracks on the floors.

We give up and just plant our garden indoors.

—Marilyn May

Mats: a must

A new hospital, nestled in a valley with one of the world's most famous ski resorts, had been in operation for two years when its housekeeping personnel retired. Replacements were needed and a professional cleaning service was contracted. Following careful measurement of the space, occupancy and conditions, and after interviews with the retiring staff members, it was concluded that twelve hours of work was required each night to clean the offices, public area, entrances and medical administrative wing. When signing the contract, the owner of the janitorial company made one explicit request: both entrances to the hospital were to be covered with vinyl-backed nylon mats running at least fifteen feet inside both entrances. There had been no mats before, because it was thought they might detract from the hospital's alpine beauty. The hospital's administrator agreed to order the doormats that day.

The cleaning company began its service and was spending twelve hours plus a few extra daily to keep the place up to standard. They wet-mopped nightly, used six treated dust-control cloths on the floor, and had to scrub some areas every week with their floor machines. Anticipating the difference the new mats would make, the cleaning company owner had the sweeping and vacuuming crew keep track of residue collected from the floors throughout the building. Each night a gallon can was half-filled with gravel, sand, thread, pine needles, and every other thing common to a resort area. Three weeks later, the mats arrived and were installed at both entrances.

The first night the mats were in place, the hours of work dropped to ten, and the sweeping residue was reduced to half a quart of gum wrappers, toothpicks, etc. After one week, the new mats reduced the cleaning to nine hours per night. The dust cloths were reduced from six to two, wet-mopping was reduced to twice a week, and dusting to every other night. Cleaning supplies were cut more than 50 percent. The mats cost $240 and were paid for in less than one week in labor and cleaning supplies saved. The hospital noted that fewer people slipped and fell at the entrances, and the mats lasted for four years!

Proper matting alone can save the average household approximately 200 hours of work a year, slow down structural depreciation, and save more than $100 in cleaning supplies. The cost of matting for the average home is about $120. But the 200 hours is big savings for you. That's thirty minutes a day cut from your chore time.

The reasons for such savings are easy to understand if you simply ask yourself, "What is it that I clean out of my house, off my rugs and hard floors, off the walls, off the furniture, etc.?" Dust and dirt are the obvious answers. Where does it come from? Almost 100 percent of it comes from the outside. How does it get inside? Eighty percent of it is *transported* in (the rest leaks through cracks, is airborne or originates inside). The average five-person home accumulates forty pounds of dust a year—dust

Mats protect your house.

75

composed of everything from air pollution particles and topsoil to dead insects and pet dander. Most dirt or residue is carried into the home via clothes and feet.

Professionals estimate that it costs $600 a pound to remove dirt once it's inside. It costs *you* even more in time:

1. You shampoo carpets because of that dirt embedded in them.

2. You strip and wax the floor because of that dirt embedded in it.

3. You change furnace and air conditioner filters more often and dust, dust, dust because of that dirt circulating in the air.

4. You wash clothes more often because of that dirt.

5. Your cleaning equipment and supplies are used up and wear out faster because of that dirt.

Proper matting will:

1. Keep your house cleaner.

2. Reduce the need for shampooing, waxing and washing.

3. Absorb sound.

4. Enhance safety.

5. Improve appearance.

All this saves you both time and money. It takes one piece of equipment and a few minutes to get dirt out of a mat. It takes ten pieces of equipment and hours to get it out of your home!

Where is your carpet the dirtiest? At the entrance, on about a three-by-four-foot square where the matting should be. It's only logical—if dirt doesn't get in, you won't have to round it up. As a person criticizing mats once said, "Bah! I hate doormats—all they are is dirt catchers!" I rest my case.

Taking advantage of good matting is the smartest, easiest and least expensive thing you can do to cut your housecleaning time. It's easier to vacuum or shake out a mat daily than it is to chase dirt all over the house. Look at the hospital. The distributed dirt and debris were reduced from one-half gallon to one pint. Mats will perform a great service in your home. Don't take my word for it—try it! You'll cry over the lost years of labor

Avoid using leftover carpet squares.

Don't use clothbacks.

Get rid of link or perforated mats.

How to mat an entrance

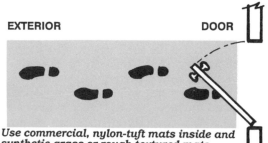

EXTERIOR　　　　　**DOOR**　　**INTERIOR**

Use commercial, nylon-tuft mats inside and synthetic-grass or rough textured mats outside. These mats are available in a wide range of colors and can be obtained in rolls or in pre-cut sizes at a janitorial-supply house. For best results, the mats should be long enough to allow four steps on each.

and money you've wasted by not getting adequate mats sooner. Instead of scrubbing your floor weekly, you could end up doing it annually. (I've even had one commercial building go *five years*, and the floor finish still looked good.)

If you have good matting, all the fine gravel, grit and dirt that hangs on the bottoms of shoes and scratches and soils things will be out of action. Waxed floors last a long time when they aren't abused by grit. Next time you go into an office building, notice the difference in the floor on the lower level as compared to the upper-level floors. Even if the traffic is the same, the upper ones will last twice as long and look twice as good because the grit doesn't get to them. Traffic doesn't hurt a floor much—it's the abrasiveness of dirt that creates havoc. Keep it out of your home, and you'll keep yourself out of the crouching, scrubbing position. Now, that's the sensible way to clean house—not to have to do it in the first place!

Here are some matting pointers that will advance your goal of gaining thirty "free" minutes a day.

Some mats to sidestep

Avoid decorative mats. We all love to see our name in print—even on a worthless rubber doormat. Get rid of it! It isn't doing much good, and the time it takes to clean around it is probably greater than the cleaning time it saves. Link mats (the kind made from little slices of old car tires wired together) are ineffective for most homes and extremely dangerous for wearers of high heels. Coco mats are more trouble than they're worth because they don't absorb well and they shed. Have you ever tried to clean a coco mat? That alone should convince you not to buy one!

For outside the house, the synthetic-grass-type mats or any rough-textured nonperforated mat with a rubber back is good. These won't rot, they're easy to clean, and they'll knock the big stuff off the shoes or boots of the person coming into your home. Try to get one at least five feet long to cover three or four steps. The exact type of exterior mat to buy depends on the space available, overhead cover (awning or porch), your home and landscaping style, and how bad thievery is in the neighborhood.

On the inside

The first thing to do is get rid of any carpet samples or scraps you're using for "throw rugs." These items are, indeed, appropriately named. The jute backing and curling edges throw their users into the hospital. They're unsafe, unattractive and, more to the point, inefficient. Get rid of them!

77

To maintain mats:

Keep them vacuumed.

When they're dirty, hose them down, apply neutral all-purpose cleaner solution, scrub a bit, and hose them again.

Squeegee off excess water with a floor squeegee or old window squeegee.

Hang mats to dry. Never use them when the back is wet.

At any janitorial-supply store, you can buy commercial grade, vinyl- or rubber-backed nylon mats. This type of mat for inside areas helps to reduce falls and trap loose dirt—the same dirt you'd be cleaning from everything in the house. They are efficient, will last up to fifteen years, and are available in a wide variety of colors. They come in widths of three, four

or six feet, and in any length. The nylon creates a static charge that actually helps pull particles from your shoes and clothes. The mats will absorb mud and water from foot traffic and hold it in their roots. They won't show dirt easily and can be vacuumed like any other carpet.

Some mats will creep a little on some surfaces, and a "rug hugger" type with a textured back can be purchased if you get tired of retrieving the carpet. Or you can get polyester "sticky pads" from a hardware or janitorial-supply store to keep your present mats from creeping or bunching.

An often-forgotten area in our homes that should also be well matted is the garage entrance. Plenty of sawdust, oil stains and project residue get tracked into the house from the garage. Fine silt, sand and gravel often get caught up in the snow that lodges under a car and falls loose on the garage floor. When it melts, the sand and grit are carried into the house by foot. Concrete dust and garage-type soils and dirt are abrasive to carpet and waxed floors.

Apartments, condominiums and motor homes need to be matted, too. The slightly smaller amount of dirt and debris that might get to the eighth floor of a modern apartment building is multiplied by the fact that it's gritty city dirt that has a smaller area over which to distribute itself—hence the soiling and damage to the dwelling can be as acute as in a large, dust-surrounded farmhouse.

A three-by-five-foot mat is an excellent all-purpose size. It's wide

> It takes one piece of equipment and a few minutes to get dirt out of a mat. It takes ten pieces of equipment and hours to get it out of your home.

enough to cover an average doorway, long enough to cover four entrance steps, and light enough to handle and to clean. An extra three-by-twelve-foot runner can be rolled up and kept for remodeling, parties or wet weather. This extra mat will be a good investment if your traffic, lifestyle and location merit it. It would be an especially good idea for a newly built home, since it's common for a family to move in before the landscaping is completed. The several months of working on the yard generates a lot of mud, and the resulting damage is often unnoticed because the house is new.

Not only will you save thirty minutes a day when you install adequate matting, but your doorways and entrances will be better looking, quieter and safer. Get mats before you start to clean, and you won't have to start as soon or work as long.

Other preventive measures

Now that you have your mats lying in wait for all that creeping dirt, you ought to set up a few more culprit catchers for the things that cause housework. Remember again, the idea isn't to get faster, bigger or better tools to beat the dirtiers. The first principle of cleaning is not to have to do it in the first place....

Cure litter

Make it a hard-and-fast rule in your home that everyone picks up his or her own litter and is responsible for personal belongings. And make it relatively simple for everyone to abide by the rule. Provide waste containers for *every* room in the

The trouble with cleaning up litter is that when you're finished you're right where you should have been before you started!

house, and outside where the kids play. Empty the containers frequently, before the contents become attractive to germs, insects and larger animals.

Make sure there are shelves, drawers, racks, hooks and toy boxes enough for everyone to put away belongings quickly and easily. If there's a place to put it, chances are 60 percent better that it'll end up where it ought to (rather than on the couch, the bed, the floor, the stairs).

Prepare

Putting a cover over or under anything that needs protection when you clean, paint, etc., will save all kinds of unnecessary cleaning. We're always tempted to skip this little step and we always pay for it later—with a lot of extra work, if not with ruined objects. So get out those tarps, dropcloths or old newspapers and use them.

Get it out of the dirt zone

What's up and out of the way won't have to be cleaned, and that's the name of the prevention game. So make sure all your unused but needed stuff is hung or cupboarded out of the way of daily traffic that will soil and abuse it.

> **Wrinkles: a condition of creased, crinkled and crumpled that we get with age, and our possessions get when not folded or hung carefully. A little prevention can save a lot of ironing.**

Animals

There's no getting around the fact that house animals create housework and cause damage, but you can minimize it. My choice, depending on the animal and where you live, is to keep it outside, but that's not always possible. If you do have an indoor/outdoor pet, consider installing a pet door so it can come in and go out at will. This saves wear and tear on the people door if your pet's a scratch-at-the-door type (and it saves you from being the animal's door person).

Both cats and dogs should be brushed regularly and their claws trimmed. Your vet can show you how to do this. Dogs should be bathed as soon as they start smelling "doggy." An inexpensive pet rake will be a big help in coping with shedding hair (see Equipment Chart, chapter five).

Vacuum pet hair off upholstered furniture. Better yet, keep animals off furniture, or designate one chair that's theirs, and keep a throw cover over it that you can wash easily.

Build your cat a good scratching post. Make sure it's tall enough for the cat to stretch full length, and weight the base so the cat can't tip it over. If you cover it with carpeting, use the loopy kind that will engage the cat's claws. But a harsh, scratchy surface like woven sisal, or even highly textured fabric like burlap, is better than carpeting of any kind.

Use a disinfectant cleaner when you clean up after animals.

Pet problems can often be traced to problems with the training process. It's important to spend as much time training your pets as you do loving them. This will reduce pet accidents to a minimum. After you train your pets, make sure that you're trained, too. If you're too tired to change that litter box or take your dogs out to relieve themselves, then you have to take the credit for the puddle on your carpet. Pets try to please you. But when they can't wait any longer, it happens. Pets demand responsibility. Don't allow your pets (and your household furnishings) to suffer for lack of it.

Mildew

Mildew looks bad and can be damaging, but it isn't really a cleaning problem. Mildew is a fungus that thrives on moisture and temperatures between 75° and 85° F. There are five ways to prevent or retard mildew growth:

1. Never put anything away wet (laundry, camping gear, etc.).

2. Well-lighted areas don't agree with mildew. Light prevents its growth and can even kill it.

3. Proper ventilation helps prevent mildew spore growth.

4. Cleaning all mildew-prone areas with a disinfectant solution will slow down or stop growth.

5. Put packets of silica gel in small, enclosed, chronically mildewed places (drawers, shoes). The gel can absorb moisture and minimize mildew growth. Reusable bags of calcium chloride (such as De-Moist) are available for larger areas such as damp rooms or basements.

Cigarette mess

One of the most effective preventive measures you can take is to eliminate smoking from your home. In commercial buildings almost 30 percent of cleaning costs stem from smoking residue, waste and damage.

All of us pay a small fortune for the smoking habit—it costs taxpayers millions of dollars daily. Smoking also causes a high percentage of fatal and damaging fires, and can make many jobs unsafe.

Smoke dirties the windows, yellows the light fixtures (so you don't get all the light you pay for), soils and ruins the acoustical tile of the ceiling, smells up the upholstery, and burns and damages the carpet and floor. Eyes water, lungs fill with smoke, clothes and hair are saturated offensively. Who would consider taking out a miniature incinerator and burning paper, leaves, and trash whenever they got the urge? But that's what a smoker does.

In trying to correct the problem, we designate special smoking areas, make better filters, bigger ashtrays, better vents and room deodorizers, better gargles and tooth polishes, develop lung transplants, etc. But this is like building a bigger drawer, closet, or garage when the others get full: The problem is still there, doing damage, it's just contained.

The simplest, cheapest, most effective approach is to de-junk the habit; then the problem will be cut off at the source.

Keep up

Finally, remember: Dirt by the inch is a cinch; by the yard, it's hard.

Don't get buried alive—clean as you go. Who wants to finish an overhaul, a paint job, or any project and have to clean the entire mess at the end? Clean and put everything back as soon as you finish using it. If you let it all pile up for a big cleaning spree, it's emotional and physical suicide.

And *don't clean things that aren't dirty.* (See "Cleaning You Can Ignore" on pages 68-69.) You can go months without doing windows and vacuuming in certain places. Too many people think they have a moral obligation to do it "every day" or "once a week" or "once a month."

You clean to prevent unhealthiness, ugliness, and depreciation. If a little dirt or dust causes none of these, darned if I'm going to flounder around with a broom and a bucket.

Design away cleaning

Cleaning faster and better isn't the only way to reduce the time and expense of cleaning and maintaining a home. How about designing it away?

You've said it, you've thought it, you've seen it. When you were working on or with something and stopped to say: "Who designed this? It's twice as hard to clean or fix this way. If it had been better/simpler I could have serviced it in minutes instead of the hours it's taking now." The women who have done most of the cleaning for so long have thought of many design ideas that would eliminate or ease some hard cleaning chores. However, men, who do little cleaning, have done most of the building, and so for centuries the same hard-to-clean, -reach, -lift and -move things are built into our homes. Maintenance-freeing design has long been needed, but is only now coming into its own. We'd all like to make things easier to care for, and the logical place to start is the place we spend so much time: our home.

"But my house is already built, so I can't have a maintenance-free home!" *Wrong!* About three-quarters of the possible time-saving changes you can make are in what we professionals call rollover items, like paint, carpeting, furniture, drapes, fixtures, appliances and decorations. In five to ten years these often need replacing anyway, so why not do it with something much easier to clean? It's a sneaky, brilliant, fun way to solve cleaning problems and get rid of the time (and agony) they take.

The more I heard women say "Why do they build things like _____?" the more intrigued I was by the subject of designing to reduce cleaning. So I asked my audiences to share their thoughts on this, and all kinds of bright ideas came rolling in on the best way of all to save cleaning time: Design It Away!

When my collection of material on this subject grew to three-box size and my daughter was working her way through school designing kitchens, we realized there was enough there for a book. After several more years of research and investigation, we assembled

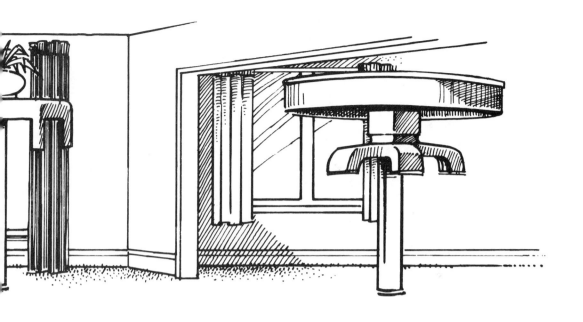

all of this material into a nice volume called *Make Your House Do the Housework*, which Book-of-the-Month Club members and tens of thousands of other people have been using to inspire them in their remodeling, redecorating and new home building. In *Make Your House Do the Housework* (check at your local bookstore), there are hundreds of good ideas for cutting cleaning through low-maintenance design. You'll learn about the wisdom of approaches like camouflage, built-in, wall-hung, better arrangement, artful elimination, and choosing the smart surface, material and color. The thrill and beauty of it all is that when you change even one single thing to reduce its maintenance requirements, those savings in time and effort are repeated day after day, multiplying even one little improvement into thousands of hours (and a lot of cleaning supplies) saved, and a lot of safety risks avoided, too.

Start thinking about it seriously and your blood will boil with anticipation. Design is one sure way to cut cleaning out of your life!

FLOOR CLEANING | PLAN I

HYDRAULIC LIFT FURNITURE

COMPRESSOR AND TANK

Check ✓ *before you clean it*

Fix those items that always slow you up and cause you to do everything more than once (or actually *add* to your cleaning chores).

Some things aren't worth doing. Some *can't* be cleaned. Others will look tacky even when they're clean and orderly. Taking care of these items first will not only make cleaning and maintenance easier, but will make you feel better (which makes everything easier). Eliminate or remove anything that bugs you—that's inconvenient, no longer functional, or that you just don't like. *Remember*: The first principle of efficient cleaning is not to have to do it in the first place. Check these things before you start:

☐ **Be sure you have plenty of convenient, roomy litter receptacles. You'll do less cleaning and picking up.**

☐ **Be sure you have enough towel racks.**

☐ **Be sure all closets have an adequate supply of hangers.**

☐ **Eliminate furniture you don't use or need. It has no value and magnifies your cleaning chores.**

☐ **Eliminate excess playthings (child or adult). Unused tennis racquets, snowmobiles, motorbikes, TV games that have fallen from favor, old hobby supplies, puzzles with "only one piece missing."**

☐ **Get anything that can be wall-mounted off the floor. It'll make cleaning a lot easier and will curb accumulation. (And eye-level things are easier to see and safer to use.)**

☐ **See that your cooking exhaust is vented.**

☐ Stop all dirt and air leakage into the house around windows and doors, etc. Cracks in the foundation, too, let dust and moisture into the house, causing damage and additional cleaning time.

☐ Make sure your vacuum works perfectly.

☐ Seal all concrete floors for easy maintenance.

☐ Paint or seal (varnish) all surfaces that can't be easily dusted, washed or cleaned.

☐ Repair/replace all damaged surfaces. Paint, patch or panel so they can be easily maintained.

☐ Alter any physical surface or appearance you don't like. Paint it, sand it, cover it or give it away.

☐ See that drawer hardware is tight and that drawers slide easily.

☐ Make sure that all doors close tightly and easily. A light sanding and two coats of polyurethane or varnish will make wooden doors bright and easily cleanable, and doortops smooth and easily dusted.

☐ Be sure that all windows slide and lock easily—and seal any cracks.

☐ Repair every leaky or dripping fixture.

☐ Fix or tighten all clotheslines, stair railings, etc. Check all the hardware around the house. Remember, a 50¢ screw or bolt can save a $5 hinge ... a $50 door ... a $500 robbery ... a $5,000 fire!

☐ Replace burnt-out light bulbs and tighten any parts of light fixtures that need tightening.

☐ Get rid of shin and head bumpers (such as sharp edges or protruding legs) on woodwork, furniture, or anything that bashes you every time you pass by or straighten up.

☐ Adjust every shelf to the height you really want and need.

9.

Don't be caught streaking windows

The dreaded task: At my house-cleaning seminars I always spring the question, "How many of you like to clean windows?" This is always good for a chorus of groans from everyone present. Occasionally, about two out of every thousand will raise an eager hand indicating that they, indeed, do enjoy cleaning windows. (Further investigation reveals why: Both have maids to do the job!) That leaves almost 100 percent of homemakers who hate window cleaning.

The reason is simple. After hours of laboriously polishing windows, you think, "At last. I'm finished!" But hope is dashed when the sun comes up or changes angle. Streaks and smears suddenly appear out of nowhere, magnified for all to see. You again give the window the old college try—and the smears and streaks only change places. Re-arming yourself with more window cleaner, rags and gritty determination, you work even harder and faster to get the windows clean, but they seem only to get worse.

Night falls, and so does the curtain, on a crestfallen and discouraged

worker. The next morning you go downtown and eye the fifty-story solid glass buildings, the huge storefront display windows, and mumble, "That glass is beautiful . . . but I never see anyone cleaning it. How do they keep it so clean?"

The reason we seldom see window cleaners isn't because those windows don't need to be done—most commercial windows have to be cleaned more often than house windows. But professional window cleaners only take minutes, not hours, to do their job. Homemakers can be just as effective on their own windows if they learn the basic techniques used by professionals.

The first move toward successful window cleaning is to rid your storage cabinet of all the "glass gleam" garbage you've been trying to make work for years. The main reason your windows streak and seem to get worse is the oily, soapy gunk (including homemade concoctions) you smear on them. Pounds of it have been put on, and only part of it wipes off. Gradually you've built up a layer of transparent waxy material that you spread around

every time you try to clean the window. It not only creates an impossible cleaning situation, it also primes the glass surface to hold dust, bug spots and airborne particles. The result is windows that have to be cleaned more often.

Take heart. It hasn't been your fault all these years. Even the chief window washers for New York City's tallest all-glass buildings couldn't get windows clean without streaks if all they used was the stuff sold to most of the public.

The right way

To recover all those lost polishing hours, let's learn to do windows professionally. Go down to the janitorial-supply store and buy a professional-quality brass or stainless steel squeegee (see Equipment Chart, chapter

Spraying and rubbing are self-defeating — as you can see as soon as the sun comes up or changes direction.

five). Ettore brand is the best! Don't go to the local supermarket or discount house and buy those recycled-truck-tire war clubs they call squeegees. These won't work well even in a professional's hands.

There are even tilt squeegees available now that are only slightly more expensive than a standard squeegee. They have a handle that enables you to tilt the blade so you can clean several windows from a single spot (you don't have to stand directly in front of each window to clean it). I saw a man stand on his front porch with one and clean all of the upper and lower story windows without changing location!

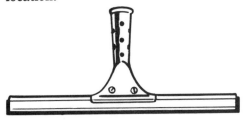

Go to a janitorial-supply store and buy a professional-quality squeegee. Make sure the rubber blade extends ⅛" beyond the frame at both ends, and keep the blade undamaged — don't do anything but clean windows with it.

Pick up some window-cleaning solution, which can be either ammonia, or ordinary liquid dish detergent. Both will work well if you use them sparingly; resist the tendency to add too

Six steps to sparkling windows

1. Put a capful of ammonia or a few drops of dish detergent in a bucket of warm water. There is always a tendency to add too much soap or detergent — this is what causes streaks and leaves residue.

2. Wet the window lightly with the solution, using a clean sponge, soft-bristle brush or window washing wand. You don't need to flood it. You're cleaning it, not baptizing it! If the window is really dirty or has years of "miracle" gunk buildup, go over the moistened area again.

much chemical or detergent to the solution—this causes streaks and leaves residue. One capful of ammonia or four or five drops of dish detergent is plenty for each bucket of warm water.

Before starting to squeegee, I always take a damp cloth and run it around the entire outside edge of the window. This removes the cobwebs and debris that collect around windows, so

3. Wipe the dry rubber blade of your squeegee with a damp cloth or chamois. A dry blade on any dry glass surface will "peep-a-peep" along and skip places.

5. Remember all those drips that came running down from the top of your clean window when you tried squeegeeing once before? Well, by squeegeeing across the top first, you've removed that potential stream. Place the squeegee horizontally in the dry area . . .

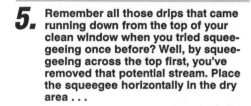
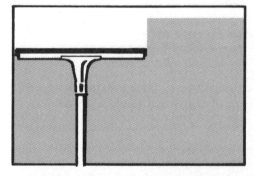

4. Next, tilt the squeegee at an angle to the glass so that only about an inch of the rubber blade presses lightly against the top of the window glass (not the window frame or the house shingles). Then pull the squeegee across the window horizontally. This will leave about a one-inch dry strip across the top of the window.

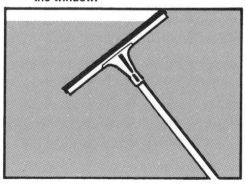

6. . . . and pull down, lapping over into the dry, clean area each time to prevent any water from running into it. Wipe the blade with a damp cloth or chamois after each stroke. Finish with a horizontal stroke across the bottom to remove the water puddled there.

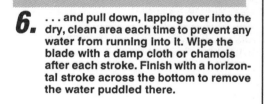
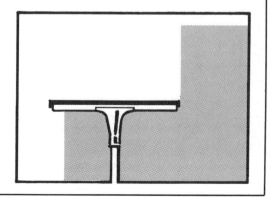

they won't end up on the window itself during cleaning.

A window can be cleaned from either side or from the top using this technique. Always be sure first to squeegee off that top inch of the glass to eliminate potential dripping. Wipe off the bottom of the window sill with your damp cloth when you're finished.

Never wash windows in direct sunlight if you can possibly avoid it. The solution will dry too fast and streak the glass. If you have to clean in bright sunlight, be extra sure not to put too much cleaner in the water, and squeegee *fast!*

How to get rid of those last spots

After completing a window, you undoubtedly will detect a tiny drop or squeegee mark or two and a little moisture on the edges of the glass near the frame. Your old tendency was to snatch a dry cloth and with a fingertip under it wipe off the edge. I can assure you this will leave a finger-wide mark right down that edge. Once you notice that, the temptation will be to wipe it again, this time with a bundled cloth. Then you'll have a four-inch mark and will have to reclean the whole window.

After squeegeeing the window, just

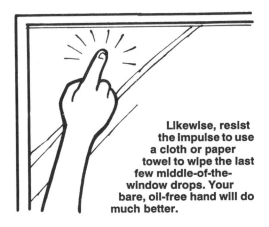

Likewise, resist the impulse to use a cloth or paper towel to wipe the last few middle-of-the-window drops. Your bare, oil-free hand will do much better.

leave those little beads of side moisture. They'll disappear and you'll never see them. Your friends won't, either, unless they bring their opera glasses with them.

As for middle-of-the-window drops or tiny squeegee lines, do not use a cloth. (*Law:* There is no such thing as a lint-free or mark-free cloth in window cleaning.) Because you've been working in the solution, your bare hand will be oil-free, and you can use a dry finger to wipe marks away without leaving a blemish.

The squeegee method really is as easy as it sounds. It's three to five times faster than the old way. It will use only a penny or two worth of cleaner and leave your windows pure and clean to repel particles and dirt.

It's worth the effort to work on your squeegee technique for a while, since it will be awkward at first. And all of that accumulated gunk might take a little extra effort to remove. Once you catch on, you'll love it and wish you had more windows to do.

Learning to clean windows quickly and effectively will change your outlook on life. You'll cherish the cute little handprints, enjoy watching frustrated insects slip off the glass, and even tolerate the sweet birdies who occasionally befoul your windows.

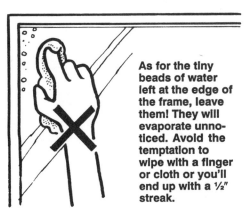

As for the tiny beads of water left at the edge of the frame, leave them! They will evaporate unnoticed. Avoid the temptation to wipe with a finger or cloth or you'll end up with a ½" streak.

Problem areas

Squeegees will work on any normal household window (but not on textured or stained glass, for instance), and they come in sizes to fit the task at hand. Squeegees can also be cut with a hacksaw to custom-fit small panes if you so desire. Pull the rubber blade out of the channel before cutting, and then cut the rubber about one-quarter inch longer than the remodeled blade (so it will extend one-eighth inch at each end).

Close quarters cleaning

There are times and places in small, confined areas where a spray bottle of fast-evaporating glass cleaner is more efficient to use (small panes, handprints on glass entrance doors, decorative doors and windows, etc.). You can obtain an inexpensive solution of this type in concentrated form from a janitorial-supply store, dilute it with water, spray it lightly on soiled glass, then buff it dry with a cotton cloth or a "hard" (read "cheap") paper towel (the soft, expensive ones leave lint like crazy). *Don't* use newspaper. Only slight sheens and streaks are left when you clean this way, and they're seldom noticeable in such small areas.

My advice regarding tiny little windows is to let them go as long as possible, because the optical illusion created by the small surfaces hides marks, specks and smudges. When they do need cleaning, depending on their size, use either a squeegee or a spray bottle filled with glass cleaner.

If you're not too particular, I'd just brush off the outside, hose them down to rinse them, and call it good. I don't think any window in a home is worth hours of work. Big windows show dirt and streaks more readily than small panes, which look more "romantic" when they're a bit hazy.

Mirrors

Once people get enthused about a squeegee, they want to use it on everything, even mirrors. *Don't!* Notice some mirrors have black circles under their eyes (black edges)? This means too much moisture was used cleaning it and the moisture dripped, leached, or otherwise worked its way to the edge of the mirror. When the cleaning solution hit the silver on the back, the chemicals oxidized it. In fact, you shouldn't even spray a mirror (or TV or computer face) with a spray bottle because of possible renegade moisture. Instead, spray into a soft cloth and then wipe. For mirrors, too, a glass cleaner is best. It's fast, inexpensive and safe (as long as you keep it off the edges!).

For no-smudge mirrors, use full-length downstrokes when you wipe. Then with a final swipe across the bottom, eliminate that start-and-stop line.

Plexiglas windows

Plexiglas should have been called plexiplastic because it doesn't clean like glass at all. Solvents can eat right through it, and anything slightly abrasive (including ordinary dust) will scratch, cloud and mar it. So "soft" is the word—soft cleaner, soft cloth, soft touch. There are special Plexiglas cleaning solutions that help clean and clear it—don't use anything else!

Don't attempt to wipe—or squeegee—Plexiglas before you rinse it well with water to remove any particles; otherwise, they will catch underneath your cleaning cloth or squeegee blade and scratch the surface. And if you squeegee, keep your blade extra clean and make sure the window *stays* wet the whole time you work on it.

Thermal windows

Many of the thermal or double-pane windows will fog up when cold, so if the streaks don't come out, check: They're probably on the inside. You can't clean them; 95 percent of the time if you want this kind of streak gone it means a new window!

Cleaning outside windows

As a precleaning precaution, look at the window carefully before whipping out your fine cleaning tools. Often the window, frame and sill are plastered with bird droppings, mud, hornet nests, and spider webs complete with dried flies. If so, give it a quick hose-down first to flush it off. It only takes a minute and makes the final cleaning neater and safer for your squeegee blade.

If you have to clean glass outside on a below-freezing day, mix your cleaning solution 50-50 with some "antifreeze"—isopropyl or denatured alcohol.

For dead bugs and other debris lying in the bottom of a sliding window channel, spray generously with neutral all-purpose cleaner and let it sit for five minutes, till it all turns soft. Then wrap a cleaning cloth around a screwdriver blade, insert it in the track, and run it up and down to dislodge and absorb the dirt. Repeat until the channel is polished clean. It sounds primitive, but it's the fastest and best method I've found.

High windows

When windows are out of reach for easy hand or ladder squeegee work, a pole or extension handle of any length you can maneuver will work on the same principle surprisingly well. Clean glass always looks good. A few tiny smudges or drips won't hurt anything, so don't try to be a perfectionist. It isn't worth the stress or time. I use an Ettore extension handle that extends from four to eight feet. Even second-story windows are quick to do, and your feet never leave the ground. You don't need a ladder and there's no safety risk.

When you use an extension pole, instead of wiping the squeegee after each stroke, just hit the pole with the palm of your hand to release excess water from the blade.

Washing high windows

When windows are out of reach for easy hand or ladder work, a squeegee handle of any length you can maneuver will work with surprising accuracy. I use a handle that extends from four to eight feet. A few tiny smudges or drips won't hurt anything, so don't try to be a perfectionist.

EXTENSION HANDLES

Second-story windows can be done easily and your feet never leave the ground. No ladder is needed and there's no safety risk.

Hard water deposits

If you have hard-water buildup from sprinkling your lawn or irrigation, don't use abrasive cleanser or the glass will cloud and scratch. If it isn't too thick and hasn't been on there too long, phosphoric acid cleaner will remove the deposit. Spray the solution on, let it work a minute, then scrub it with a white nylon scrub sponge until it dissolves. Rinse and repeat if needed. If you have a real accumulation welded on, it'll take several applications, with the phosphoric acid left on for a longer time. Don't lose patience if it doesn't wipe right off. If after all this it's still white and opaque, your window may be etched and damaged. No cleaner I know of can repair this. Replace the glass or draw the drapes. Keep hard water off your windows with regular maintenance or an adjustment in your sprinkling system.

Keep your eye on the blade

If your squeegee blade gets damaged and starts leaving a line of solution on your windows, pull it out of the channel, turn it over, and snap it back in. When the blade finally wears out, just buy a new blade and snap it into the squeegee channel. (Be sure ⅛ inch of the blade extends beyond each end of the channel.)

When window casings and trim get older, paint and putty chips catch under the squeegee blade and make cleaning miserable. New aluminum or well-maintained wood won't give you any grief. Taking the time to sand and repaint or reglaze will save you many cleaning hours.

Window scraping woes

A lot of window damage is done when paint, labels or mortar are being removed from windows. Here's the right way to go about cleanup operations on glass:

1. Before you start scraping a window with anything, try to soak the foreign material off with plain water. Then try a solvent such as De-Solv-it.

2. Always keep the glass surface wet when scraping.

3. Use only razor-sharp blades or flat razor-type tools in a one-way forward motion, then lift the tool off the glass and make another forward stroke. Never go back and forth. Pulling the tool back and forth will eventually trap a piece of grit or sand behind and under the blade, which will scratch even a wet window. (You'll never rub *that* one off with a de-oiled bare hand, either.)

Dragging a scraper backward or back and forth can trap sand or dirt under the blade, causing it to scratch the glass.

4. Don't use abrasive scrub pads or compounds on window glass.

5. Be *careful.* Too much pressure, or an abrupt or careless motion, could get you a nasty cut as well as a broken pane.

In general, windows are high-maintenance areas, and there's a lot more than glass to keep clean and dust-free. Fortunately, just as professional window-washing methods can have glass looking its best with minimum effort on your part, a little attention to technique can keep your screens, blinds and curtains looking sharp.

How to clean . . .

Drapes

Buy good-quality drapes, and check regularly to make sure they stay hung properly. Vacuum drape tops and sides occasionally. When you clean the floor near full-length drapes, protect them by slipping the bottom of the panel through an ordinary clothes hanger and hooking the top over the rod.

You can refurbish drapes not dirty enough to be cleaned by running them through the clothes dryer on a cool setting. (*Don't* do this with fiberglass drapes; they'll leave an irritating residue in the dryer that will transfer itself to clothing.) Be sure to remove the

A simple coat hanger will protect drapes from damage during carpet-cleaning.

drapery hooks first.

Since drapes are relatively inexpensive to dry clean, get estimates from different shops. It's often less of a hassle than doing them yourself.

Check your drapes by slapping them in the sunshine. If they've been collecting dirt, you'll see it. If they're faded and threadbare and the dirt is all that's holding them together, it's time to go shopping.

Shades

If window shades are going to come clean, a dry sponge (see page 159) will do it. The sturdier plastic or plastic-coated shades can be damp-wiped with a neutral all-purpose cleaner. Remember that shades get sun-rotted and discolored over time, so don't be disappointed if they don't look resurrected when you're finished.

Screens

When your screens become embedded with dead bugs, tree sap, dirt, bird droppings, and other unsightly debris, take them down. Carry them outside, spread out a big cloth, old rug, or piece of canvas, and *lay them flat* (this is important to avoid damage) on it. Mix up a light neutral cleaner solution and scrub them with a soft-bristled brush. Rinse the screens with a hose, give them a sharp rap with your hand to jar most of the water loose, and let them finish drying in the sun.

Blinds

Whether the old venetian type or the newer minis, blinds are such a pain to clean that some homemakers have cheerfully given up the privacy and easy light adjustment that blinds undeniably provide. If you haven't yet reached that point, you might never have to if you clean blinds this way.

The big secret of blind maintenance isn't any "magic fingers" you send away for. It's simply dusting often enough that the dust doesn't have a chance to blend with airborne oils into that stubborn, grimy coating we all know and hate. This means at least a monthly run over the blinds with a lambswool duster (see Equipment Chart, chapter five), making firm contact with the surface. Close the blinds before you start, and when you've done one side, close them in the other direction and do the other side.

Vertical blinds don't collect dust and airborne soil as swiftly as the horizontals. But they should be dusted frequently too (quarterly might be enough here), for the same reason. Cloth-covered verticals should be done more often because their soft surface will absorb dirt, which if left on will soon be baked in by the sun. Don't use a lambswool duster or treated dust cloth of any kind on cloth-covered blinds—again because of their absorbency. Vacuum them with a dust brush attachment instead.

Sooner or later blinds will need to be washed. Don't try to do this without taking them down; washing blinds in place is slow and messy, and you'll curse yourself for attempting it. Don't wash them in the sink or bathtub, either. Take them outside. Find a slanting surface, such as a driveway, if you can; if not, flat will do. But you *must* lay down an old quilt, blanket or piece of canvas first, and then lay the blinds on it to prevent them from being damaged.

Let each blind out to full length and close it, making sure the louvers are flat. Lay the blind down on the cushioning cloth and scrub in the direction of the slats, using a soft-bristled brush and neutral all-purpose cleaner. Then reverse the blind and wash the other side. The cloth will get soapy and help clean the blind.

Hang or hold the blind up and rinse it with a hose (a helper is very useful at this point). Shake the excess water off and let the blind dry thoroughly before rehanging it.

There is a nice little tonglike tool called a "Tricket" we professionals use on jalousie windows that makes quick work of washing vertical blinds, since you can do both sides at once. You wash them with the sponge inserts, then squeegee them with the miniature squeegee blades.

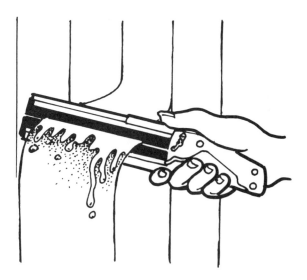

A tricket makes quick work of washing vertical blinds, since both sides of each blind are cleaned with a single stroke.

Clean cloth-covered verticals a couple of times a year by taking a cloth dampened with carpet shampoo solution and lightly wiping the surface.

The most painless way to clean blinds is to send them out to a professional for ultrasonic cleaning. (Just look in the Yellow Pages under Blinds—Cleaning.) This gets the slats, ladders, cords—*everything*—sparkling clean.

10.

Floors under your foot & rule

The floor, more than any other part of the house, projects the overall image of your home. The chances of anyone's noticing that all-day sucker stuck to the patio door, the half-eaten wiener on the bookcase, or the cobweb across Grandpa's picture are lessened if the floors are clean and brilliant. Fortunately, maintaining beautiful floors is one of the simplest jobs in the house. (Trust me.)

The term "hard floors" didn't originate as a description of the effort needed to clean them; it's simply used to distinguish them from soft floors (carpets). Hard floors include vinyl, linoleum, wood, ceramic and other tiles, terrazzo, cork, dirt (nothing under it) and good old concrete. All hard floors have their purpose, and they all have to be cleaned and maintained.

Proper floor care can be a lifesaver for you physically and emotionally. There are four reasons for you to learn and apply good floor care:

1. Appearance
A beautiful floor is an exhilarating experience for the beholder and a reward for the homemaker.

2. Protection
Even the hardest surfaces will scuff, wear and dull with grinding foot traffic, spills and chemical cleaners. A wax or other protective finish covering the surface lessens abrasion and other damage and lengthens the life of the floor. Even "no-wax" floors need a dressing or finish to prevent an eventually dull and damaged surface.

3. Cleanability
Soil, dirt, spills, marks of all kinds and abrasive residues are much simpler to clean from a smooth, well-waxed or finished surface. Sweeping a well-used unwaxed or unfinished tile floor will take you 25 percent longer than sweeping a highly polished one. A coat of wax or other finish on the floor is like a coat of varnish on a bare wood picnic table: It keeps soils and oils from penetrating the surface. Wiping something from the top of a protective nonpenetrable finish takes only seconds. It sure beats spending hours trying to scrub it out once it has soaked in and stained.

4. Safety
Contrary to what most people think, shiny, well-waxed and properly maintained floors are generally much less slippery than bare floors. Bare, porous, worn floors have a slick, flint-hard surface whether wet or dry. A coat or two of wax or acrylic finish actually cushions the floor. This could be compared to laying a thin cloth or cover over a bare plastic tabletop: it creates a surface that won't let things slide around. Thus a coat or "cover" of wax makes most floors less slippery.

A waxed floor is safer

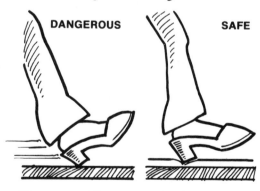

DANGEROUS   SAFE

Clean, waxed floors are safer than bare, untreated floors. Wax "cushions" the surface and actually helps prevent slipping.

Another reminder: Floors require less cleaning if you provide adequate entrance matting (see chapter eight). Hundreds of hours of floor problems and worries will disappear if you install adequate matting at entrances to stop dirt and abrasives from getting into your house. Some discoloration and wear of waxes comes with time and exposure to sunlight. But most discoloration of wax or finish and deterioration of flooring material comes from dirt penetrating into the wax and eventually to the floor surface. Keeping the surface clean will greatly prolong the life of the finish.

I'm often asked whether hard or soft floors are easier to keep clean. The answer is, it depends. In high-traffic or high-abuse areas, hard flooring is better. In low-traffic, low-abuse areas, carpeting is easier and faster to care for.

How to clean hard floors

Again, the most important factor in saving time and keeping maintenance of your floor to a minimum is simple: Keep it clean! That doesn't just mean removing roller skates, cat toys, coins, combs and clothes, either. It's the dust, grit, gravel, sand, food crumbs and other such substances that remain on floors, abrade them, and eventually get ground into powder and embed themselves in the surface that cause your cleaning woes. Once all this "dirt power" is on the loose, it will destroy a floor rapidly. Keep hard floors well swept (even when you can't see dirt and dust).

You can, of course, vacuum a hard-surface floor, and it does get all the dust and crumbs from corners and hard-to-reach crevices, but on a large hard floor (wood, tile or vinyl) vacuuming is slow, noisy and inefficient. However, on small areas of hard-surface floor right next to other vacuum jobs, it's smart maneuvering to just hit it with the vacuum while you're at it (and it saves stooping with a dustpan). Don't use a vacuum with a beater bar

on a hard floor, especially wood—even if the beater doesn't dent the floor it can, at its rapid rotation rate, fling grit or gravel into the floor and chip the surface. The wide brush head on a canister is designed for hard floors.

Where possible, use a commercial twelve- or eighteen-inch treated dust-mop. It's faster, more effective, and will last much longer than anything you can pick up at the supermarket. Brooms stir up dust all over the place and leave fine unseen particles that will be ground into your wax and eventually destroy the finish. A good dust-mop is much faster and does a much better job than a broom. There's no comparison, especially if you have a good-quality commercial dustmop with a full-circle swivel head. It will cover a lot of ground quickly and is flat enough to get under furniture. It will gather gravel, paper clips, gum wrappers, safety pins, and the hundred other items that find their way to the floor. It will also pick up and hold the dust. A dustmop is unbelievably effective on sealed concrete basement and garage floors, especially if it's treated to pick up dust.

The care and feeding of dustmops

Treat your dustmop by spraying the head with a little Endust, furniture polish or commercial dustmop treatment, or by taking the head off the frame and pouring a few tablespoonfuls of furniture polish into the pocket. Let it sit overnight (at least twelve hours) before mopping.

Before you start, use a counter brush or angle broom to detail the edges so you don't leave a lingering buildup in the corners. If you use a broom to do this, run it along the tops of the baseboards too and use the angled point to clean out corners.

When you mop, use "s" strokes and keep the mop in contact with the

Dustmop

Get dust and dirt off the floor regularly—preferably with a dustmop.

A 14–18″ commercial-quality dustmop will pay you dividends. It cleans hard-surfaced floors better and faster than any broom.

floor, but don't bear down on it; pressure isn't necessary. The mop will turn and swivel under furniture (one of the advantages of the professional-quality mop). Always lead with the same edge and don't lift the head from the floor until you're finished or you'll lose your dust load. Mop next to the baseboard last.

If you have only a small amount of hard flooring, do it by hand with a cleaning cloth (see chapter fifteen) or dust cloth. You won't need a commercial dustmop.

When you need to sweep

The corn broom has been around a long time, and can serve well if you remember it's only for dry work. If you do sweep anything wet, don't set the broom on the straw end to dry or it'll develop a permanent curl.

I've switched to the nylon angle head type. The bristles have fine split tips, to get up even the most minute stuff, and lots of springy strength to pull the rocks and toys along, should you need to sweep that hard. The angled head reaches into corners better, and it suits our natural sweeping stroke better. And these plastic brooms shed less and last and last (which is easier on the pocketbook and

our dumpsites)—water, snow, chemicals, or chasing the chickens won't hurt them. I wouldn't be surprised to see the witches switch to them soon!

For outdoor or rough-surfaced expanses of hard flooring, a push broom is what you want—with an eighteen- or twenty-four-inch nylon bristle head and good, sturdy handle braces.

To pick up the final whisk of dirt that the dustpan and broom won't get, I grab a piece of paper out of the garbage, or from an old newspaper or magazine, and wet it (if no one's looking, I just lick it). Then I wipe the area with it, and those tiny particles all stick to the wet paper. Not a speck will be left on the floor.

An angle broom suits our natural sweeping stroke better.

Damp-mopping

The most important operation (after sweeping) is damp-mopping, which is done to remove the light layer of dirt, settled airborne grease and sticky spills that accumulate from daily use.

The equipment needed to wet-clean your floors depends on the amount and type of hard-surfaced floors you have. During the last twenty years, wall-to-wall carpet has found its way into more and more of the new homes built, often leaving only kitchen and bathroom with hard floors.

If a hard floor is in the center of the house where considerable travel over carpeted areas is required to reach it, that hard-floor finish will last for months, if it's kept clean. You could do it by hand in about fifteen minutes a year. A sponge mop (see Equipment Chart, chapter five, for the superior professional model of these) is adequate damp-mopping equipment in 80 percent of modern homes.

If you have several rooms of vinyl, linoleum, quarry tile or wood floors, as well as a big game room, garage, converted patio or storage area, some basic labor-saving floor tools would be a good investment. The Equipment Chart in chapter five outlines what I'd suggest. Get a good twelve- or sixteen-ounce string mop, preferably a rayon/cotton Layflat, and a good mop bucket (the built-in roller wringer types are good, and so are the small versions of the commercial handle squeezer type). Wheels on a household mop bucket aren't necessarily what you want, since we rarely move the bucket when we just mop the kitchen floor; besides, wheels make a bucket heavier and more awkward. But you do want *something* to squeeze the moisture out of your mops so you don't have to tromp on them with your foot or do it with your bare hands. Wringing mops by hand is finger suicide: The things your mop picks up—pins, glass, etc.—will lacerate your hands. The price of a small commercial mop bucket might shock you, but gasp once or twice and buy it anyway. It will be a time-saver and greatly contribute to the quality of work you can do.

How to damp-mop

Dipping a mop in a bucket of plain or soapy water and swabbing the place down is not mopping. It gives the floor a temporary wet look, but when it dries it won't look much better than it did to begin with. Magnificent moppers remember these basics:

1. Use the right solution.
Mopping with plain or vinegar water is an exercise in futility, wasted wear and tear on a good mop. Without a surfactant (chemical that helps the solution to penetrate) and emulsifier (to help break up and dissolve the dirt), moisture alone does little to a floor or to the soil on it. On the other hand, too strong a solution will degloss the floor and cause filming or streaks. So use just a bit of neutral all-purpose cleaner (one ounce per gallon of warm water). You want to cut the dirt but not the wax or the finish.

2. Sweep or dustmop the floor thoroughly before you start.
Even better, vacuum it. (By failing to do this, more people soil their floors mopping than by any other method.)

3. "Frame" the floor first.
Run the mop around the edges of the floor, to a point ten to twelve inches from the baseboard. Then when you mop the middle (see number four following), stay ten to twelve inches away from the wall. This eliminates the buildup that mopping can deposit along the baseboard. Slapping the mop on the baseboard is a bad idea that will result in a filthy edge.

4. Mop all the rest in a "figure 8" from side to side out in front of you.
Mopping like this is less fatiguing because you use the big muscles of your

Figure 8 pattern for damp-mopping

midbody and hips, rather than your wrists and arms; it also covers more ground in less time. You also overlap more, so there are fewer missed spots.

5. *Keep your mop clean.*
Always wring the dirty water into a slop bucket before you dip the mop back into the cleaning solution.

6. *Flop your mop!*
Or turn the mop head over, often. Water is heavy, so when you pick up water with a mop it will always accumulate at the bottom of the mop as you work with it. This is why you need to flip the mop over every two or three strokes, to get a drier side. When you use a mop to apply solution or "scrub," you flop it to get to a cleaner side. When you've flopped the mop several times and it won't pick up any more water or it's completely dirty, then wring it out.

7. *Go over the floor twice.*
Make *two* passes over the same surface:

the first to wet and dissolve, the second to remove. So first spread the solution out over the floor (but don't flood it), and let it sit on there a minute (or a little longer if the floor is extra dirty) so the cleaner can attack and emulsify the dirt. Then wring the mop dry and go over the whole area again, removing all the moisture and dirt possible. If you've mixed up the solution right—not too much cleaner—and mopped the floor good and dry on the second pass, you'll be done. If you put on too much solution and leave it on too long, it'll cut the wax. And if you don't make a second pass to remove your cleaning solution, there'll be lots of detergent residue when the water evaporates, leaving the floor sticky and cloudy.

Mop miscellaneous

- The telltale four: If you find more than four mop strings in the bottom of the bucket after cleaning the

floor, it's time to get a new mop head. With all the time they spend wet, they do disintegrate after a while.

- Why do you want a rayon/cotton rather than all-cotton mop? Because the strands will be stronger, so there will be fewer of them left behind on the chair legs and in corners.

- "Damp-mopping" means what it says. Wring all the possible moisture out before putting mop to floor. Excess water runs into cracks and corners and down to the subfloor, and it won't do any good for anything in any of these places.

- Keep a green nylon scrub pad handy when you mop so you can make quick work of stubborn "glued-on" spots and spills.

- Watch the handle when you raise a mop to put it in the wringer. Pro cleaners know only too well that you can wreck ceiling tile, break light fixtures, and be injured by falling glass.

Wax it!

As I said earlier, most hard floors need a protective coating. Floors will wear out much faster if they're not protected. Floors claiming to be "no-wax" will also dull in traffic areas if not protected by a finish of some kind. The "never need to wax" claim just doesn't hold up. If you expect such a floor to stay shiny in heavy traffic areas, it needs a dressing.

First, take the old wax off

Once the hard floor is prepared by sweeping and you know the old wax or finish is due to come off, it's time to make that hard job an easy one. Arrive at the scene with two buckets: an ordinary bucket and a mop bucket.

Fill the mop bucket three-quarters full of clean water; don't put cleaner in it. Mix some warm water and wax stripper in the ordinary bucket. A detergent cleaner will do fine for a light scrub, but if you want all the wax off, use a commercial wax remover. Ammonia cuts wax, but it can also cut the plasticizers in the floor if you leave it on too long! A nonammoniated commercial wax remover will do the best and safest job.

Dip your fresh mop into the solution and apply to the floor generously so that the solution can attack the old wax or dirt. Cover as large an area as you feel you can clean and take up before it dries. (About ten by ten feet—you'll learn how much to do if it dries on you once.) Remember, use the basic principle of cleaning explained in chapter six. As soon as the solution is on the floor, old wax and dirt begin to be dissolved and suspended and can soon be wiped off easily.

This may be a bit optimistic, because chances are you have some spots where wax is built up thick as cardboard and hard as a bullet. It will need scrubbing or scraping, and possibly another application or two of solution. If so, scrub (and not on your hands and knees, either). Get a hand floor scrubber (see Equipment Chart, chapter five). It has a long handle with a plastic "gripper" on its end that holds a five-by-ten-inch nylon pad. Edges, especially, are easy with one of these little gems. I think one hand floor

> Do all your hard floors at once if you can. Whether you mop, wax or vacuum, it's a lot more efficient to get out, clean up and put away all your equipment just once. (Cleaning up the wax applicator, for example, can take as long as waxing one whole floor.)

The right way to remove old wax

1. Spread solution on floor in an area you can handle at one time . . . about ten by ten feet. Then let it sit to dissolve old hard wax.

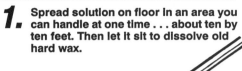
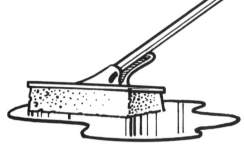

2. Now scrub with a hand floor scrubber or floor machine with a stripping pad. Go over the area twice.

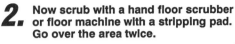
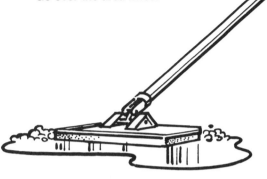

3. Test the floor with a fingernail to see if all the old wax is dissolved.

4. With an old squeegee or a floor squeegee (*not* your window squeegee), squeegee up the dirty mucky slop water.

5. Then scoop up the sloppy puddle into a dustpan and dispose of it.

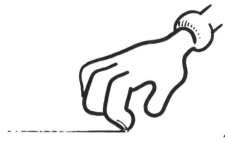

6. Now rinse. Use a little vinegar in the water to neutralize the floor. This is important because the stripper is highly alkaline and if the surface isn't neutralized the new wax won't bond to it.

scrubber could outdo five of those small electric twin-brush scrubbers. If you do use a floor machine, the single-disc models are at least twenty times better than the little double-brush units. Watch the classified section of your paper and you might find a $350 twelve- or thirteen-inch commercial unit for $40 or $50. Use nylon scrubbing and polishing pads under a floor machine for best results. Brushes are almost worthless. For wax removal, the brown or black pads are the best.

When the solution on the floor looks gunky and creamy, it means the dirt and old wax are coming loose. Before you clean off the stripper and gunk, check the scrubbed floor with your fingernail. If, after a scrape across the floor, your nail looks like your son's, wax is still there. Use more solution and if necessary scrub a little. If you're on the verge of passing out from exhaustion, you're in an ideal frame of mind to resolve not to let your floor ever get in this condition again.

Most floor-cleaning time is spent trying to get wax off unused areas, such as under the lamp table and TV, and off the edges of the floors. Previously, when you rewaxed the traffic paths or worn areas that needed it, you also gave the edges, the areas beneath furniture, and all the other places that didn't need it a generous coat. This system of application was repeated year after year. A traffic pattern area will come clean easily because there's no buildup, but the thick areas will need lots of work to get the buildup off. Next time, don't rewax the floors where you don't use them. Once you've given the entire floor one coat of wax and more coats are to be applied, put the additional coats *on traffic areas only.*

Now, back to cleaning the floor. The floor is soaked and scrubbed, the wax and dirt are loosened, and it's a mess. Don't pull out that mop and try

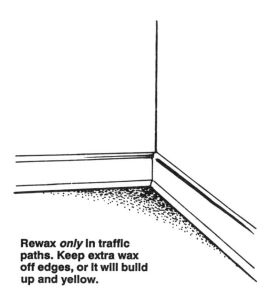

Rewax *only* in traffic paths. Keep extra wax off edges, or it will build up and yellow.

to sop or slop it up. Instead, reach for a simple, inexpensive tool called a floor squeegee (see Equipment Chart, chapter five). Or you can use an old window squeegee you have lying around (not your nice new one, which should be used only for windows). Squeegee the gunk into a puddle on the uncleaned area (mind you don't squeegee it down a heating vent), and use an ordinary dustpan and empty bucket to quickly scoop the gunk up. (I once met a woman who uses her turkey baster to suck it up, but I'm sticking with the dustpan.) The squeegeed area (except for a possible drop or two from the squeegee lap) will be almost perfectly clean. A squeegee will do a great job on all hard floors—even fairly rough concrete, or vinyl floors with relief designs (the little crud-catching indentations or pits that really are the pits to clean). If the floor has some deep bad cracks between tiles you can use a wet/dry vacuum with a squeegee attachment to pull the liquid out.

Now for the mop. Rinse it in clear water and then damp-mop the area. Add a little vinegar to the mop water to neutralize any alkaline residue from the cleaner so the wax will apply better. If the floor was really gunky, rinse again with clean water. Let the floor dry, and that area is ready to wax. Repeat this process until the whole floor is finished. All the gunk will end up in one bucket to be dumped in the toilet (*not* the sink). The mop water will remain fresh and work for the entire floor because it only rinses the squeegeed floor. (And just think: You never had your hands in filthy water.)

When the floor is dry, apply a first light coat of wax to the entire floor. Put two more thin coats on your traffic paths; don't rewax areas that don't get heavy wear. I'd use a good commercial metal interlock or polymer finish, obtainable at any janitorial-supply store.

Wax wisdom

- Just because it shines doesn't mean it's clean. Those mop-and-shine products lay a gloss on top of your floor that reflects light. When you're finished, where's the dirt? Under the wax. Likewise, be sure to remove the grimy scrub water before applying any finishing product, or you may just have shiny dirt.

- Pros wax floors with a clean string mop, but a full-sized (thirty-six-ounce) mop is huge. The next time one of your small mops gets older or hardened at the ends, trim it to six- or eight-ounce size and wax with it, just as if you were damp-mopping. It's faster than an applicator and it applies wax perfectly. Rinse well with hot water afterward or you'll have a plaster-hard wax mop!

- Most floor finishes and waxes are delicately balanced chemically. Mixing them with water or other wax—or even waxing over an un-rinsed floor—will cause them to yellow, powder, streak and perform poorly. Use them pure.

- Three's Better than One: When applying floor finish or wax, remember that several (two or three) thin coats beat one big heavy coat. It's better for looks, durability and even drying!

Tile floors

There must be four hundred brands, five hundred styles, and at least a thousand different colors and patterns of clay and masonry floor tiles to choose from. And it's pretty clear from all the calls, letters and questions I get concerning "their new tile" that everyone thinks they picked the wrong one. Seldom does any tile give you all you expected, but many tile problems can be cured with a little adjustment in approach and cleaning product, especially by simply coming to understand and accept just what you *do* have in the floor tile you have now. Tile in general has a very hard surface made to take abuse and wear and to require a minimum of maintenance. Generally it does just that, but the stickler is that tile comes in everything from a slick, glossy surface to a dull, porous one. Your tile could be one of these or of the many variations in between.

Lots of people who have bought the shiny tile call me and say, "I don't like the shininess. It shows every streak or bit of dirt. What can I do?" Well, that is the tile's nature and personality, the way it was designed—its slick surface reflects light and so the shine. Shiny surfaces also won't hold finish or "wax"; it powders and flakes off because the surface is too slippery to bond to. But that same slick, hard surface won't allow dirt or spills to penetrate and is easy to clean. (As to how to avoid streaks, see point #1 following.)

The next most frequent question I get about tile floors is, "I can't make my 'Mexican tile' floor shine!" That's right. Unglazed clay or quarry tile like this was designed rough and porous to provide traction, and it absorbs rather than reflects light so it won't shine. If you put enough coats of sealer and finish on, some shine will come, but it takes a lot of applications and continual maintenance. Again, you won't change the personality of the tile.

A few more truths about tile

1. Remove the residue

Two of the most common mistakes on shiny tile are mopping in a way that leaves soap residue behind (which kills the luster), or mopping with plain water, vinegar and water, or something that doesn't cut the grease and dirt so the floor stays dull and sticky. You have to mop or scrub a tile floor with a good cleaner (such as neutral all-purpose cleaner), making sure you mix it up exactly as the manufacturer recommends, no stronger—and then make sure you get rid of all the traces of that cleaner when you're done. To accomplish this, rinse-mop with plain water afterward or add a little vinegar to the rinse water (it doesn't clean, but it will neutralize any alkalinity left on the floor). Check this out if your ceramic tile isn't as sparkling as you want it. If I had lots of tile I'd get a little thirteen-inch single-disc floor polisher from a janitorial-supply store and, with a white nylon pad, buff or "burnish" the tile after it's been cleaned to remove hard water and other stubborn stains or deposits and bring up its natural luster. It only takes a minute or two.

2. Coat it

If you have one of the more porous types of tile and insist on some shine, you can put a coating (sealer or finish) on it to fill the pores, prevent dirt penetration, and give it a bit of a glow.

Since I don't know which of the five hundred tiles you may have out there in Stamford, Miami, Albuquerque or Billings, I suggest you go down to the local janitorial-supply store and ask what they would recommend for tile of your type or what the local contractors use to enhance floors like yours. Then you'll know what you can use and where to get it. But be sure the floor is properly prepared first—well cleaned, rinsed and neutralized if necessary, or the finish will quickly flake or powder off. Finish will also fail to adhere over any greasy or oily spots.

3. Grout

On most tile the grout is the biggest problem. The mortar between the tiles gets porous (or was that way to begin with), so dirt and stains get in it and, when you clean, they don't come out. Any untreated masonry like this, just like a plain cement garage floor, will absorb everything and quickly get cruddy. Clean and rinse your tile floor well, especially the grout (you may need a degreaser to get out all that embedded oily dirt). Then get some grout sealer (Color Tile stores have it), take a little brush and seal the grout; it will be well worth it. The sealer, usually a silicone, fills the pores of the grout so that it resists dirt and buildup.

4. The secret of intelligent selection

All of you who were going to get a tile floor, don't panic! I was once very gun-shy on tile, but now I'm putting mostly tile floors in the maintenance-free house

I'm building. The secret is that for years my wife and I viewed tile that was already in use. Some tile, especially in shopping malls, always looks beautiful, and with little maintenance. Contact the architect of the place with the tile you admire and find out what it is — "showroom selection" is often maintenance masochism.

> **If you have carpet butting up against ceramic tile flooring, be sure to replace any metal bar in your vacuum beater with another brush. The metal bar (great for bouncing the carpet to loosen soil) can chip your tile if you happen to lap over onto it.**

Coping with concrete floors

Dust-mopping concrete floors is a trick most of us haven't heard of. Concrete floors, believe it or not, are almost equal in square footage to carpet in many American homes. Unfinished full basements are common. People often intend to finish them, but they wait many years — "until we can afford to finish those two bedrooms and a family room in the basement." Two-car garages are also a mass of concrete flooring. Both of these areas bear a constant flow of traffic back and forth into the "finished" part of the house. Concrete absorbs and holds stains and marks and produces much destructive material (dirt, grit, sand, etc.), so it's responsible for more cleaning time than you might realize. The surface of concrete (which is made of sand, cement, lime and additives) will perpetually "bleed" dust and grit, which if not cleaned up regularly eventually circulates through your house.

Go get your broom right now and sweep your basement or garage. Leave the pile of residue, and go back and sweep again just as carefully. The second pile will amaze you, as will the third if you sweep again. Because concrete is textured and porous and "bleeds," vacuuming it is really the only way to get it dustless, and after use, it will again be dusty. If you want to eliminate hundreds of hours of direct and indirect adverse results from concrete floors in your home, seal the concrete. You've walked on many a sealed floor in supermarkets, malls, stadiums, on ramps, around pools, etc. It looks like it's varnished. Sealed concrete is easy and practical to maintain and will last for years.

You can seal your own concrete floors

Concrete has to cure at least twenty-eight days after pouring before it's ready to seal. It's best to seal it before it's used, because oil stains and other fluids may penetrate and will be difficult or impossible to remove, and the seal will magnify any pre-existing marks.

On either old or new concrete, sweep up all surface dirt and remove everything possible from the floor (furniture, tools, etc.). Mop on a solution of strong alkaline cleaner or, better still, etching acid diluted in water. (Your janitorial-supply store or paint store will have these.) Let it soak in awhile. It will break and release the lime and debris on the surface of the concrete, leaving a good, firm, clean base. If the floor is old and marked, scrub it with a floor machine (or your trusty hand floor scrubber). Even if you don't scrub, apply the solution and let it sit. Then flush the solution off, using your floor squeegee. Rinse with a hose. Allow the floor to dry for five or more hours.

You can get penetrating seal at paint or janitorial-supply stores. The

latest generation of water-based concrete seals are wonderful! Apply the seal, according to directions, with any applicator that will distribute it in a nice, thin, even coat; let it dry. Most concrete seals are self-leveling so it should turn out okay, but I'd advise a second coat to make sure all the "etched," rough surfaces are filled. (Don't try to save the used applicator. It isn't worth cleaning out.)

Once the seal is dry, you have a shiny, glossy, smooth (not slick) surface that can be waxed and maintained just like any hard floor. Stains, oil spills, etc., can be wiped off without leaving the usual ugly penetrating mark. Sealed concrete finish wears well. Chips and scrapes can be touched up with a small paintbrush or cloth.

Wood floors

Homeowners are in awe of their wood floors; literally thousands of them have written or called me with fears and worries about wood.

Wood is a warm, handsome surface that will last and look good indefinitely if you treat it right. The old way to maintain wood floors is to apply a penetrating oil and then put a layer of solvent (or "spirit") wax over it. This does protect the floor to a degree, but it doesn't give it a hard, permanent, waterproof coating. It's also a lot of work, and the floor always looks like an Alaskan barroom floor needing only a layer of sawdust and a moth-eaten moosehead to complete the atmosphere.

The better way to go is to apply two or three coats of polyurethane-type finish or varnish to a wood floor. Like a thin sheet of glass, this will seal the wood off from moisture, wear and abuse. Any maintenance you do after that isn't going to touch the wood itself. Water doesn't hurt well-sealed wood if used wisely, which means used sparingly and not left on for long. Be sure the sealer or finish is intact (no cracks or worn spots), because once moisture gets into wood it swells the grain and pops off the finish; it can even discolor and warp the floor.

Once the floor is well sealed, pick any spills up quickly, dustmop or sweep it frequently to keep it free of dust and grit, and damp-mop it occasionally with a light neutral all-purpose cleaner, getting that water on and

Keep wooden floors covered with a protective polyurethane or resinous floor finish. If moisture penetrates wood it will swell and pop off the finish; then the wood deteriorates rapidly.

off quickly.

Even a well-varnished floor will look dull when it's worn and scratched, so that's why I personally like to wax them. You can use paste wax, but it's slow hands-and-knees stuff—a nice liquid acrylic with 23 percent solids (such as Top Gloss) will work as well with much less effort. The wax keeps the polyurethane (which is protecting the wood) from getting scratched. But don't try to wax freshly sealed wood, or the finish won't stick. Use the floor for a month or two to reduce the gloss, and the wax will adhere.

Refinishing wood floors

Shy away from sanding wood floors except as a last resort. An eighth of an inch of wood taken off a three-quarter-inch floor really affects its performance. Cracks, crowns and cupping will appear and squeaks will develop.

Sometimes, especially if you're rehabbing a much-abused old house, you'll have no choice but to sand down the floors. But chances are, if your wood floors are old and ugly-looking, the problem's not the wood, but the layers of yellowed, cracked finish. If you sand it down, the old finish will

gum up the belts of the sander, and it will be a mess. Plus, you lose part of your floor. Instead, try this: Buy a gallon or two of varnish or paint remover and apply it generously to the floor. The old varnish will instantly crumble and release its hold on the wood. Scrape it well, then use your trusty floor squeegee and dustpan to pick up the mess. This should leave the floor bare. If some old varnish does remain, use a little more remover and scrape some more; it will come off.

Then go over the entire floor lightly with a screen-back sanding disc. Apply one coat of polyurethane or varnish—thin it down so it will soak into the wood—and then one or two coats more, the number of coats depending on the condition of the floor. Soft or cracked wood generally needs two coats to achieve a good gloss.

You won't believe how good your floor will look or how easy the job will be. Just be sure to read all the directions that come with floor care products, and don't be afraid to ask the dealer questions.

P.S. It's clear to me that a small book on the subject of caring for wood in a home—especially floors—is really needed. I'm working on it, so be sure to send *me* your questions and concerns about wood so I can include them.

To move heavy furniture and appliances easily without scratching the floor—

A thick towel slipped under each leg will help the unit slide for easy cleaning access.

Remember daily maintenance for protection

After you've expended all the time and effort to get your floors clean and shiny, keep them clean daily and they'll last for years. Remember, it's the spills, crumbs, sand, dust, etc., that create the conditions that make you work. If a few black marks get on the floor, they'll be on top of the wax, and easily removed with the moist nylon cleaning pad on the end of your hand floor scrubber. The most efficient way to keep hard floors clean is to dust-mop them daily.

A few final words about floors

Remember, good matting at exterior and interior entrances will save you more floor work than all the gimmicks, tips and miracle floor formulas combined. Avoid "one-stroke" miracle combinations that clean and wax your floor at the same time. And if anyone in the family has shoes or other footwear that leave black marks, I'd make a quick Salvation Army donation of them (the shoes, not the person!).

Some floors are much easier to maintain than others, so don't break your neck trying to match your neighbor's shine. Some floor material, because it's cheap, damaged, porous, discolored or just plain ugly, is almost impossible to make look good. When you put in new flooring, stick to

A quick review of floor care

VINYL OR LINOLEUM

All vinyl, asphalt and even "no-wax" floors must have a coat of wax or polish applied so that dirt and debris from foot traffic won't damage them. Keep such floors dustmopped and damp-mopped regularly, even if "they don't look dirty." Damp-mop with a light neutral all-purpose cleaner when soiled; rewax regularly in the traffic patterns.

WOOD

Make sure wood floors are sealed with a good resinous or polyurethane "membrane" finish so moisture and stains won't penetrate the wood. Then treat wood floors like any hard flooring. Sweep, dustmop and damp-mop to maintain, but go light on the water, and don't let it puddle on the surface.

tested, reliable surfaces.

Some floors need three or four coats of wax to build them up to a gloss. A good shine will hide a multitude of sins. If a floor won't shine, or is difficult to maintain, consider replacing it or carpeting it.

Pick a good-quality flooring. Remember that solid colors are tougher to maintain and keep looking good. Try to avoid flooring with grooves and indentations—it's literally the "pits." Smooth-surfaced floors are nicer—and much easier to keep clean.

The basic principle of good floor care is to provide the flooring with a surface that will protect it and from which dirt can easily be cleaned. Most floors are maintained in much the same way. *All* floors will deteriorate if not cleaned regularly and coated with protective finish.

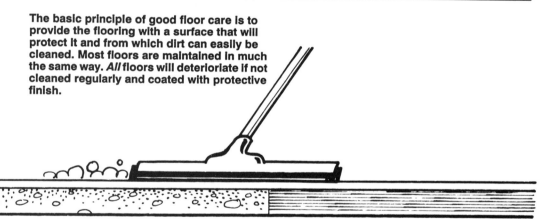

CONCRETE

Raw concrete will "bleed" dust and sand. Once interior concrete has cured, it should be cleaned thoroughly, let dry, and then sealed with a concrete seal. The resulting protective finish lets it be maintained like other floors. Never paint concrete floors, because most paints will peel and chip off concrete.

STONE, BRICK, CERAMIC OR QUARRY TILE

The dozens of types of tiles available make it difficult to recommend a single method. If you have one of the more porous kinds of tile and are unhappy with it, ask the dealer (or your local janitorial-supply store) for a sealer or finish appropriate for your kind of tile. Remember that tiles intended to have a highly textured or "rustic" look will never shine no matter what—so don't waste your time and energy.

11.

How to clean carpets for a softer life

"Never shampoo a carpet before you have to, because once you do, it will get dirty faster." (Old Wives' Tales, continued). That's like saying, "Never wash your socks after the first wearing, because they'll get dirty faster." There are plenty of soothsayers around quoting great carpet wisdom to the homemaker, most of which costs you time and money. With some simple professional techniques, you can get the job done, keep your carpets looking sharp, and minimize your maintenance time. My company cleans and maintains several million square feet of carpet every night. What I've learned in the process applies to household as well as commercial carpet.

Buy quality carpet

"Which carpet is best?" If I had a dollar for every time I've been asked that, I could carpet the parking lot at your favorite mall! Carpet is so much better today than it was twenty or thirty years ago that if you stick to a good, reputable dealer and a Stain-Master, Stainblocker or other soil-resistant type, it'll be hard to go wrong. The fierce competition in the carpet industry has forced the quality up; almost all of it is nylon now and stain-resistant, and it's good! Don't bargain for the basement cost—better carpet is better, period! Pay the few extra dollars per yard to get the better grade, and have it installed professionally. You'll get thousands of dollars of benefit in comfort, durability, enjoyment and ease of maintenance. Choose what you like, but make sure you get good stuff.

Selecting carpet color, style and material is generally a personal privilege, but living with it (especially maintaining it) may not be a "privilege" if you don't choose wisely. For example, commercial carpets are so tightly woven and low-pile they're now referred to as "soft floors," not carpeted floors. Don't get too commercial-minded and buy the "wear like iron" style. Believe me, it *feels* like iron when you roll around on it with the kids or tackle a "living room floor" project. Go for the highest-quality domestic instead, and you'll be better off all around. The feel and the looks are a large part of the value of home carpeting. Much low-pile or indoor-outdoor carpet is difficult to maintain, not because it gets any dirtier than a thicker, plusher carpet, but because of its short pile and the solid colors it usually comes in. Every tiny piece of litter or trash is highly visible on it, and little bits of thread and similar material resist being vacuumed off; a good, deep pile can tolerate, undetected, just about anything from crumbs to catcher's mitts. There's nothing wrong with letting your rug help you out a little—as long as it isn't physically destructive to the carpet.

A homemaker will often spend hours selecting an exact shade, not realizing that once it's in place and in use—under different light conditions, and underfoot being soiled—the color won't be the same as the color you chose for even a tenth of the time the carpet is in service. Color is one area where you should be cautious.

There's no way you can keep airborne soilants from industrial burning, home heating gases, family cooking or foot-borne street oils from any carpet. All carpets will get soiled with time. Light golds, yellows, whites, pastels or flecks will serve you well if you live "el plusho" and your house is only a showplace. However, if you have children, grandchildren, animals or home-study groups, those elegant light carpets will be a disaster. Light solid colors show soil and are difficult to shampoo, and often show "cow trails."

Patterns and textures tend to hide soiling and wear.

Use common sense when you choose carpeting. Think of the maintenance. Deep pile is harder to vacuum than medium pile. Although the old standby, wool, is lovely, I'd choose nylon, a synthetic, ten times over for stain resistance, wear and cleanability. Oriental, Indian and woven rugs must *always* be cleaned professionally. These and other area rugs *cause* housework: Area rugs present two surfaces (instead of one) to clean. They're always being kicked and wrinkled, and they're easy to trip over. But they *are* beautiful. If you have to have them, hang them on a wall.

Kitchen and bathroom carpet

I'd *never* have carpet in a bathroom. There is a 100 percent chance that moisture (new and used) will get on the carpet, as will hair spray and other grooming residue. It will stink, harbor germs and look ugly. Bathroom carpeting takes much more time to care for than hard-surfaced flooring, and it deteriorates rapidly. Don't do it!

And in the kitchen? Where bread always falls jelly/mayonnaise/salami side down? Where meat juices run over the edge of the counter and dirty dishwater splashes out of the sink? Where pressure cookers of potato chowder explode and casseroles of baked beans are dropped? Don't you have better things to do than clean carpet?

High-abuse areas such as bathrooms, kitchens, garages, studios and workshops should have the lowest-maintenance, easiest-to-clean flooring possible. It will certainly save you time and grief, and probably money as well.

If you're in doubt anywhere here, my daughter and I did a book called *Make Your House Do the Housework*

which covers carpet from every angle for looks, durability and ease of upkeep.

Regular maintenance is important

Carpet in a home or lightly trafficked commercial area is easier to take care of than a hard floor if it's maintained properly. Its biggest problem is neglect. A carpet that looks okay is often used and abused, going unnoticed until it's too late. Then the owner of the neglected carpet says, "Huh, I wonder why the fur is all falling out" or "I can't remember what color it used to be. It must be time to clean it." At this stage most people wake up to the fact that carpets have to be maintained. But by then it's too late. Cleanup attempts are generally futile, and the owner becomes displeased with the carpet, unjustly blaming the problems on the salesperson or manufacturer.

You might think that carpet wear and damage result only from foot traffic. Wrong! Excessive carpet damage or wear results from a combination of foot traffic, furniture pressure, and residues (such as sand and grit) that are allowed to remain in the carpet. Any sharp, abrasive particles or articles on or at the base of the carpet fibers are, as the carpet is walked on, ground against each other. In time, the fibers that aren't cut or damaged are soiled. The carpet wears out and gets soiled from the bottom as well as the top. Thus, to maintain your carpet properly, you've got to keep off or remove surface litter, dust, grit, wet soils and the old airborne soils before they become embedded in your carpet. Another reminder: Good matting will eliminate a big share of this, especially wet soils and grit. Airborne dust you have to live with. Litter you can pick up or vacuum. The real culprit is embedded dirt.

Enter the vacuum . . .

Vacuum cleaners were invented to get surface dust, embedded dirt and litter from carpets efficiently. Few vacuums make as much impression on the carpet as they do on the user, who thinks noise, chrome and suction are the ultimate. For ages, vacuum sales-people (all equal in wind velocity to their products) have unloaded shiny, overpriced machines on customers fas-cinated by suction and attachments. Neither of these is that important in maintaining your carpet and saving yourself housecleaning hours. After showing you how a vacuum can do everything but brush your teeth, the sales approach is to drop a steel ball on the floor and suck it up into the vacuum. The gullible potential cus-tomer thinks, "If that vacuum can get a big steel ball off the carpet, sand and gravel will be a snap!"

Wrong! First, the steel ball trick is a volume maneuver that any vac-uum, weak or strong, old or new, can do under the right conditions. Just get a steel ball slightly smaller than the hose and the ball is easily slurped up. Now take a piece of thread and mash it onto the carpet so it has a little static bind. A vacuum cleaner strong enough to pick up a piano bench will

Rugs and carpets must have good reg-ular care with a beater-brush vac-uum to keep dirt out of the roots.

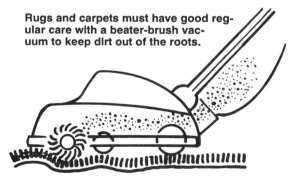

often have trouble picking up the thread because there's no "displace-ment lift." We've all tried to get up a thread, haven't we? Likewise, suction alone won't remove the embedded par-ticles of dirt, grit and sand. It will remove only the surface soil because, as with the thread, the displacement lift isn't there. The carpet fibers stand in the way to effectively hold the em-bedded dirt, grit, and all those other villains grinding away at your carpet. A good "beater brush" vacuum is what's needed to pull those babies out of the pile.

Beat it!

Vacuums with a beater brush, or beater bar, are distinguished by a rap-idly rotating brush that beats, combs and vibrates the carpet. This loosens and dislodges embedded dirt and soil so the suction can pull it up into the vacuum. Most beater brush heads will adjust to different heights and won't wear out carpet under normal use. On some models of vacuums the beater bar may be called a "brush roll," and on canister vacuums it's usually con-tained in a "power wand" type of at-tachment.

Are you the one in seven?

National studies show that one out of every seven homemakers needs a new vacuum cleaner. If you're that one, get it before your spouse spends the money on a new router or a fancy new computer program he'll use just once or twice during the rest of his life.

A vacuum is indeed "the" tool of cleaning. But which one should you own? A good question, since there are hundreds of them, all shapes and sizes—and a lot of them are excellent. A lot of them are also too big, too small or too expensive. Many fill some special need better than another, but for all-around, all-purpose use in a home we want one that's easy to use, maintain and repair. I like uprights the best, and I've used Eurekas at work and at home for more than thirty-five years. The ideal? I would buy two vacuums: first, an upright beater-brush type. (I hate canister-type vacuums that drag behind you like a ball and chain.) Go a step further and get a commercial upright. These are almost like the regular model sold downtown—except they generally have stronger motors, longer cords, a heavy-duty beater bar, a more durable turn-on switch, and a better-quality bag. Just be sure you choose a model you feel comfortable handling. You should be able to buy a first-class commercial upright for $250 to $350.

Resist buying a boxful of extra attachments that do everything from painting to pan-frying. Most of them are trinkets, and gradually the gadget accessories break or get lost, and eventually the machine is only used for what you needed it for in the first place—to vacuum! Ninety-five percent of your vacuuming can be accomplished with just two or three basic tools.

My criticism of attachments is well documented by your own experience. That big display box of nickel-plated gizmos to hook up to your vacuum is a dandy selling point. But it gets shuffled, unused, from closet to closet for years until the box disintegrates. Then the tools themselves are banged around but never used. Finally, after twelve years, you need the goose-necked anteater attachment to vacuum the glove box of the car. Then you can't find it. If you're buying an upright, forget the attachments.

Just get a sturdy, simple upright. Do be sure to get a vacuum with a long cord—who among us has not wished a hundred times that the vacuum cord was "just ten feet longer"? An extension cord is a pain and cuts

your efficiency greatly. Every time you need to use it you have to hunt it down from the family member who borrowed it for some other purpose.

For your second machine, invest in a tank-type wet/dry vacuum. You'll be money and time ahead.

Commercial uprights are available with either cloth or disposable paper bags; some have a second type of cloth bag that zips open so you can replace the paper bag inside. Cloth bags are reuseable, so you aren't always buying disposables and then having to find a place to store them (due to popular demand, some uprights such as the Eurekas now have a bag holder right on them). I like cloth bags best, but it's a matter of taste. Disposables, on the other hand, can be changed more quickly, don't make a mess when you do, and keep you from handling all the germs, pollen and dust that fly around when you empty a regular vacuum bag. Disposables can be popped out and put right into the trash. In seconds, you're back on the road again.

If you use good doormats, you'll cut down vacuuming intake considerably, and a cloth bag will last a long time. Cloth bags need to be emptied *before* they're a third full and shaken well to keep them from becoming impregnated with soil. If you lack a suitable alley, north forty, or yard to do the airing, disposable bags might serve you better. When bags get too clogged, you'll smell dust when you click the vacuum on. If you see dust pouring out when you start the vacuum up, you've waited too long.

There is a trick to easy cloth bag emptying. After you remove the bag, turn it upside down, holding your hand over the opening, and shake the bag vigorously for a minute or so. All of the clinging dirt within will fall to the top of the bag, and then you can just hold the bag over a waste container, slide off the bag clamp, and let the ball of dirt plop into the waste can. This way there'll be minimum spills, and you won't get dust all over.

Watch a cloth bag while the machine is on. If it blows out like a big balloon the pores are beginning to fill up with dust and the air flow is being constricted. This means reduced suction and pickup. It's time to replace the bag. You can vacuum the bag inside and out, but sooner or later, you'll have to replace it. Don't try to wash the bag, either—it'll negatively affect its operation, and the bag will still have to be replaced soon.

The wet/dry vacuum

A wet/dry is a vacuum that can be safely used to pick up both dry material and liquids. Generally this is accomplished by a simple filter adjustment. Wet/drys are great! They are the vacuums to buy a few attachments for, and the first one should be an extra-long hose.

A wet/dry will not only clean up floods and spills and empty the fish tank, it's great for carpet edges, drapes, floors, furniture, rafters (another reason for a long hose), car upholstery, campers, boats ... the list could go on and on.

A small (ten-gallon capacity) wet/dry is the best size for the household. Those twenty-gallon units will tempt you, but stay with the small—remember, you'll be carrying it full of toilet overflow, diluted doo-doo and other unpleasantries better not slopped out of the tank when you go to empty it. And getting out and muscling around a jumbo wet/dry is a job you'll start wanting to dodge. Wet/drys range in price from $49.95 (on sale) at K-Mart to $120, or you can go high society and get a deluxe stainless steel tank

type at a local janitorial-supply store for several hundred dollars. I warn you, when your neighbors and relatives see what a wet/dry can do, you'll have to buy them one for Christmas, so shop accordingly!

The upright and wet/dry vacuums together are approximately a $500 investment and will take care of all your basic vacuum needs.

Special-purpose assistants

The following helpers make special vacuuming jobs a snap:

- Hand vacs, for quick pickup of little messes like a few cracker crumbs on the couch or the litter the kitty kicked out of the box. We're much more likely to clean it up *now* if we don't have to get out a whole big vacuum rig and plug it in. There are even hand-helds (like the Eureka Step Saver) with beater bars that can handle things like embedded stair tread grit.

- Self-propelled vacuums are not just for the weak or lazy. When they first came out, I wouldn't use one. (After all, John Wayne would never use a self-propelled vacuum.) I have two now, and they're nicer than cruise control.

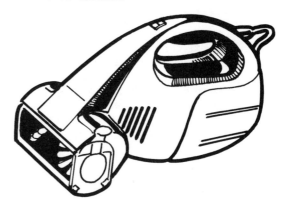

A hand vac with a beater bar, the Eureka Step Saver.

A full-size cordless vacuum.   **A wide-track vacuum.**

- Full-size cordless vacuums like the Eureka Freedom are battery-powered and can go up to thirty minutes without recharging. Light, quick and easy to use—all the advantages of a cordless vac in a larger size.

- Wide-track vacuums like Eureka's wide-track upright with a sixteen-inch head (instead of the usual eleven or twelve) zooms over the carpet in no time. If you have a big home with lots of carpet, like my wife and I, it'll cut a third off your

vacuuming time. This is one secret that janitors with their acres of carpet have known for years.

Cord control

Two ways we pros keep vacuum cords out of the way: (1) Hold the cord in your free hand, or (2) drape it over your shoulder and vacuum your way into a room or area instead of going all the way in and then vacuuming out (fighting the cord all the way).

Built-in vacuum systems

These beauties—also called "central vacs"—are still one of the best-kept secrets on the market. Watch them take off in the next ten years!

My first experience with a built-in vacuum came when I opened a closet in a house we were cleaning. I winced in startled fright at what I thought was a giant coiled python ready to strike. Its sedate reaction identified it as the longest vacuum hose I'd ever seen. "Wow, there must be some hunk of a vacuum to fit this baby," I thought. The owner later showed me the little wall receptacle where the hose inserted and turned into an instant vacuum. In the next year or so I only encountered or heard of a few more, but the more I saw of them, the more I liked them. And all of their owners seemed to be in love with them.

As I met ever more homemakers across the nation in my seminars and tours, "What about central vacs?" became a question I was asked at every other stop. I began to seek out sources of the central vacuum and had a hard time finding one or two, and my builder and supplier were as uneducated as I. Now in the '90s at least seventeen companies are hard at work selling America central vacs.

Installation is what most of us wonder about, but the vacuums fit easily in new homes and without much difficulty in the already-built ones. Dealers have videotapes to show you how to install them yourself, or they will do it for you. A central vac averages around $1,200 installed, but that's a bargain considering the time and energy it'll save over the years. I'm putting one in the maintenance-free house I'm building in Hawaii and in my twenty-five-year-old masonry home. If you need a source, write to me and I'll send you a list of companies who can direct you to local distributors.

Here are the pluses of the central vac:

1. It saves wear and tear on the house (the vacuum hitting furniture legs and baseboards, etc.).

2. It's the cleanest vacuum going. Residual dust has no home here—it goes out of the room.

3. Since the motor's far away in the basement or garage, it's amazingly quiet.

4. All you handle is a light hose, so it's super easy to use, especially for those once-a-day pickups or once-overs.

5. It's a permanent investment. You can buy one regular vacuum after another and end up with nothing to show for it, but installing a built-in is like putting money in the bank. It's there for good, and it increases the value of the house.

But the nicest thing about central vacs is their simplicity—no vacuum to drag out, no canister to drag around, no cord to keep flipping over furniture (or pulling out of the socket). Central vacs also have *lots* of power, so don't go sticking it on your skin to test the suction.

If you're installing a central vac

The hose of one of these is a little awkward if it's too long; I'd put in a few more receptacles so you can use a short hose.

And here, too, you'll want beater brush action to bounce dirt out, and the manufacturers do make a beater brush head for the hose. If you get the air-driven type of beater head you won't have to worry about needing an electrical outlet at or near each receptacle, to plug the power head into. Be sure to put a couple of outlets in the garage and anyplace you have stairs.

Put the receptacle in the garage near the exterior door, as three-quarters or more of your vehicle vacuuming will be on the driveway, not in the garage.

Mount all the receptacles and switches high—it'll save a lot of bending over.

A vacuuming in time. . .

A good carpet-cleaning program will free you from hours of work and emotional anguish. Clean carpets look and feel better, and they last longer. A regularly maintained carpet means less frequent shampooing, less time expended on carpet care, a longer life for the carpet, and more compliments from your guests!

The ideal carpet care plan is to (1) keep all possible dust, dirt and abrasive material from getting on the carpet—the job of good matting; (2) regularly remove all litter and extract harmful embedded debris from the carpet—the job of a good vacuum; (3) keep grime cleaned off the top of the carpet so that it doesn't have a chance to penetrate—the job of effective surface cleaning.

Install a good set of mats as explained in chapter eight, and vacuum carpets and mats regularly. Don't wait until you can see the dirt. Just because it's possible to camouflage crumbs, dog biscuits, pins, pennies and peelings in deep pile doesn't mean you should overdo it. Keep all materials detrimental to carpeting out of the carpet. I've seen homes go for ten years before the carpets needed shampooing, all due to good matting and regular maintenance. Avoiding unnecessary shampooing is wise because shampooing is expensive, whether you do it yourself or have it done professionally.

Professional secrets of better, faster vacuuming

Always police the area first, to get any large debris off the carpet. A quick bend to pick up an object by hand is a lot faster and smarter than wasting ten minutes—and who knows how much repair shop money—trying to dig it out of your vacuum.

When possible, plug in to a strategic location that will allow you to vacuum the maximum area and avoid backtracking.

You don't have to vacuum every square inch every time. Spend most of your time on the traffic areas—that's where the dirt really is. Under and behind furniture and other out of the way or unused areas can go for two weeks or more without hurting a thing (including your honor). Likewise, don't sweat the edges—where the vacuum won't reach and the foot never treads. Once every two weeks or so before vacuuming, sweep along the baseboards to flick anything there out to where the vacuum can reach it. Occasionally run over the corners and edges with your canister vac and crevice tool or dusting brush. Any dirt (mostly dust) there won't wear out the carpet, since we don't walk along the walls.

Slow, deliberate strokes pick up better and are faster in the end than zipping over one area three or four times. Let the vacuum work for you. It needs time for the beater bar to loosen the dirt and for the air flow to suck it up. If you watch a lot of vacuumers, you'll see that much time is spent in overlap. This is a waste of time if you have a beater brush assembly on your vacuum. Overlap each stroke an inch or so, but avoid running the machine over the same area twice, except as might be needed in badly soiled, high-traffic areas.

If you have a room that's especially dirty, you may have to resort to overlapping, up and back vacuuming strokes. But this takes a lot of time, tires you out, and usually isn't necessary. In rooms or halls that are too small for effective maneuvering, instead push the vacuum to the end of the stroke and then pull it back to cover the next strip of carpet. After you've pulled the vacuum all the way back, push it forward again and repeat the process. This method is quick and will do an effective job 90 percent of the time.

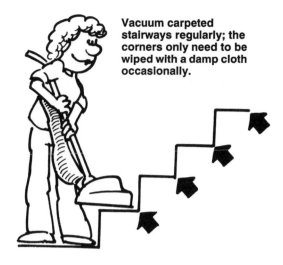

Vacuum carpeted stairways regularly; the corners only need to be wiped with a damp cloth occasionally.

Stairs

Don't get on your hands and knees— vacuum the center traffic areas of the steps with your beater brush vacuum. This will remove even deeply embedded dirt. As for the edges and corners that rarely are tread upon, just wipe with a damp cloth to pick up the visible surface dust, and occasionally hit 'em with your canister when you do the edges in the rest of the house.

● Area or throw rugs

Take them to a nearby carpeted floor for vacuuming. If you stand on one end of the rug and vacuum away from you, it won't get sucked in.

● Vacuuming carpet fringe

Those fringes on area rugs and carpets are just laying there waiting to be sucked up and jam your beater brush. Outsmart them by quickly sweeping them out of the way (over onto the rug they're attached to); then you can vacuum by and pull up that previously hidden dust and dirt. Or you can bleed off the vacuum suction (that means open the little valve on the hose so the vacuum won't have as much suction).

Edges are only a visual problem because traffic wear is impossible.

Sweep when they're dusty.

It will then pull up the dust bunnies, but not the fringes. You can use the suction adjustment when you vacuum drapes, too.

Always keep your vacuum on carpeted area while it's running. I've ruined a beautiful wood floor by running a low-adjusted beater bar type vacuum over it. The metal part of the bar thumped the floor on every rotation and dented it (at great expense to me, since our insurance covers liability but not stupidity).

Don't abuse your vacuum

Eighty percent of vacuuming problems are caused not by a loose nut on the machine, but by the loose nut running it. The personality and habits of the user can take a great toll on vacuums. For example, I gave two heavy-duty commercial vacuum cleaners for Christmas in 1965, one to my mother-in-law and one to another relative. My mother-in-law's vacuum still looks and works like new (she's had it twenty-six years now). The other one lasted less than thirteen months.

The unintentional (or sometimes intentional) vacuuming of coat hangers, Scout badges, marbles, overshoes

Never feel under a beater vacuum to see if it's working.

Make sure the beater and belt are working properly.

WRONG! Kicks dirt out and away from vacuum.	RIGHT! Pulls dirt under vacuum to the intake.

and scissors is what hurts vacuums. Those clicks and clanks you hear when the vacuum picks up one of these or similar articles generally means the (usually plastic) blades of the little gizmo that generates suction, called the impeller or the turbulator fan, are being sheared off. If you're vacuuming more and enjoying it less (getting up less dirt), you had probably better re-

place the fan. It's not uncommon to have a fine-running vacuum without suction, and a beat-up $5 fan is generally the reason. (If it's not the fan, then it's probably the beater brush.)

Note: A strong bar magnet screw-mounted to the front of your upright vacuum will pick up tacks, pins, needles, scissors, can openers, or any other metal object you might miss before vacuuming. It will save injuries to crawling babies, wrestling kids and nice, new vacuum cleaners.

Vacuum health check-up

The biggest secret of efficient vacuuming is *keeping your vacuum well maintained.* Your vac is your second most important set of wheels, so take care of it and check it regularly, just like your car.

● Don't let your bag "overeat." Anything more than 50 percent full will sap your vacuum's cleaning energy and strain the motor. Keep cloth bags emptied and shaken out so the pores in the cloth won't get clogged. To avoid leaks, keep the bag clip tight.

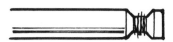

- Never run over the cord or pinch it in doorways. Avoid using extension cords; they lower your vacuum's performance.

- Protect the plug. Remove it from the receptacle with your fingers, not by pulling on the cord.

- Tighten the screws in the handle every so often or they'll work loose and fall off. Keep the handle clean — it's easier to grip, and healthier too.

- Keep the rubber bumper in place to protect your vacuum as well as your furniture and baseboards.

- Make sure the brushes on the beater brush aren't worn to nubs (if they are, you can slip in a new brush insert — it's easy). Check the beater occasionally for cracks or jagged edges that can snag carpet pile.

- The right pile adjustment on your vacuum gives the beater brush room to move to loosen deep dirt. It also ensures that the suction will be able to carry the debris into the bag. Set the brush to its highest setting, completely up off the floor, and turn the vacuum on. Lower the setting gradually until you hear the brush come in light contact with the carpet. If you set it lower than that ("I'm really gonna chomp the carpet"), you cut off the air flow and slow down the beater.

- Make sure the belt is tight and that it's on right. If it's worn, replace it. Don't buy cheap imitation belts, only genuine original manufacturer's parts for your make and model. If the belt runs hot, clean the motor pulley of threads, glaze and accumulated dirt.

- Make sure the beater or roll bar turns easily and is free of thread, string and shoelaces. String wrapped around the bar will pres-

sure the bearings and cause them to turn harder and even heat up. Hooking the point of scissors under them is the best way to remove things like this.

- If you seem to have a lot less suction these days, have a vacuum repair shop check the fan. The fan is what creates the suction, and the blades might be worn down or broken. For a few dollars you'll have your vac like new again.

A new vac fan

A worn vac fan

- Dust the exterior of the machine, and wipe off the power cord occasionally!

Soil retardant

If your carpeting isn't one of the newer types with soil resistance built right into the fibers, it's generally a good idea to treat with soil retardant.

A soil retardant is a chemical treatment that helps carpet resist soiling and helps prevent water- and soil-based spots and spills from becoming hard-to-remove stains. Water-based soiling agents especially, such as soft drinks, milk, coffee, mud and winter slush, cause big maintenance problems as they soak into carpet fibers and backing, rapidly deteriorating appearance. Soil retardants can be applied to *clean* carpet, old or new. (It's often applied during manufacture, so chances are your new carpet has it. Ask, when you buy a carpet.)

The best-known brand of soil retardant is Scotchgard, made by the 3M Company. If applied correctly, it can be a real boon. After spending time in the 3M testing labs observing control blocks of carpet, treated and untreated, I was impressed. Apply Scotchgard yourself following the directions on the container, or have your dealer do it for you. You can even purchase carpet and upholstery shampoo containing Scotchgard.

But just because carpet is protected by a soil retardant doesn't mean you can relax. You must still keep up your regular schedule of cleaning and maintenance. The chemical types of soil retardant have to be reapplied every time you deep-clean (shampoo) the carpet. Carpets with soil protection locked right into the fibers themselves must be cleaned according to the manufacturer's instructions, or you can undo their stain resistance and void the warranty.

Antistatic agents

Static electricity is the mild shock produced when you touch a metal object after walking across a carpet. It's the result of friction. While not harmful—unless you have a home computer that will go on the blink—it can be irritating. And static electricity can actually pull dust particles from the air. By eliminating static, you keep your carpet cleaner.

Some carpeting contains a small amount of stainless steel fiber to dissipate static electricity. For carpeting that lacks this feature, applying an antistatic agent to the carpet periodically, or simply increasing the humidity in the room, can help the problem.

Shampooing the carpet

There comes a time in the life of all carpet, regardless of how faithfully you have vacuumed, removed spills and spots, and kept mats at the doors, that it will have collected enough dirt and soil deep in the pile that it just has to be washed or "shampooed" out. Some people shampoo the carpet every year (which is probably too often), and some every ten years or when they can see it start to twitch and move by itself. The grime usually sneaks up on us, like weight gain or weeds in the garden—by the time we realize it, it's too far gone. Its location, color, and the amount of traffic it receives will have a lot to do with when a carpet needs to be cleaned, but there are several ways to determine when shampooing is needed:

1. Look for a clean place (under the couch, a saved remnant, etc.) and compare it with the rest of the carpet.

2. Feel it! Yes, dirty carpet feels heavy, matted and sticky.

3. Rub it with a white towel dampened with carpet shampoo. The dirt and soil will show up like a red flag.

4. Smell it. Musty, dusty carpet has a smell we all know too well. Get down on your knees and sniff a few times.

5. You can see a three-foot grimy circle around the TV chair or the dust storm that follows you when you walk across the carpet!

Okay, it's ripe. Besides that, company is coming, and you're holding your third daughter's wedding reception at home. You have two basic choices to get the job done: Do it yourself, or call a professional. (And once it's clean, start a regular surface cleaning program—see page 129.)

I'm the first to push independence and "doing your own thing," but I caution you about the pitfalls of shampooing your own carpet. It's not necessarily a complicated job, but don't be deceived by the propaganda of trouble-free, money-saving, automatic, do-it-all machinery. The operator of the machine has to have some knowledge, the ability to adapt to different carpet-cleaning requirements, and understand how much moisture and chemical to use. Otherwise a poor cleaning job, overwetting, or fiber and backing damage will result. It amazes me that people will spend $2,500 for a carpet, then attack it with powerful cleaning gear without any experience whatsoever.

Another pitfall is cost-value miscalculation. Take, for example, a 14×20-foot living room carpet, which a professional might do for $30. A pair of homeowners (one of whom is missing a fishing trip) will drive ten miles across town to rent a big steamer or rug outfit for $15. Then they'll buy $5 worth of chemicals, skin up the family car getting it all in, and drive another ten miles home. They'll unload the

heavy equipment, grunting and groaning. Then they'll move furniture, read directions, spend most of Saturday cleaning carpet, and probably will have to drive back for more shampoo. The results will be questionable.

Once they're finished, it's a repeat performance of loading and driving to return the equipment. At the end of the day, they've spent $35 on gas, rent, shampoo, etc.—not to mention their time. They are dead tired; have

experienced a smashed hand, three arguments, two dogfights—and come Sunday night the carpet still isn't dry in places. I've cleaned carpets for thirty-five years, and always do my own because I know how and have easy access to the equipment. But I would never do my own if I had to round up and rent the mediocre machines available and go through all that. I couldn't afford it and wouldn't enjoy the hassle.

If you insist on doing it yourself, see pages 127-128 for some ways to improve your results.

Professional carpet cleaning

There are also pitfalls to having your carpet done. Not all so-called professionals *are* professionals. Some "carpet cleaners" are opportunists who were franchised or hired for a big kill; their training has been by trial and error. The method used in shampooing carpets is important. That TV before-and-after demonstration of a great contrast once a little foamy carpet shampoo is rubbed on is deceptive. That isn't cleanliness you behold, but the "optical brightening" most carpets exhibit when wetted. After a light foam job, many carpets appear to gleam and sparkle, but they can still be filthy.

This has been the story with most home carpet-cleaning and is in fact the reason you so often hear: "Never shampoo your carpets, for once you do, they will get dirty faster." They *do* get dirty faster, but only because the surface was grazed with a dab of shampoo, and the dirt and soap were carried by the moisture down to the bottom of the fibers, only to emerge quickly when the carpet is in use again. (Remember—ask yourself, when you clean, where the dirt goes.

If you can't figure it out, the dirt probably isn't coming out.) Also, many shampoos leave a soil-attracting residue on the carpet fibers.

Great deals?

You will be approached by mail or by phone with the "mist" method, the "dry-foam" method, the "liquid" method, the "dry-powder" method, and the "steam" or "extraction" method. I would be cautious of any of these on my carpets because they are all in some way obsolete or ineffective. For example, "steam" isn't what it's cracked up to be, but when steam cleaning hit the market, it positively revolutionized carpet-cleaning. It wasn't the steam itself but the extraction process that was so valuable: Hot cleaning solution is pressure-injected into the carpet, and a super-strong wet vacuum is used immediately to pull almost all the moisture back out.

It's my opinion that steam extraction alone generally won't clean an old, dirty carpet. I know the water extracted from the carpet is impressively muddy, but remember that the dwell time between the solution's being injected and removed is so brief that it can't dissolve much of the goop adhering to the fibers. Rotary motion or scrubbing action is needed after the solution is applied to loosen all the dirt and deep-clean the carpet. This should be followed by extracting (rinsing) to remove all dirt, soap, etc.

If you do decide to have your carpets done rather than do them yourself, first make sure there's a good, professional carpet cleaner in your area. (*Always* check references.) They'll do a better job than you can, and probably save you money over doing it yourself.

Be sure to get a firm price quote. And ask which method they use. If they say "steam" or "extraction," request a truck-mounted unit that heats the solution to 150° and has the power to actually steam-clean your carpet. Request that they prespot and prespray any stains.

If they say "rotary," make sure that after they've scrubbed the carpet it is rinsed with hot water by the extraction method. That means, if nine gallons of liquid go into the carpet, they get eight-and-a-half gallons back out. Some professionals call the combination of rotary scrubbing and hot water extraction "showcase" cleaning. It's the most expensive but does the best job.

How to do a better job if you do it yourself

All kinds of places carry rental shampoo equipment, from the simplest to the two-gorilla size guaranteed to beat up your car and give you a hernia loading and unloading. Companies such as Bissell and Sears also sell scaled-down hot-water extraction units.

Equipment like this doesn't have the horsepower to truly deep-clean the carpet all the way down to the roots—suction isn't strong enough and the water doesn't get hot enough. These units are probably better suited for surface cleaning (see page 129). If you follow the manufacturer's directions, the best you can expect is a fair job of shampooing. Let me give you some better directions, whether you use them to surface clean or shampoo. You can do a couple of important things at home with a small extractor that will double your shampooing speed and efficiency.

When you shoot the cleaning solution in, the filthy water you pull right back out gives the illusion that your carpet is really getting cleaned, but that dirty water is just the easy surface dirt that comes off as soon as the carpet is wet. The little sprayers shoot the solution in, but before it can attack

the tough, stuck-on dirt—the aged dog doo, the smashed raisins, the ground-in jellybeans—the vacuum pulls it back out. We pros call this problem not enough "dwell time"; in other words, the solution isn't in the fibers long enough to exert any chemical action, only to dissolve the loose, easy dirt.

Protect carpet when shampooing. Block furniture legs with pieces of cardboard or waxed paper.

If an imprint remains . . .

Rub the area with a bit of clear water.

Brush up and let it dry.

The good professional carpet cleaner using an extractor system does one of two things, either of which you can do:

1. Scrub the carpet briefly before you start to extract, using a rotary floor scrubber or "buffer," or even just by hand with a cleaning cloth or towel. Just dip up some shampoo foam (not lots of water) and work it into the carpet so it can attack and emulsify the dirt clinging to the carpet yarn. Then when you come behind, with the extractor shooting hot water into the carpet and pulling it out, it's like a flushing rinse; a lot more of the dirt comes out, a lot faster.

2. Use a carpet prespray solution at least five minutes before you start shampooing. *Lightly* spray the carpet, using a hand spray bottle or even a weed sprayer, if the job is a big one. You don't want to soak it, just mist it to wet the surface, where most of the dirt and airborne oils are. Spray a little heavier in the traffic patterns where the dirt is thicker and worked in. The solution will loosen and release the soil and as your carpet lays there, panting and wounded, you pass over it with your trusty extractor unit— *snort, bobble, squeak*—your water will *really* be dirty now, and you can sigh confidently that you do have most of the dirt.

Rental extractor units such as Rug Doctor have a little scrubber built into the head, which is fine. But even with these it's better to first apply the solution lightly with the scrubbing tool but not the vacuum; then, on the second trip, give it the full business, all controls on. This way you'll have given the shampoo time to "deterg the dirt."

If you do a lot of shampooing, go to a janitorial-supply store (or see page 44 for a mail-order source) and

A home-size hot water extraction machine.

get a gallon of shampoo concentrate. It's much cheaper than the stuff they sell with the machines.

Surface cleaning to delay shampooing

Most homeowners put up with increasingly dirty carpet until they can't stand it anymore, then they spring for an expensive steam-cleaning job. They could learn something from those who maintain carpeting in commercial buildings. These people have learned the value of regular surface cleaning to keep carpets looking good and to stretch out the time between deep cleanings. Surface cleaning is just what it sounds like—a spiffing up of the surface of the carpeting, as opposed to deep cleaning (such as extraction cleaning or shampooing), which takes more time but cleans the carpet clear down to the base of the fibers.

There are various ways to surface clean carpeting, and a home extraction machine, as described earlier, is one. Dry powders (Host, Capture and Amway dry carpet cleaners are some good ones) can be applied by hand or with a machine (purchased or rented) specially designed to scrub them in; with many models you have to use a regular vacuum to remove the powder afterward. There is also the system professionals use called "bonneting." This is a process of taking a yarn bonnet (a yarn pad or disc two inches or so thick) dampened with a special solvent cleaner and simply rubbing it on the carpet. Or if you have a floor machine, you can use it to massage the surface of the carpet with the yarn bonnet. We use it at night on the traffic lanes of commercial buildings, and they're dry in an hour. Bonneting

doesn't deep-clean and it does leave a speck or two of residue, but it's widely used in the professional field and I use it in my own home. I've been in a Bell System office in Pasadena, California, that has used this method for seven years. The carpets, even in the reception area, are clean and new-looking, though they've never been shampooed.

The bonnet treatment is fast, easy and inexpensive. After you moisten the bonnet with carpet-cleaning solution, you wring it out in your roller mop bucket, then mount it under the floor machine and run it over the carpet. The machine moves the pad in a rotating motion on the carpet, and the bonnet picks up and absorbs surface grime and soils. When the pad becomes dirty, turn it over and repeat the process. When both sides are dirty, rinse the bonnet clean in the mop bucket, wring it out and repeat the process.

In a home, a once-a-month bonnet-

A few more do-it-yourself carpet-cleaning cautions

- Vacuum well before you start.
- Don't let the solution sit too long before you extract it.
- Don't overwet! Keep the wand moving and only make one pass to wet the carpet. Overwetting can cause the backing and pad to rot, mildew or even shrink.
- Use a good-quality shampoo in the recommended dilution. Using cheap shampoo or too much shampoo can cause rapid resoiling.
- Ventilate!
- Long-napped carpet may need to be raked or swept to a stand-up position to dry.

ing would be plenty. It does take a certain solution such as Argo Sheen to produce the best results, so check with a professional supplier if you plan to try the bonnet system. A janitorial-supply store can direct you to the right chemical to clean with and a bonnet to fit your floor machine.

You can also use a plain old terry towel or a hand applicator (a dustmop-looking tool), such as that made by Argo Sheen, to bonnet. (The Oreck Company also now produces a little twelve-inch oscillating scrubber perfect for bonneting.)

I like surface cleaning because it holds carpets to a consistent level of cleanliness and replaces the old inefficient up-and-down approach to cleaning. There is something spiritually uplifting about a clean, fresh expanse of carpet.

Spots and stains

Spots, stains and spills on carpet are just as upsetting in the home as they are in the commercial buildings I clean.

There are two basic approaches to take to carpet spots:

One way is to keep just two different spot removers on hand: an all-purpose spotter for water-based substances (food, blood, etc.), and a solvent spotter for tar, grease and oil stains. (If a particular problem keeps recurring in your household, you may want to select in addition to the two spotters and keep on hand—bacteria/enzyme digester, for example, if you have pet "accidents" or children in toilet training.) These spotters are available at janitorial-supply stores, and are very effective. If there's a stain they won't remove, you can call in a professional to get the spot out chemically or to doughnut-cut that piece of carpet and plug in a new piece.

If you're a do-it-yourself type, keep handy a spotting kit (see page 132) and consult the stain chart following. A janitorial-supply store will carry any of the items not available at the supermarket or discount store. Both the kit and chart are useful in the laundry room, too.

Remember, keep cleaning solutions and tools safely out of reach of little children. I would suggest you store your spot removal tools and supplies in a small plastic carrying tray. This will organize your supplies for quick attack on spots.

It's important before you try to deal with it to know what a stain or mark on the carpet *is*. What base is it—water or oil? You must match the base of the stain to the base of the cleaner—for instance, a water-based detergent solution won't make much of an impact on oil, but a petroleum-based solvent spotter will dissolve it immediately.

Smelling and feeling a spot will help you determine what it is. You can also ask other household members (nicely) if they know anything about how the spot got there. If a spot is darker than the carpet, you have a chance of removing it; if it's lighter, that means the substance bleached the fibers and the spot will need to be plugged (unless you can rearrange the furniture).

Bleaching a stain—even with the relatively mild hydrogen peroxide—is a last resort, and I don't generally recommend it, unless you want a little adventure or a new *white* spot as a conversation piece. Before you bleach, *always* test the carpet or fabric in an unobtrusive place.

Red stains—from barbecue sauce to Kool Aid to melted cherry popsicles—have always been among the worst. But now there are special professional products such as Red Out designed just for this purpose, so if you have a stubborn red blotch somewhere,

How to remove carpet stains

1.  Catch the spot or stain when it's fresh. Chances for removal are 75 percent better.

2. 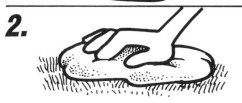 Carefully blot or scrape the entire stained area thoroughly before applying any solution. If the spot is very large, use your wet/dry vacuum. Avoid using liquids before you've blotted up all you can; they might spread the stain.

3.  Before using any chemicals, test carpet in a small, inconspicuous area to make sure damage or discoloration won't occur.

4.  Don't rub the spill; it might spread the problem. Work spot cleaner from the outside of the stain toward the inside to avoid spreading the stain.

5. 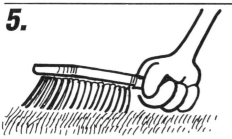 After treatment, blot up all moisture. If you used a detergent or ammonia cleaning solution, rinse the spot with cool or lukewarm water. Blot again. Dry with a terry towel and brush the nap to a standing position after the stain is gone. Be sure you blot with a clean *white* cloth.

6.  After final blotting, if you feel there is still too much moisture, place a stack of white cotton towels about ¾ inch thick over the spot and weight them with a heavy object. Leave for five hours. Then brush up the nap.

check with a pro carpet cleaner.

The critical difference in spot removal on carpet as opposed to other fabrics or hard surfaces is drying. Carpets are low and there's no such thing as air circulation under them, so whenever you wet them you better pull that moisture back out with a dry cloth (blot) or even a wet/dry vacuum, if necessary. Get out all the moisture you can, and if it's still wet place a fan near the spot. If carpet stays damp it will rot, mildew, breed bacteria, smell, and the floor underneath can even warp and buckle!

If you have wool carpet or upholstery, try to avoid wet-cleaning it. Use dry-cleaning solvents whenever possible. Call your dealer for advice.

Be patient—give the chemicals time to work. Don't expect all stains to come out immediately—most take some time.

Most old stains and spots can't be removed, and some chemical stains are permanent damage that can't be reversed, so don't get your hopes up too high about that three-year-old acne medicine stain you've had the lamp table over. It might have to remain until you replace the rug!

Spot removal kit

Bear in mind that there is no one miracle stain remover; most stains require a combination of chemicals and a several-stage attack.

Keep the following things on hand to attack fresh spills: (1) a spotting brush (available at janitorial-supply stores) and a scraper (a dull butter knife will serve the purpose); (2) clean white terry cloths (you always want a *white* absorbent cloth when working with stains so you can check for colorfastness and see if the stain is coming out or not); (3) neutral detergent such as liquid dishwashing detergent (dilute 20:1 for spotting); (4) clear household ammonia (don't use on silk or wool); (5) white vinegar (dilute 1:1 with water for cotton, linen and acetate); (6) solvent dry-cleaning fluid such as Energine, Carbona or Afta; (7) hydrogen peroxide (3 percent solution) for bleaching; (8) enzyme digestant such as Biz (soak washables in a solution of digestant for up to an hour; mix into a paste with water and apply for 15 to 30 minutes to dry cleanables); and (9) denatured or isopropyl alcohol. If you have pets, stock a bacteria/enzyme digester also, such as Out! Pet Odor Eliminator.

Pretreat whenever possible. Apply a laundry pretreat or just some liquid laundry detergent, or powdered detergent made into a paste, to the stained area for 15 to 30 minutes prior to washing. This will loosen the stain so the washer can flush it away. You may need some gentle persuasion, too, which means a little physical assistance or "agitation." A stain is generally locked or lodged into the fibers of any fabric; you usually need to gently push or pull it out.

If it's a mystery stain, first try a dry solvent. If it's still there then try a water-based spot remover.

In the following instructions, the terms "sponge" or "feather" are used frequently. Their meanings are as follows: **Sponge**—Lay the stained article face-down on a pad of clean, white, absorbent cloth and use another such pad, dampened with the spotter, to push the spotter through the stained fabric into the pad below. **Feather**—Rinse and dry a spot from the outside in, to blend in the edges and avoid leaving a ring.

Don Aslett Spot Removal Chart

STAIN/SPOT	METHOD
Alcohol (Liquor, Beer or White Wine)	*Blot up all you can and sponge the spot with water. Sponge with vinegar; blot; rinse. If stain remains, use digestant, and if that doesn't do it, bleach with hydrogen peroxide.*
Blood	*Blot or scrape up all you can; soak old blood stains in salt water or digestant for several hours. Blot with cool water. Blot with ammonia; rinse. Bleach with hydrogen peroxide if necessary. If stain remains, try commercial rust remover from a janitorial-supply store.*
Candle Wax/Crayon	*Scrape off all you can first with a scraper or butter knife. Put a clean, absorbent cloth over the spot and iron with a warm iron to melt and absorb the wax into the blotting cloth. Remove remaining residue with dry-cleaning fluid.*
Chocolate	*Scrape off all you can. Sponge with dry-cleaning fluid. Sponge with detergent solution; blot; rinse. If stain remains, bleach with hydrogen peroxide.*
Cigarette Burns	*For slight discoloration, rub with dry steel wool, vacuum up the debris, then apply detergent solution. Trim off blackened tufts with scissors. For bad burns, have a professional "doughnut cut" the damaged area out and plug in a new piece.*
Coffee	*Blot with detergent solution; rinse. Blot with vinegar; rinse; air-dry. If stain remains, sponge with dry-cleaning fluid. Bleach any remaining stain with hydrogen peroxide.*
Grass	*Sponge with water. Sponge with alcohol (exception: use vinegar if you're working with wool, silk or acetate). If stain remains, use digestant, then sponge with detergent solution; rinse. Bleach with hydrogen peroxide if necessary.*
Greasy Foods	*Gently scrape off all you can. Sponge with dry-cleaning fluid. Sponge with detergent solution. If stain remains, use digestant, then sponge with detergent solution; rinse. Bleach any remaining stain with hydrogen peroxide.*

STAIN/SPOT	METHOD
Gum	*Use aerosol gum freeze from a janitorial-supply or dry ice to harden the gum and make it brittle. Break into pieces by striking and scraping with a dull butter knife, then pick up the pieces. Remove residue with dry-cleaning fluid.*
Ink (Ballpoint)	*Sponge with detergent solution; rinse. If stain remains, saturate with cheap hair spray and blot. If still there, try alcohol, acetone or non-oily nail polish remover and a bleach safe for the fabric, in that order. If yellow stain remains, try commercial rust remover from a janitorial-supply store.*
Lipstick/Shoe Polish	*Gently scrape off all you can, being extra careful not to spread the stain. Blot dry-cleaning fluid through the stain into a clean, absorbent pad. Sponge with detergent solution; blot. Sponge with ammonia; rinse. If stain remains, try alcohol, then hydrogen peroxide.*
Mildew	*Dry-brush to remove as much of the mildew on the surface as possible. Sponge with disinfectant solution; blot. Sponge with ammonia; rinse. Bleach with chlorine bleach if safe for fabric; if not, use hydrogen peroxide.*
Milk/Cream/Ice Cream	*Sponge with detergent solution, then with ammonia; rinse and air-dry. Sponge any remaining stain with dry-cleaning fluid. If stain remains, use digestant, then sponge with detergent solution and rinse.*
Mustard/Catsup	*Scrape and blot to remove all you can. Sponge with detergent solution, then with vinegar; rinse. If stain remains, bleach with hydrogen peroxide.*
Nail Polish	*Blot acetone or non-oily nail polish remover through the stain into a clean, absorbent pad (test first for fabric damage — use no acetone on acetate, modacrylic, silk or wool.) For sensitive fabrics, use amyl acetate (banana oil), available at pharmacies. Flush with dry-cleaning fluid; air-dry. If stain remains, try alcohol, then hydrogen peroxide.*
Oil	*Absorb fresh oil with cornmeal or fuller's earth (available at pharmacies), then sponge with dry-cleaning fluid. Feather edges to avoid leaving a ring. If stain remains, sponge with detergent solution; rinse and feather.*

STAIN/SPOT	METHOD
Paint	*If fresh, flush with either mineral spirits for oil-based paint or detergent solution for latex. If dry, soften with lacquer thinner or paint stripper (test first for fabric damage), then flush with appropriate solvent.*
Rust	*Use commercial rust remover. Home remedies such as salt and lemon juice are slow and not always effective.*
Soft Drinks	*Blot up all you can. Blot with detergent solution; rinse; air-dry. If stain remains, soak with glycerin for thirty minutes and rinse.*
Tar/Grease	*Scrape up all you can, then remove residue by blotting with dry-cleaning fluid. Blot with detergent solution; rinse.*
Urine/Pet Stains	*Scrape up all the solid matter you can and blot out all liquid possible by placing an absorbent towel on the spot and standing on it. Apply a bacteria/enzyme digester according to directions. When dry, remove any remaining stain with detergent solution; rinse.*
Vomit	*Scrape up as much as possible, then rinse the spot with water. Blot with detergent solution. Blot with ammonia; rinse. If stain remains, use digestant, then sponge with detergent solution; rinse.*

Remember, when spills or stains occur, you need to act immediately. Get those spots when they're fresh and manageable, before they can set. For complete stain removal instructions for even the toughest stains, see my book, *Don Aslett's Stainbuster's Bible.*

My free catalog lists a full array of professional supplies and books to help with your every cleaning need. Write to me: Don Aslett, P.O. Box 39-H, Pocatello, ID 83204; or phone (208) 232-6212.

12.

What to do about furniture

"What should I do about furniture?" is a question homemakers ask me repeatedly. My own attitude toward furniture is, "I dislike moving it, and I dislike buying it even more." A woman has a finer appreciation for furniture because she's often the one who chooses it, plus much of her time is spent maintaining its appearance.

In an attempt to eliminate both my furniture frustrations, I designed most of the furniture out of a home we built in the resort mountains of Sun Valley, Idaho. Our living room had an octagonal conversation pit padded with vinyl cushions. Twelve or thirteen people could sit and visit comfortably. A plush padded two-stair landing where ten or twelve more visitors could sit

faced into the living room. This house didn't have a single piece of furniture except for the beds and the dining room set. I built the stereo and bookcases in, to eliminate cabinets and stands. Pedestal beds were built to the floor and other such adjustments were made to eliminate the clutter and upkeep of furniture. Our home was not only beautiful but usable for family and groups of up to forty, and I didn't have to buy or move furniture!

But for most of you, furniture not only must be bought and moved, it must be cleaned. So the question becomes, "How do I keep my furniture looking nice without a lot of time and effort?"

Attempts to answer this question

have greatly stimulated the sales of "miracle" furniture polishes. Think about the messages given by thousands of TV furniture polish commercials: "fast and easy"; "polished clean and lint-free"; "see yourself reflected"; "Brand X shines your dingy furniture better than Grandma's beeswax and turpentine and it smells woody, lemony and expensive."

Furniture care isn't that simple. There *are* some ways to cut the time spent caring for furniture and make it last longer. Notice I said "ways," not "way." It isn't done with a squirt of magic aerosol furniture polish as a TV or magazine ad might suggest.

My approach to furniture-cleaning is more preventive than maintenance-oriented. Buy high-quality furniture — well-manufactured furniture, though it may be expensive to buy, costs less in the long run. Cheap furniture loses its crisp, elegant look rapidly and becomes conspicuously dull and shabby-looking. Once in this decrepit condition, it takes a lot of time and supplies to maintain it. And it rarely looks any better cleaned and polished than it did

before you started. Select carefully and get good quality. Paying a little more cash will save a lot of your most precious commodity, personal time.

Choosing furniture with an eye to cleanability

The design and style of furniture you choose will determine how many hours per day, week or year you will have to give to maintaining it. Elaborate grooves, carvings and decorations take more time to keep looking good. And the more kinds of material furniture is made of (or a room is decorated with), the more time and types of equipment and supplies it will take to clean.

You are the sole judge on this one. If the prestige or decor of your home calls for the elaborate unit, you have to decide the long-range value of own-

Which chair leg would you rather clean?

ing it. No matter what you have in mind, check the furniture and make sure all the surfaces *can* be maintained. The wood should have a finish—not just an oiled surface or a colored stain, but a transparent varnish-type coat, called a "membrane finish," to prevent dirt and cleaning materials from penetrating into the wood. Natural or bare wood that needs constant "feeding" or oiling is a pain to maintain and will look dull and discolored before long. Lighter wood furniture shows less dust, is easier to make look good, and remains that way longer than darker furniture.

Metal should have a smooth finish, not be pitted or engraved. It should have a baked enamel or other hard-surfaced coating. Stainless steel and chrome are durable, but require a lot of effort to keep clean and bright.

Glass used as an overlay on a desk or table looks good and doesn't show dust, fingerprints, etc., too badly. But clear glass see-through units—coffee tables, end tables, breakfast tables—act like a magnifying glass. *Everything* shows—a piece of lint will look like a caterpillar carcass.

Is it cleanable?

Fabric will generally be the most used and abused part of furniture. Spillage on furniture is as common as on carpet, believe it or not. Some fabrics look superb, but stains and marks on them may never be removed. Ditto with unfinished cane and wicker furniture. But if you have your heart set

on it, spray-enamel or spray-polyurethane cane and wicker the minute you have it inside the door; this will make it somewhat cleanable (depending on what you spill on it).

Scotchgard, which you can buy at the supermarket or hardware store and apply, is a lifesaver for most upholstery and for you personally. It is an excellent protection for most fabrics, making them more maintainable, because the fibers are protected. But if a big bowl of borscht gets upended and sends a tidal wave of red over the table and onto a Scotchgarded seat, you'll probably need to consult the spot and stain removal chart (pages 133–135).

Is it restorable?

Some fabrics look great when new, or newly cleaned, but after a few people sit on them, they become matted or shiny. You've all seen velvet or fur-type material after it has been sat on: a rump print remains, and you have better things to do than go around brushing up cushions to make them look good. Pick a fabric that "restores," or comes back to life, after use (or that doesn't need to "restore"). Select a hard-finish fabric for dining room chairs that are used constantly. White or light-colored fabrics (especially solid colors) show and accent every spot. Fabrics with some color blend or a pattern hide dirt better. Again, this is a matter of taste—but try to make it easy on yourself. Remember, furniture exists for your use and comfort.

Keeping furniture looking nice

Convinced that the secret of furniture maintenance is in the bottle or can of polish, the majority of us use too much of it. We build up layers of gunk, which result in more work and sometimes even surface deterioration. A treated cloth that leaves no oil or residue, yet picks up dust, is the best way to go. Throw away your feather dusters (alias dust spreaders). They are the least effective duster going. You can purchase treated paper dust cloths at your local janitorial-supply store. They're called Masslinn cloths, and they'll last and last; when they're dirt-saturated you can throw them away.

The pro approach might give you new ideas about furniture cleaning. My company cleans thousands of desktops, tabletops, chairs, stands, racks and cabinets every night throughout the United States. In most of our cleaning, we wipe with Masslinn cloths to remove dust. When finger-marks have to be removed, we use a light spray of neutral all-purpose cleaner or a water-damp cloth to wipe, then dry-buff to a natural sheen. We avoid using polish where the finish can maintain its own luster. You could also use a solution of one of the oil soaps made for wood, followed immediately by buffing with a dry cleaning cloth.

If you use an aerosol polish, use it seldom and lightly. Select one type of polish and use it consistently. The reason for this is simple: Often your furniture surfaces will come out dull and streaked because your new polish isn't compatible with the old polish.

Types of polish

● Clear oil treatment

Usually some kind of oil (mineral or vegetable) and solvent blend, used to "feed" bare wood. Has a wet, glossy look when applied, but a dull sheen after it soaks in. Will become an oily, sticky film if used on varnished or membrane-finished wood.

● Liquid or paste solvent

Hard to apply. Excellent water and abrasion resistance. Low gloss, but durable.

● Oil emulsion polish

Cream type with same drawbacks as clear oil.

● Water or oil wax emulsion (aerosol or spray)

Contain a variety of waxes, silicones and polymers, generally in a water base. They have all the components of a good polish: they protect your furniture, enhance its beauty, and make it easy to dust. Used once a year or so they *are* good, but if you use them every time you clean they'll lay a thick layer of gunk on your pretty wood.

If you have raw or natural wood surfaces in your home, they'll need to be "fed," or treated to keep them from drying out and cracking. Rub on clear oil treatments such as lemon oil. Take your time so the wood can absorb it, then wipe off the excess.

However, I think feeding wood is a ridiculous waste of effort and material. Besides, if grease or ink get on bare wood, it's ruined. Either low-gloss or satin-sheen finishes are available that seal the surface, forming a glass-like membrane through which that beautiful grain will still be bright and clear and fully visible. Marks and stains will end up on the finish instead of on the wood.

If you wish to apply (or reapply) a varnish or polyurethane membrane coat to ailing wood surfaces, it's easy. First, clean the surface with a strong cleaning solution—a strong ammonia solution, wax stripper or degreaser if it's been sealed; solvent if raw—to take off all dirt and oils. Let it dry until any swollen grain goes down. Take care of any nicks or raised spots with a few strokes of superfine sandpaper, then wipe with a tack cloth or a cloth very lightly dampened with paint thinner to pick up any dust or lint on the surface. Finally, apply the varnish or polyurethane, paying attention to the directions on the container. It may take two coats.

your furniture shows dust, and how finicky you are.

Dust causes more mental anxiety to you than it does physical damage to your dwelling, so don't get your duster feathers ruffled. Dust is visually offensive and may strain your emotions when visitors drop by, but it does little harm unless someone in the family has an allergy. (Dust on floors, carpets and electronic equipment, however, *does* cause deterioration.) If I had a place I had to dust more than weekly, I'd move!

You can reduce dusting to a minor duty if:

1. You place and maintain proper matting.

2. Your vacuum works well and you use it. Empty your vacuum bag frequently, because if you vacuum when it's full you'll *create* dust.

3. You clean or replace your furnace and/or air conditioner filters regularly.

Dusting

One of the simplest ways to keep your furniture looking nice is to keep it dusted. The frequency with which you need to dust depends on how dusty or polluted your area is, how readily

4. Your home is weatherproofed (door and window seals, caulking, etc.); weatherproofing keeps dust out, too.

When you dust, don't use clouds of aerosol polish or puddles of oily wood treatments, because after a while, you'll create a waxy buildup that will not only look bad and be sticky and more difficult to clean, but actually attract and hold dust. Dust high places first. This gets the dead flies and other crud off the ledges onto the floor, from where it can be vacuumed easily. Always dust *before* you vacuum so that the crumbs and ashes and orange seeds in the corners and crannies of the furniture won't end up on a neatly vacuumed floor.

> **Dusting drill: (1) Dust before you vacuum; (2) work top to bottom; (3) a weekly once-over-lightly is enough for the average house; (4) monthly, hit door frames, window blinds, valances, light fixtures; (5) dust lofts and rafters at least twice a year, using an extension handle.**

Use the right dusting tool. *Don't* use a feather duster. The air movement a feather duster causes will blow particles all over and you'll chase dust for hours. Instead, use one or more of these tools:

1. A Masslinn cloth. This is the disposable chemically treated paper dustcloth I mentioned earlier. It picks up (in fact, attracts!) dust and small particles and is excellent for fine furniture. It will snag on rough surfaces (but any surface that rough should be vacuumed). When a cloth becomes saturated with dust (after about three months of daily use in the average-sized dwelling), simply pitch it and use a new one. These cloths leave a nice nonsticky luster on wood and other finishes and cost only pennies. They're available at janitorial-supply stores.

2. An electrostatic cloth. I'll admit its name—the "New Pig"—is ugly, but the cloth isn't. It's made of a new electrostatic fabric developed by DuPont. Without any oil or treatment of any kind it picks up and holds dust and lint and even gnat eyebrows. When it gets filthy (which it does because everything clings to it), just toss it in the washer. It can be laundered and reused one hundred or more times—now *that's* a dust cloth! I was skeptical at first, but it really works.

3. A water-dampened soft terry cleaning cloth (see Equipment Chart, chapter five). Make sure it's thoroughly wrung out so it's only slightly damp. A damp terry duster won't damage surfaces or create extra work; it will hold and remove dust and other residue. Make sure, when you use one, to keep switching to a clean side so it won't become a dust distributor. When it's dust-saturated, use another cloth. On glossy surfaces, buff behind the damp cloth with a dry cloth.

4. A lambswool duster. This is a fluffy ball of (sometimes synthetic) wool on the end of a long handle. It

> **Cobwebs come off easily if you flick them off, rather than rub them in. The lambswool duster is the best tool for the purpose.**

looks like cotton candy on a stick, but almost magically picks up dust and fine particles by static attraction. It's especially good for dusting high and low cobwebs and venetian or mini blinds. Shake it outside after use, and vacuum it when it gets dust-saturated. Lambswool dusters can be bought at a janitorial-supply store or a local housewares store.

Becoming a dust detective

The big trick to dusting is learning where the dust collects: the corners, tops and bottoms of walls and furniture, light fixtures, wall hangings, and any horizontal surface, is the answer. The greatest amount of dust isn't at eye level, as most of us imagine. Natural air currents in the house deposit dust and dirt eighteen to twenty-four inches from the ceiling, and two or three feet up from the floor, and this happens even if no one is in the house! There's plenty of it down low where our feet kick things around, and pets lounge, and the fluff from higher-up settles. The floor (especially a carpeted floor) is full of it, and as we stir it up it lands on the lower rungs and lower half of furniture legs. Take a good look down there and see.

Dust one room at a time with a lambswool duster. Hit the higher areas first, using the side of the duster like a large paint brush, taking care to cover the whole surface and overlap a little. Don't forget those havens for dust known as screens and lattice that may look okay at first glance. Dust and cobwebs really snuggle in here; you have to look close. Even those who dust the top of the door casing trim usually forget the inside of the frame down both sides of the door. Static electricity accumulates here as people, pets and air pass through, so you'll usually see lots of fuzz there. As for that low dusting: with that long

handle on a lambswool duster, you hardly even have to bend at the belt.

Cleaning fabric upholstery

As part of your routine cleaning, keep both vinyl and fabric upholstery vacuumed. Use your upright on the seats of couches and chairs as you vacuum the carpet, or go over the whole piece with the upholstery attachment of a wet/dry or canister vac. Slight surface dirt or hair and skin oils on fabric or vinyl can be removed with a cloth dampened in a carpet shampoo solution. Then wipe with a damp rinse cloth and rub dry with a towel. This kind of surface removal works well if you do it often enough that the headrest, armrests and seat don't have a chance to get too dirty.

When upholstery really gets dirty, you probably ought to call a professional if you want to clean it right. But it *is* possible to do it your-

Most lampshades can't really be cleaned. They're stained, or the light has faded them or cooked dirt onto them. If vacuuming, dry-sponging, and gently spotting with dry-cleaning fluid won't work, I'd go shopping for new ones!

self. If the fabric is thoroughly soiled, it should be washed with an upholstery cleaning solution or shampoo, then rinsed out. This is where problems arise in a do-it-yourself upholstery cleaning job. Cleaning solution is scrubbed on the dirt and the upholstery fabric seems to be cleaner. Actually, the surface dirt has been loosened and has sunk deeper into the fabric along with the cleaning solution. The fabric appears clean, but it isn't. The fabric is soaked with chemical, which leaves it sticky and matted down. The dirt and moisture have to be removed with an upholstery extractor attachment or a good wet/dry vacuum. Soon after the cleaning application, rinse with clear water and use the extractor again. But be sure to use water sparingly—don't get the backing or filling material wet!

Napped fabric should be brushed upright (all in the same direction) before it dries.

To remove stains on upholstery, apply the same principles you do with carpet (see chapter eleven). A surface spot can be wiped or cleaned with an applicator dampened with cleaning solution and dried with a dry, absorbent cloth. Spotting kits with professional instructions are available from most large carpet distributors or a janitorial-supply store.

Always be sure to check manufacturers' cleaning instructions. If your upholstery has been treated with soil retardant, it will usually have to be reapplied after deep-cleaning.

Appliances

One of the most important principles in cleaning appliances, as in any cleaning, is to keep them up. If you let your oven or refrigerator go forever, of course it's going to be a depressing and time-consuming chore.

Frequent, easy, spray-and-wipe cleanups will keep your kitchen appliances looking new indefinitely. Most appliances have an enamel surface: acrylic, porcelain or baked. It's tough and stain-resistant, but not tough enough to resist abrasives. So don't use scouring cleanser, metal scrapers, or steel wool or abrasive (colored) nylon scouring pads on your appliances; these are damaging to enamel, stainless steel and plastic surfaces alike. *Do* use the following: a solution of neutral all-purpose or heavy-duty cleaner (or even plain old hand dishwashing detergent and water) in a spray bottle; a soft white nylon scrub sponge; and a dry cleaning cloth (see page 161) to polish the surface dry right afterward. For those stubborn, dried-on, cooked-on spots, spray and let the solution sit awhile to soften them. Remove and soak the removeables: grills, drawers,

Things looking dim around the house? It may not be a reflection on your cleaning; it might just be dust, grime and cigarette smoke coating your light bulbs. Fluorescent tubes, for example, lose 40 percent of their glow if they aren't kept clean; but the loss is so gradual you never notice. Dust and wash them today. (Be sure to turn the light off and let the bulbs cool down first. A cloth dampened with neutral all-purpose cleaner should do it.) It'll brighten up the whole place.

drip pans, covers and kickplates. If you want an appliance exterior to really shine, use glass cleaner to polish it. To clean under and behind appliances, just use a radiator brush or vacuum dust brush—but unplug any appliance before you start poking around in back of it (so you'll be sure to live to enjoy how clean it is). Now for the particulars:

Stoves

Spend more time soaking, and you'll spend less time scrubbing. Remove the burner pans and any other parts you can, and dump them in hot, soapy water while you clean the rest of the unit. (If you really need to, you can use a green nylon scrub sponge on the pans to remove the baked-on crud.) Spray and wipe the top, back and sides of the stove. Stop right here if you have the wonderful new solid elements—and consult your owner's manual. Some of them are cast iron, which can tolerate abrasive scouring pads, but others, like some flat-surface ranges, are downright delicate and can even be scratched by a dirty sponge!

If you come across a hardened spot or spill that doesn't come off an ordinary stovetop easily after the

De-slob your knobs!

Knobs—yes, knobs and dials on stoves—are undoubtedly some of the dirtiest things in the house and are rarely if ever cleaned. They really get bad because they're grooved or serrated for easy grip and often have other little ridges and crevices that catch and hold the crud. *Surprise!*— most knobs and dials slip right off or only need a little simple screw loosened so they can be removed. Toss them into the dishpan (do them right away so you don't forget about them) and give them the "old toothbrush" (scrubbing) treatment if necessary. Then clean that greasy spot *under* the knob or dial before you put it back.

spray-and-sit-for-awhile treatment or even a workover with a white nylon sponge, scrub it gently with a plastic or stainless Chore Boy-type scrubber (keep the surface wet while you scrub). Rinse the pad well in hot water afterward, or grease and grime will harden in it.

Ovens

All of us who still have the old-style ovens clean them the same way, and it's always a tough job. Don't forget to wear rubber gloves, and make sure there's plenty of ventilation—oven cleaner is nasty stuff (for nasty work). I like to put a dropcloth or blanket on the floor in front of the oven when I clean it. Newspaper too often just strains any spills, which end up "eating" your floor. Apply oven cleaner, and wait, and wait some more. (I'm a "wait-over-nighter," myself.) This is the most important step; the chemical needs time to loosen and dissolve all those drips and spatters and stone-hard lumps. When you've tested for the fourth time and the stuff finally seems to be coming off, wipe off the bulk of the now-brown, murky cleaner with paper towels that you can just throw away. By now you should almost be able to see the actual surface of the oven. Reapply cleaner to any black patches that remain, and let it work through them. Don't scrub— just keep applying oven cleaner as long as you need to and let the chemical do the work for you. Simply wipe away the dissolved mess after each application.

When you're done, be sure to remove all traces of oven cleaner with a damp cloth rinse so your next quiche won't reek of chemicals.

Refrigerators and freezers

If you wipe up leaks and spills as soon as they happen and do a quick shelf once-over every week or so with a sponge dipped in clean dishwater, you may be able to avoid the all-out, all-over-the-floor cleaning routine altogether. Regular reconnaissance in there will also keep your hard-earned food dollars and carefully saved leftovers from being wasted. An open box of baking soda in the fridge will help keep odor away, and three tablespoons in a quart of water makes a good deodorizing solution for an overall wipedown. A neutral all-purpose cleaner is fine, too. Let the solution soften hardened-on food; don't scrub except with a white nylon scrub sponge. Wipe dry with a cleaning cloth. Wash all removable parts in the sink and thoroughly dry them before you put them back.

Stove hoods and exhaust vents

These can cause fires if they get too grease-laden, so don't neglect them. Check the manufacturer's instructions if you can. Generally, you take off the grill, remove the filter, and unplug the unit if you can. Soak the aluminum mesh grease filter in hot dishwashing detergent solution (stubborn deposits might require a strong degreaser solution), or wash it alone in the dishwasher. Rinse in hot water. While the grease filter soaks, use paper towels to wipe off the worst of the sticky, fuzzy grease inside and outside the hood and on the fan blades. Then use a cloth or, if necessary, a white nylon scrub sponge dampened with heavy-duty cleaner or degreaser solution. Deeper cleaning might mean removing the motor and fan assembly; never immerse these parts or spray anything on them or allow water to drip inside. But do wipe off the fan blades and remove the grease and lint from the motor housing. Dry everything, replace the filter and reassemble.

13. Shorter visits to the bathroom

The restroom in the commercial building was a sight to behold. A line of sinks stretched to infinity, and the toilet stalls looked like the starting gate at Santa Anita. This huge restroom was used by 250 people, and it just radiated cleanliness. The chrome glistened, and the porcelain of the sinks and toilets sparkled germ-free — and the matron only spent an hour per day to keep it that way.

Clean your bathroom in 3½ minutes

Considering the average home bathroom's size and use, and that matron's production time, you should be able to keep your bathroom in that same immaculate condition in 3½ minutes a day! Sound impossible? Not if you put some professional techniques to work. The "commercial approach" to cleaning your bathroom is simple and will save you time — the secret, of course, being to spend a few minutes each day keeping it clean rather than indulge in a big once-a-week clean-and-scrub siege. The preventive approach here — maintaining your bathroom regularly and efficiently — is smart.

Again, tools and supplies are important. You'll have to bite your lip and disregard most of the old standbys such as abrasive cleansers, deodorant sprays, magic toilet spices, perfumed blocks, wonder wicks and blue bowl seltzers. The following is a regular cleaning program that eliminates the need for these.

Essential supplies

To avoid wasted time, damage to fixtures and poor results, go to the local janitorial-supply store and purchase scented or unscented disinfectant cleaner concentrate — it's what hospitals use. (Get a *quaternary* cleaner; its active ingredient is ammonium chloride. Avoid the phenol-based cleaners; they're too toxic for home use.) This liquid, if diluted according to the directions on the bottle and used correctly, will clean quickly and efficiently, and eradicate or retard bacterial growth. This will eliminate not only smells but the need for the expensive perfumed preparations you've been using.

I and most other pros use this kind of disinfectant cleaner (nicknamed a "quat"), but if you clean *often* enough, most cleaners sanitize pretty well. So you could use pine cleaner or (if you live in a hard-water area) phosphoric acid cleaner, too. The secret is regularity, not letting soap scum, dirt and mineral deposits build up to stone hardness and thickness.

While at the janitorial-supply store, pick up one plastic spray bottle for each bathroom so the bottle can be left in the room. Once the spray bottle is filled with the water and disinfectant cleaner in the correct proportion, the only other tools you need are a cleaning cloth and a two-sided scrub sponge of cellulose and white nylon mesh (for dislodging any persistent residue).

Your daily bathroom cleaning routine should be something like this: Spray and wipe the mirror if it's spotted. If not, leave it alone. Next, spray the hardware, sink and countertops (spray ahead so the cleaner will soften and break down soil); wipe and buff the surfaces dry. They will sparkle. Do shower stalls and tubs next. Do toilet stool last. (See pages 150-151.)

Once the upper fixtures are clean, fall to your knees (one minute won't hurt you). Spray the floor and, with the already-damp cleaning cloth, wipe it up. This method is a lot faster and better than mixing up mop water and fumbling around with a mop in a fifteen- or twenty-square-foot area.

For daily bathroom maintenance

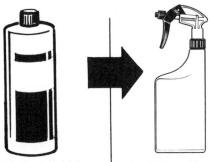

Use germicidal or disinfectant cleaner diluted from concentrate.

Dilute according to directions into a plastic spray bottle. When spraying disinfectant cleaner in a confined area like the bathroom, adjust the nozzle so the droplets will fall when you spray. If the mist is too fine, you'll inhale particles and irritate your throat.

Spray the mirror, fixtures, sink and countertops. Wipe and buff dry. Next do the shower stall and tub. Then the toilet (base last!) and floor. Remember that odors are caused by bacteria. A clean bathroom won't need deodorant.

The benefits of preventive maintenance

It takes only minutes to clean a bathroom the spray-disinfectant way, and if you leave a spray bottle and cloth in the room, you can get your bathroom spotless while you wait for Junior to go potty or for the sink to fill up. The system works only if you clean the bathroom regularly, however. This keeps hard water deposits, soap scum, toilet bowl lines and other soils from building up and cementing on. The basic reason you needed abrasive cleansers and acids (and dynamite) to clean the bathroom in the past was that buildup accumulated to the point of no return and had to be ground off instead of wiped off.

Don't use powdered cleansers and steel wool to grind dirt off surfaces. In most of the many thousands of houses I've cleaned in my career, the sinks, tubs and shower units—porcelain or plastic—have had damage from improper use of acids, cleansers and abrasive pads. The grinding abrasion that removes spots and stains also re-

moves chrome and porcelain. This is a great reason to use the disinfectant cleaner/spray bottle system from the start. Your chrome, plastic, fiberglass, marble and porcelain will remain bright and sound.

If you have damaged fixtures, you'll have difficulty no matter what you use, because porous surfaces collect gunk quickly and clean up slowly. Many of these surfaces—especially the shower area—will benefit from a coat of paste wax, which helps repel the scum and hard water buildup. (Just don't wax the shower *floor!*)

A squeegee in the shower is worth a truckload of "de-limer"

After attending my seminar, many a housekeeper minimizes the problem of shower buildup by simply hanging a 14-inch squeegee in the shower. It takes only fifteen seconds for the user to leave the wall dry and clean after a shower. (Besides, squeegeeing in the nude is a unique experience!) But if you let hard water dry on your bathroom surfaces over and over again, the built-up minerals practically need to be chiseled off.

It's not a bad idea to wipe the shower chrome (faucets, etc.) too while it's still wet. Use your bath towel to dry it after you dry yourself, and you'll leave it nice and shiny and prevent mineral deposit buildup!

What if you already have hard-water buildup on your walls and fixtures? A professional-strength phosphoric acid "de-scaler" (for home use you don't want anything stronger than 9 percent) will dissolve it faster and better than supermarket de-limers.

For old, stubborn soap scum, try the above first (often the hard-water deposits on a surface create little "shelves" of mineral that hold scum). If that doesn't work, use a degreaser

or soap-scum remover from a janitorial-supply store.

Be careful with those things the hint-and-tip books tell you to soak in tubs and sinks overnight (such as oven grills, blinds, crusted camping gear, tools, etc.). Extended exposure to some

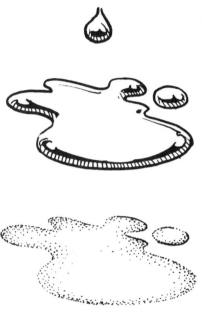

When a drop of hard or soapy water lands on a surface and dries, the minerals and other residue dissolved in it collect at the base of the drop when it evaporates. Every time the surface gets wet, new drops add to the accumulation—and this will keep building up into a hard, solid deposit. That's why it's smart to clean regularly (especially showers and windows) and not give buildup a chance to happen.

Hard water is fast and easy to clean up when fresh, but like cement if you wait!

normally harmless cleaners will often pit the fixtures.

Keep your drains running free by pulling out the stopper every month or so and cleaning the collected hair off it (encouraging hair care to be practiced elsewhere than over the sink can prevent this). Boiling-hot water poured down a drain periodically ought to handle any soap scum buildup that might slow drainage down.

Cleaning toilets

Briskly scrubbing inside a toilet bowl with a bowl brush for a few seconds each day will retard buildup and remove discoloration and lines. When you do your daily spray-cleaning of the bathroom with disinfectant cleaner, spray and wipe the entire outside of the toilet from top to bottom. Contrary to popular belief, it's the outside of the toilet that's most unsanitary. Be sure to do the base of the toilet last. This will prevent you from transporting the worst germ concentration to the faucet handles. Every couple of weeks, pour a little disinfectant into the bowl, swish the water around, and let it sit awhile. Remember, it's the *outside* of the toilet—under the seat and around the rim—that's germiest and will begin to smell if not cleaned frequently. The cold water that enters the bowl with every flush discourages bacterial growth there.

If you need to remove old buildup in the toilet, do it right. Don't pour steaming acid into the water-filled bowl and slosh it around. Dilution with water neutralizes the power of any bowl cleaner. Instead, a couple of times a year, grasp a swab (see Equipment Chart, chapter five) and push it quickly up and down in the bowl toward the "throat" of the toilet. All the water will vanish (no free advertising intended). Then give the swab a light

Basic bowl cleaner technique

For daily maintenance, scrub briskly inside the bowl with a bowl brush. You only need to use acid bowl cleaner a couple of times a year. When you do . . .

Don't pour bowl cleaner into the water.

Do force the water out of the bowl with a swab or bowl brush.

Soak the swab with bowl cleaner, lightly coat the bowl—and flush to rinse.

150

application of bowl cleaner and coat the inside of the toilet bowl. Let the cleaner sit on there a few minutes, then flush to rinse. Reapply, let sit, and rinse again as necessary until all the deposits are gone.

If a ring remains, don't get excited and acid-bath the whole unit. The ring is the result of hard water deposit that's left as water in the toilet evaporates. A pumice stone will remove almost any ring (be sure the surface is wet or it will scratch).

Remember to swab the bowl regularly to prevent buildup. And don't stake your hopes on "miracle" toilet cleaners that promise to make the job fun and easy—there's no such animal out there yet. The "automatic bowl cleaners" that go in the flush tank are a help in keeping things sanitary, but aren't a substitute for periodic deep-cleaning. Even if you can't see the ring, it's still there—you just can't see it because it's bleached white. You still need to get in there with your bowl swab now and then to keep it from building up.

> **Still finding hair clinging to the bathroom toilet, sink and walls after cleaning? Before you start, wet a dab of toilet paper and swipe up all the fugitive hair first.**

How to get rid of bathroom mildew

When warm, humid weather and spores of mold team up, those little black spots of mildew can grow on everything, including drawers, closets, books and shoes. But aside from the basement, mildew's favorite home is the bathroom.

For the first twenty years of my life, I thought mildew was something that only appeared on roses and alfalfa. Since entering the cleaning business, I've been bombarded with the mildew question: "How do we get rid of it?" The best way to get rid of it is to prevent it. See chapter eight for household-wide tips for preventing mildew.

Using disinfectant in the bathroom and shower areas discourages mildew growth there. Chlorine bleach kills mildew, but won't prevent it from returning; you can only do that by altering conditions favorable for its growth. But drying out a bathroom that several people bathe and shower in every day is difficult, so all you can really do is keep cleaning with disinfectant—and hitting mildewed grout with a weak chlorine bleach solution (1 part bleach to 5 parts cool water), as long as the tile isn't made of plastic and you're careful not to get the bleach on anything that is.

Doorknobs, purses and telephones

If people were asked to list the most unsanitary objects in the home, most of them would remember the toilet but forget doorknobs. It wouldn't hurt, while armed with a spray bottle of disinfectant cleaner, to go through the house and spray and wipe all the doorknobs occasionally (and the light switches, chair backs and telephone receivers).

Another unsanitary item that all women should be aware of is the purse. Purses are often placed on dining tables (right next to the salad fork) after having been set on the floor alongside the toilet in a public restroom. Avoid this unappetizing practice! Set your purse by your chair—and use the purse shelves or hooks provided in public restrooms, when available.

14.

Success in high places

One of my customers had a husband full of ambition and desire to clean, but he was terrified of high places. She would hire me to wash all the high areas, saving the low stuff for him. One year while doing his low section, he was on a plank just a foot off the floor when he was seized by the phobia. He lay down on the plank, dug his whitened fingertips into the wood, and froze. His wife, unable to talk him down from that dizzying height, ended up calling the fire department (siren and all!). They finally dislodged the husband's death grip on the plank and got him onto floor level safely, but he was never sound enough emotionally to assist in cleaning again.

Be sure to adjust or limit the reaching of tall areas to fit your resources, age and nerves (and your helpers' bravery!). But don't be buffaloed by hard-to-reach areas. "Once I got up there, it only took ten minutes" is the wail of many "end-of-the-day" housekeepers. The many hours it takes to get going is the bane of cleaning in high places. Easy access contributes greatly to success in such cleaning, yet the shaky old ladder and unsteady step stool are about the extent of most homes' scaffolding. More energy, time and emotion are used going up and down the ladder or stool than actually doing the job. And all of our effort, worry, tool procurement and arrangement seem to be focused on the few minutes we'll actually perform the job, instead of trying to save the hours getting in position to start it.

As a professional housecleaner, I have to weigh the same factors a homemaker does. The equipment needed to reach the work has to be light enough to be manageable, and small enough to fit in tight areas and keep from scratching walls and woodwork. It must be *sturdy* and *safe* enough to ensure no falls. The following is the basic equipment that more than thirty years of housecleaning have taught me to use.

A good ladder

A plain old common ladder is one of your best all-around tools. It's versatile, manageable and safe . . . if you choose the right model. For household use, the perfect stepladder height is five feet. Four-foot ladders are too short to work on 8-foot ceilings; a 6-foot ladder is too high, and it nicks up the house when you carry it around. A 5-foot ladder is just right for most household cleaning operations. Instead

A five-foot ladder is just right for household cleaning.

4-foot	**6-foot**	**5-foot**

of buying several creaky wooden ladders for $20 each during your lifetime, buy a 5-foot heavy-duty commercial aluminum ladder for $35 to $50. You'll never regret it. It's strong, safe to use anywhere, and will probably outlast you, even counting the ten years it may add to your life. It can be used outside on rough terrain, and neither bad weather nor dry storage will hurt it.

For higher reaches every household should also have a tall ladder such as the ones firefighters use, and I feel the perfect one for this purpose is an 18-foot, two-piece extension ladder. It will collapse to 10 feet for storage in the laundry room or inside the stairwell and lengthen out safely to 16 feet—enough to get the cat out of the tree, put up the aerial, or paint the trim every five years. Aluminum is lighter, but in an extension ladder for home use, I prefer wood or fiberglass for safety and electrical protection. Don't paint wooden ladders; paint hides breaks, cracks and flaws and is slippery when wet. Instead, use boiled linseed oil to maintain wooden ladders. It penetrates the wood, keeps water out and slivers in. A coat every five years will keep a ladder happy.

Make yourself a box

To reach high cabinets, curtain rods, etc., people usually climb on the harmless-looking kitchen stool or bench. These have a narrow base and a deceptively sturdy top. But they're too unbalanced and risky to use as a standing or cleaning tool. To replace the old bench—and the equally unsafe chair, which has battered many a body—a simply constructed box of three-quarter-inch plywood is inexpensive and far superior. I'd suggest dimensions of $15 \times 20 \times 28$ inches or smaller (see opposite). The telephone companies have a similar unit they've used safely and effectively for years. It's called a "three-position stool." Laid flat on its side or end, it gives you three low heights to work from. Hand holes can be cut in the box's side to move it, and it can serve for storage when it's not in use. It can also serve as a baby crib, an extra chair when company comes, or a place to hide the puppy on Christmas Eve.

Walk the plank for safety

The last and most useful tool to help you conquer the unreachable places is a sturdy, ordinary 2×12-inch plank eight to ten feet long. Purchase it at a lumberyard and make sure it has no loose knots, cracks or weak areas. Redwood is good because it's light and rot-resistant. (Pine and hemlock will also work all right, but they're not nearly as light.) Sand off the corners and rough edges for ease of handling, and it's ready to use. Don't paint or varnish it or it will be slippery when wet. You'll use the plank for many things. It is one of the best "under $20" investments you'll ever make. The idea is to combine the stepladder, extension ladder, box and plank in a number of ways to reach your working area easily, safely and without wasted motion. If you need to reach higher areas than can be reached with this combination, rent the necessary equipment, because you'll seldom use it around the house.

A plank, though it may be scary at first, is safe to work on if you're reasonably awake. You'll soon get used to the slight spongy "give" you'll feel. Planks were only fatal to blindfolded pirates when they had to walk

This simply constructed box is inexpensive and a far better way to reach the high places. I'd suggest dimensions of 15″ × 20″ × 28″. You can make it larger or smaller to custom-fit you or your stepladder.

Materials needed:
1 4′ × 8′ sheet of ¾″ exterior plywood
1 pound of No. 8 finish nails
1 bottle of wood glue
sandpaper
1 pint of clear varnish or polyurethane

Just lay out the following plan and assemble per directions. If your husband has traded in his $300 power saw to buy a new vacuum, no sweat—a $39.95 sabre saw will work fine!

Laid flat on its side or end, it gives you three low heights to work from. Hand holes can be cut in the box's side to move it. Use it for storage when it's not in use.

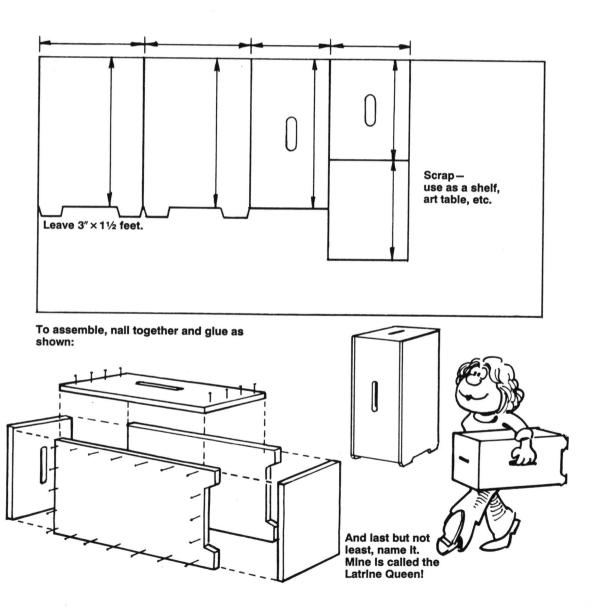

Scrap—
use as a shelf,
art table, etc.

Leave 3″ × 1½ feet.

To assemble, nail together and glue as shown:

And last but not least, name it. Mine is called the Latrine Queen!

For maximum stability, be sure your plank extends a few inches beyond the end of the box and beyond the ladder rung it's set on.

off the end. Looking up at the ceiling and moving toward the box end of the plank puts you in the same circumstance as the pirates. That's why you should always keep an extra sponge or empty bucket at the end of the plank so a nudge of the toe reminds you to stop walking. (This is a case where "kicking the bucket" is an aid to longevity.) The plank-and-ladder combination is especially effective to use in high stairwells. On stair landings and other open areas, you can figure out a combination (such as the one on the page opposite). It will make you love yourself for your brilliance.

You're usually only about two feet off the floor when you do ceilings in a house from a ladder. When in a stairwell, you are higher over the stairs, but with the walls of the narrow landing on both sides of you and with a ladder at both ends, there is little risk of falls. I've seen twenty ladder accidents for every plank-and-ladder accident.

Regular or extension ladders must be tilted at the proper angle to keep them from slipping down or tumbling over. One foot out from the base of the wall for every four feet up is just right. Keep your cleaning solution, tools, paint, and other working materials as close to you as possible by wearing a pocketed apron or by setting your

Be sure to adjust or limit the reaching of high areas to fit your age, nerves and bravery. If you have an overwhelming fear of heights, don't do it—you'll get hurt. If you have no fear of heights, get smart—you *can* get hurt. If heights make you shake in your boots, find a couple of daredevils and bake them some cookies. Let *them* climb to clean off that flyspeck, change a light bulb, paint or wash the ceiling.

To clean a stair landing

Lean your extension ladder (padded with a towel or dry sponges) against the wall with the base angled into the stairs. Open your stepladder at the top of the stairs. The plank, set across a lower rung of the stepladder and a rung of the extension ladder, puts you in a safe, convenient position to clean or paint the walls. Padding the "wall" end of your plank if it touches the wall will protect the wall.

To use a ladder safely: Angle one foot from the wall for every four feet of height. Never stand on the top rung.

gear on the plank. Ascending or descending a ladder or plank for every dip depletes strength, wastes time, and exposes you more often to mishap.

One "trick" I've tried without much success is moving a stepladder without moving the buckets or tools off it first. I bat about 60 percent. The other 40 percent has cost me wet carpets, skinned shins, painted faces, and trips back to the starting gate. It is also extremely risky to tie or lay a plank on planters, metal railings, fireplace mantels or other trim. Most of these were designed to be looked at, not to support 150 pounds or more of plank, cleaning tools and person. Place

ladders and planks on supports where strength is certain.

A cleaning towel (see chapter fifteen) slipped over each of the ladder's upper legs will keep it from marking up your walls. A dry sponge (chapter fifteen) under each leg will prevent it from slipping if the surface the legs rest on is questionable. Tennis shoes on your feet will prevent *you* from slipping, too.

A final word of advice: put your name on your ladders and planks. When your neighbors spot them, they will be only too happy to try out your new way of reaching high places.

15.

Simplified wall & ceiling cleaning

I once bid to wash walls in six large offices, a long hall, lobby, entrances and storage areas in a Massey-Ferguson tractor dealer's office. Back in the '60s when a dollar was a dollar, I was the low bid at the price of $275. Our new crew was busy on the scheduled day, so I tackled the job alone. Seven hours later, I had it finished and more than a few compliments on the quality of the job. On another occasion, I washed all the walls, ceilings, and woodwork in a modern three-bedroom home in less than one day—alone. Now, I'm no more a "super" wall and ceiling cleaner than you are. In fact, I'm certain that many of you could keep up with or beat me on my best day, if you'd use the same approach I did.

There are two reasons why wall and ceiling cleaning will become one of your favorite housecleaning tasks when you do it my way: (1) It's easy and trouble-free, and (2) the delight of seeing the surface come clean is great! In fact, you'll find washing your walls and ceilings so easy and satisfying, you'll want to wash your friends' walls and ceilings just to show off. Your days of struggling with a bucket of grimy wall-washing solution will end as you finish this chapter, if you follow the simple principles it sets forth.

We outlined the basic principle of cleaning—eliminate, saturate, dissolve, remove— in chapter six; here's how that principle applies to the technique and tools of wall-cleaning. Your height, your arm strength, and the degree of dirt accumulated doesn't make much difference in the time and effort it takes to clean walls and ceilings. Using your head and the right tools *will* make a difference.

The versatile dry sponge

One of the first and most important (and least-known) tools of housecleaning is a rubber sponge, called a dry sponge. It works just like a rubber eraser, removing and absorbing dirt. Dry sponges are generally tan or red and come on handles, or as flat 5×7×½-inch pads. The pad is by far the better way to go because it has a larger number of usable surfaces.

Dry sponges come wrapped in cellophane, and when you unwrap them they feel dry and spongy. Never, *never* use water on them or get them wet—not a drop—or they will become useless for cleaning. Most people use dry sponges for cleaning wallpaper. (Now more of you will know what I'm referring to.) They are excellent on wallpaper—much better than "dough" wallpaper cleaners that crumble and stick!

On ceiling acoustical tile and on most flat oil- or latex-painted walls, one swipe of a dry sponge will remove the dirt. It won't remove fingerprints or flyspecks or grease—only the film of dirt. In most homes, dry-sponging the ceiling will leave it perfect. I've washed behind a dry sponge many times, not believing that the sponge could get all the dirt out, but it did— every bit of it! In fact, on many porous walls or painted surfaces, even where the dirt is embedded deeply, a dry sponge is superior to washing. Even on walls that are smoke-damaged, ten minutes of dry-sponging the room prior to washing will reduce washing time and expense by more than 50 percent. When dry-sponging, you don't have to stop to dip or rinse. Just get to the surface and swipe in four-foot lengths (or shorter if your arms are shorter). The sponge will absorb the dirt and begin to get black. It will hold the dirt as you clean along, but as soon as it reaches its saturation

Dry sponges are great for cleaning wallpaper, oil paintings, and smoke or soot damage. Dry sponges also work well on acoustical tile ceilings, masonry surfaces, and most flat-painted walls and ceilings. The proper way to hold a dry sponge (illustrated here) utilizes each pad's eight surfaces.

point, turn and/or refold the sponge and keep going. The residue that falls from the sponge won't stain or stick and is easily vacuumed up after the job is done.

Each pad-type sponge has eight good surfaces, if used correctly. (The handled dry sponges are great, except that once their single cleaning surface is saturated, the sponge is no longer usable.) When a dry sponge is black on both sides, throw it away. Washing it doesn't work. Dry sponges cost less than $2.00 and are worth ten times that for the job they do and the time they save.

A dry sponge won't clean enamel or greasy surfaces, so don't be disappointed when you make a swipe across the kitchen or bathroom wall and nothing dramatic happens.

If you go into the bedroom and make a swipe across the ceiling or outside wall and can't see where you've just been, those surfaces don't need cleaning, and the rest of the walls probably don't either. Just clean the light fixtures and the woodwork and take off the rest of the hour you allowed for bedroom cleaning.

Once the dry-sponging is out of the way, the remaining areas, not cleaned with a dry sponge, will have to be washed. You can accomplish this rather simply if you use the right tools and methods.

Your rag is your worst enemy

There is no question that the most famous household cleaning tool is the simple little item known as a "rag." Your rags have been salvaged from ancient sheets, tattered curtains, worn-out jeans, feed sacks and other fabric scraps. Using a rag to clean with is like using a rake to comb your hair: ineffective. For five hundred years cloth manufacturers have worked to develop fabrics that repel liquids and stains. They've succeeded, and we have scores of fabrics today that resist moisture—which makes them terrible cleaning tools. Yet we can't seem to resist saving trouser legs, old tricot slips, and a thousand other unsuitable fabrics for cleaning rags. Don't do it!

I'm certain that one thing that makes the professional a three times faster—and better—cleaner than the homemaker is the fact that homemakers are hung up on rags. Rags are only good for paint cleanup, stuffing rag dolls, blowing your nose, attracting antelopes in the Wyoming desert, or signaling surrender when the cleaning gets you down. Henceforth, the term "rag" must be banished from your housecleaning vocabulary and from your basket of cleaning tools. The rag in your housecleaning tool bag will be replaced with an item called a "cleaning cloth."

The noble cleaning cloth

A cleaning cloth is made from a new or salvaged heavy Turkish (cotton terry) towel. I've had a lot of questions as to what kind of toweling to use. The big worry is that the poly/cotton blends aren't as absorbent as the old pure cotton towels. Not so! They're an improvement! The polyester is used for the base fabric and the cotton to make the pile (nap). Moisture rarely gets to the base anyway, and the polyester dries faster and resists wrinkles. (A wrinkle-resistant cleaning cloth—now *that's* class!) But do be sure to use toweling with a high cotton content.

First cut an eighteen-by-eighteen-inch piece of toweling. Then fold it over and sew the long side together, leaving it open on both ends like a tube. By

How to make a cleaning cloth

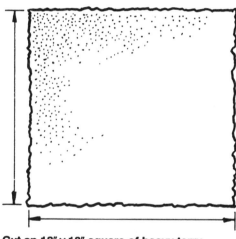

Cut an 18″ × 18″ square of heavy terry.

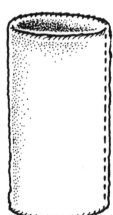

Fold and stitch together on the long side; hem the edges.

It will be hollow like a tube.

How to use it

Fold once—

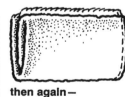

then again—

and it will just fit your hand.

Soiled cleaning cloths are simply washed and tumble-dried for reuse.

By changing sides and turning it inside out, you have sixteen sides to clean with.

folding the tube twice, you have a hand-sized surface of thick, absorbent terry that will efficiently cover every inch of surface it passes over—even get down into bumpy-textured walls and floors. It's not like the old linen bedsheet that just streaks and smears the film around. (We wouldn't think of drying *ourselves* on a piece of sheet after a bath.)

If you refold your cleaning towels correctly and use both sides, you have eight efficient surfaces to use; turn the towel inside out and you have eight more. Sixteen surfaces on one little cleaning cloth! (Terry cleaning cloths are great to protect the hands from scrapes, cuts and ripped fingernails, too.) I often clean all the walls of a large room using only three cleaning cloths. When you finish and the cleaning cloths are damp and dirty, throw them in the washer.

You don't have to use much detergent, because the towels will be full of the cleaner you've been using. If you wash the towels while they're still wet, they'll come out as clean as they were before you used them (although in time they'll get dingy and battle-scarred; they'll still be clean, just stained). Be sure to tumble-dry them! If you hang them on the line they'll be stiff as a board and impossible to use the next time: Twenty cleaning cloths will clean your entire house and, if washed properly, will last for years.

Your basic wall-cleaning tools

The dry sponge and cleaning cloth are the main professional tools you need for your wall-cleaning, so don't prepare a long list of materials and equipment. The rest of the items you probably already have around the house, so round them up: one empty bucket (plastic won't skin up the furniture or sweat like metal does); one bucket half full of warm water; an ordinary cellulose sponge (preferably about 1½ inches thick; make sure the other dimensions fit your hand); and some neutral all-purpose cleaner (I always add a little ammonia to cut grease—besides, I like to see my hands shrivel up!). That's it!

I know what you're thinking now. "Man, wouldn't a two-compartment bucket be great!" No, it wouldn't. They are, without question, one of the most worthless instruments ever palmed off on a housecleaner. Just try to pour dirty water out of one side and keep clean water in the other—or to carry the thing without any intermingling!

Mix your cleaning solution following directions on the container. Make sure your cleaning compound is one capable of cutting the dirt you want to remove. Ammonia or neutral all-purpose cleaner will be fine unless you're dealing with an extremely grease-laden kitchen, where a little degreaser added to the solution will make the job much easier. For bathroom walls, you might want to use a disinfectant cleaner.

Before beginning, reinforce your attitude. I've read books and articles on cleaning house that say, "Allow yourself a day to a week for each room." You're going to clean it, not rebuild it! If you hustle, you should be able to wash a room in thirty minutes, but you'll probably want to allow yourself an hour (maybe more if you anticipate being interrupted). Prolonging a simple job will wear down your initiative and determination.

Cleaning procedure

You have your ladder or scaffolding in position, and now you're ready to begin my method of wall-cleaning. You won't have to cover everything because there will be little or no dripping. (If you have a grand piano that a drop might hurt, don't take the chance—throw a dropcloth or sheet of light plastic over it.) Upholstered furniture can usually be moved out of the way rather than covered. A drop of cleaning solution won't hurt anything if it's removed immediately; if it's not, it may spot or ruin the finish.

Placing your bucket of solution in the right place is extremely important; it should be where you don't have to climb thirty feet to dip your sponge. *Always keep it as close to your working area as possible.* Spilling solution was a major problem in my beginning housecleaning days. I finally learned to set the bucket next to me near the wall—not in back of me, nor on a table, nor in the middle of the floor. Be sure to set it in a visible spot. The most common spillage problems involve tripping over buckets or knocking them over while moving a piece of furniture. If you do spill it on carpet, run for the wet/dry vacuum and get all the moisture out you can. Then rinse with clear water to get the ammonia (or other cleaning agent) out. Again, remember to fill your buckets only half full (if you fill them to the brim they'll be top-heavy and can easily spill), and keep the dirty bucket dumped in the toilet regularly (after each room), for if it spills you'll have a tough cleanup problem.

Take your sponge and dip it into the solution about one-half inch (not all the way in). This will give you plenty of solution to wet the wall or ceiling, yet leave the rest of the sponge dry enough to absorb any water that otherwise would splash into your eyes or run down your arms, down your back and into your shoes.

I know all the books say to start at the bottom of the wall and work up, because if you dribble on the lower unwashed wall from the top, it might stain: an old wives' tale. Anyone who tells you that doesn't know how to wash walls. In extreme cases with, say, fifty-year-old paints or spectacularly dirty walls, it might be wise, but I think it's discouraging to start at the bottom, get it clean, then go on to the top and dribble on the clean wall. I can't stand to back up and redo an area I've already done. So I start at the top and recommend that you do the same.

How large an area you work on at one time depends, of course, on (1) your reach; (2) how soiled the surface is; and (3) how fast the solution will dry on the surface. A three-by-three-foot section is just about right for the average person. Quickly cover the section with the solution on the sponge. Don't press hard or water will spurt out and drip on the carpet and your head. Gently spread the liquid on the surface. By the time you get to the end of the section, the initial application of solution has worked the dirt loose. Now go back to the starting point and again go over the area gently. Don't squeeze the sponge! By now, the dirt should be loosened by the chemicals in your cleaning solution and will come off and soak into the sponge. In the other hand, folded to perfection, is your cleaning cloth, with which you quickly wipe and buff the area before it dries. No rinsing is necessary. The wiping will not only remove the remaining cleaner and dirt, but will polish off the scum that so often streaks washed walls.

Now the critical procedure: Hold the sponge over the empty bucket and *squeeze*, don't wring (you only wring your hands or a chicken neck). When you squeeze the sponge, the dirty solution will go into the empty bucket, leaving the sponge damp and clean. Again dip the sponge one-half inch into the bucket of cleaning solution and repeat the process until the room is

To clean a wall

  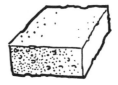 

A bucket half filled with a warm ammonia or neutral cleaner solution . . .

an empty bucket . . .

a sponge . . .

a cleaning cloth.

1.

Dip the sponge about ½ inch into the solution.

2.

Start at the top of the wall and spread the solution to dissolve the soil. Then go back over the wetted-down area with your sponge and wipe to remove the soil.

3.

Wipe the sponged area with a folded cleaning cloth.

4.

Squeeze (don't twist) the dirty sponge into the empty bucket.

Then dip the sponge into the solution again and repeat.

5.

When you finish, the bucket that started out empty will be full of dirty water.

Your cleaning solution will stay crystal clear—the chemical will always be working full strength.

Go easy on the solution. You'll be shocked what too much will do for you!

bright and clean.

You'll notice that the empty bucket is beginning to fill with filthy black gunk, while the cleaning solution is still crystal clear. The sponge you dip into the bucket of solution each time is a squeezed-out hungry sponge (not a sponge full of dirty cleaner), so the dirt never touches your cleaning solution. This means that every drop going on each new section of wall is powerful, unpolluted cleaning solution that will do most of the work. The old method you once used—scrubbing, dipping your sponge in the solution, wringing it, and scrubbing again—always left your cleaning water murky and filthy and thus without full cleaning power. It would streak the walls and have to be changed every fifteen minutes, taking up a lot of time and wasting a lot of cleaning solution. With the two-bucket method you don't spend time scrubbing, just applying and removing. And the towel dries and polishes walls three times as well as the old rags you once used.

"Outside walls" (the inside surfaces of exterior walls) will be dirtier than inside or "partition" walls, so don't be surprised. If you can't see where you're going when you wash, forget it—it doesn't need washing!

Two-bucket benefits

Besides doing a 70 percent faster and better job, the two-bucket wall-cleaning technique has two more great "Life After Housework" savers:

1. You'll never dump and refill another bucket of solution. One bucket of water and fifty cents worth of solution will do all the walls in your house!

2. The dirty water . . . you will love it. In fact you will have a special relationship to it. Before, all your evidence of toil and accomplishment went down the drain; now you have it for show. I've seen people save it for days. (Bottle it and place it on the mantel.) I guarantee it will be the best, most heartwarming exhibit in your housekeeping museum.

Enameled walls

When cleaning enamel-painted halls, kitchens or bathrooms, use the same procedure, with one simple adjustment: Keep the drying towels cleaner and drier, because enamel needs more polishing with a drier buffing cloth than flat paint. Wipe marks won't show on flat paints, but they will show even on perfectly clean enamel. Those circular wipe marks that you can't see when you finish (but can later in certain light) are caused by rags; rags can't/won't buff-dry your walls. I was called back on many jobs during my first year of cleaning to remove streaks that weren't there when I left. Since that day twenty-five years ago when I began to use terry cleaning cloths I haven't been called back for a single case of "enamel streak."

P.S. Plain sheetrock can't be washed. It's just paper over gypsum

How to clean:

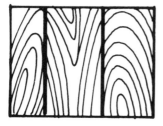

PANELING. Same procedure as for painted walls. Use neutral all-purpose cleaner or oil soap solution, keep the sponge nearly dry, and then, buffing with the grain, dry completely with a cleaning cloth.

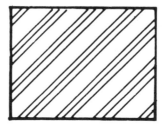

WALLPAPER. Use a dry sponge and clean with the flow of the design.

VINYL WALL COVERING. Use the cleaner recommended by the manufacturer, keeping the sponge nearly dry. Use no harsh or abrasive cleaners. Then dry thoroughly with a cleaning cloth.

TEXTURED WALL COVERINGS. Any textured wall covering will have dust and dirt resting in the thousands of little pockets of the design, which will spread out all over when the wall is wet or rubbed. Vacuum walls like these first before wet- or dry-cleaning.

and the joints are taped compound with emulsives—it'll just turn to putty if it's wet. Paint it with two coats of enamel and next time you'll be able to wash it.

What to do about wall spots

When you run into marks and spots on the walls that don't come clean when you wash them, just leave them until you finish. Then come back and try to remove them by rubbing hard with a cleaning cloth and a little solution. Toothpaste, peanut butter or abrasive cleansers will get them, but will also take off the paint or at least kill the sheen on the wall. Don't try to clean spots before you wash down the whole wall—they might come off with the first washing. *Let the solution do the work!*

Most wall marks can be removed by simply finding a cleaning agent with the same base as the spot. On a tar spot, for example, you can scrub and rub with high-powered cleaners, sweat and swear, and not get the spot; a little turpentine or paint thinner will remove it in three seconds and not hurt the wall. Use your head, not your hands—you won't scour off the paint or streak the surfaces.

Cleaning woodwork

You can wash the woodwork or baseboards while doing the walls, but I seldom do, because woodwork is covered with lint, hair, dead gnats, etc., that will get into your sponge and be difficult to get out. Before you start washing the room, use a damp paper towel to wipe the baseboard and pick up all the residue, then just dispose of it. Use a damp cleaning cloth to finish it up, if need be, streak- and lint-free.

How to clean paneling

Remember that raw wood must be coated with a finish so that moisture won't penetrate it. Then you'll be cleaning the finish, not the wood itself—it's faster, and much easier on the wood and you!

Don't be like the homemaker who decided to leave the wood paneling in her new home unfinished. She loved that natural wood look because it looked warm and homey. But then one afternoon, her children got into the Crisco and the crayons, and a generous percentage of the mess ended up on the wood wall. No matter how she scrubbed or what formula she tried, the spots and marks remained visible.

She should have finished the wood with a low-luster varnish or polyurethane. This would have formed a protective shield on the surface of the wood that would keep grease and marks from penetrating into the wood and staining it. A flat or satin resinous or polyurethane finish will dry with a low sheen and preserve the natural look of the wood. (Follow the instructions on the can, remember to stir well, and keep your work area as dust-free as you can.)

On wood paneling with a sealed surface, or vinyl paneling (much "imitation wood" paneling is actually vinyl, or vinyl-coated composition board), use only a mild oil soap or neutral all-purpose cleaner solution, and apply it sparingly with a sponge. (I use an oil soap that I had a chemical company formulate for me; you could also use one of the vegetable oil soaps on the market such as Murphy's.) Then, going with the grain, dry-buff it

with a cleaning cloth. If you dry with the grain, occasional streaks will never be noticed. A clean, dry surface on a paneled wall is much better than covering the paneling with "El Gunko" panel polish or cleaners that leave a sticky surface to collect and hold handprints and every passing particle of dirt and dust. The oil soap cleans the wood surface and leaves a nice shine.

Clean ceilings

Ceilings are always tough, even the easier-to-clean types like enamel, with no texture or special finish of any kind. There is good news and bad news for you women who for years have had aching arms and back and neck from working above your head. The bad news first: A physiologist told me that the muscle structure of a woman's torso is built to transfer to her shoulders the weight of a child carried during pregnancy. When a woman works above her head, she pulls against these muscles, so overhead work is much more difficult for her than it is for a man. The good news is: what an excuse to get a man to do the high work (such as ceilings)!

You don't have to wash the ceiling every time you wash the walls (ceiling-washing is hard work, even for experienced experts). Ceilings only need cleaning about one-third as often as walls (unless you have a ceiling heat vent or exhaust fan, and then you can just clean the area around it and feather the cleaning line). Except for fireplace soot and cigarette smoke, ceilings just don't get the abuse that walls do. They don't have the fingerprints, crayon marks and everyday spatters, so they can go several years between cleanings.

For fairly smooth ceilings with washable paint (gloss or semigloss enamel), use the same two-bucket technique described for wall-washing. If the ceiling is greasy or nicotine-coated, use heavy-duty cleaner or degreaser solution rather than neutral all-purpose cleaner.

Most flat-painted ceilings can be cleaned quite well by wiping with a dry sponge. Should a few flyspecks remain, dip a cotton swab in white shoe polish or matching paint to mask them. Flat paints are not very washable, no matter what the label says. You almost always leave streaks and lap lines when washing them. It's usually faster and easier to just roll on another coat of paint, especially if you're faced with heavy smoke or water stains, hanging lamp scars, etc.

When you clean the ceiling, take down any ceiling light fixture diffusers or globes first, pour cleaning solution on them, and let them soak in the sink while you clean the room. This keeps you from cutting your arms on them as you clean the ceiling. After you finish the room, use a cleaning cloth to wipe the loosened film and dirt from the plates. Rinse with hot water, dry, and put them back up immediately.

Textured or acoustical tile ceilings

Builders often leave textured ceilings unpainted in a new home. When five to seven years later the ceiling needs cleaning, it can't be washed because the texture (which is a water-based compound) will dissolve when water touches it. If you rolled one coat of latex paint on when the ceiling was new, it "filled" the texture and left the ceiling looking fantastic. But five years later when you try to wash it, the moisture gets to the compound (which turns brown when wet) and you have a streak. So always paint two coats on an unpainted ceiling and it will be sealed enough to clean.

If you have either "cottage cheese" or those sparkly ceilings, your cleaning choices are limited. You can try vacuuming them with your extra-long hose and soft bristle attachment, or maybe you can dry-sponge them. You should also resolve never to hire any architect or contractor who uses the stuff.

Acoustical ceilings generally won't show dirt until it's too late to clean them. Clean annually with a dry sponge; it will only take a few minutes. A badly dirtied acoustical ceiling can be resprayed with an acoustic finish or cleaned by the bleaching or oxidation process—you could do this yourself with supplies from a janitorial-supply store, but it's safer to have a professional do it for you. If you paint an acoustical ceiling, you'll ruin the looks and the acoustics.

Washing closets

I'd wash the inside of the closets once every twenty years or so; most of them are closed, so they don't get dirty. Closets generally take longer than the whole room, and besides, nobody ever sees them anyway. But when you paint your closets, use a hard-finish, light-colored enamel so they'll be easy to clean whenever you do wash them.

Don't forget the doors

Our doors get much more use than any other part of the house, yet we spend very little time keeping them clean and looking sharp. Doors are so taken for granted we seldom appreciate their contribution to a neat, attractive house.

I once gave my wife a rest and got the house in top shape. When I finished my cleaning marathon, for some reason the house still looked unfinished. When I looked everything over, I found the floor glistening, the walls clean, no dust anywhere—but the *doors* had marks all over them. Marks from hands, scratches from carrying suitcases through, the black marks from kicks, mop and vacuum bumps, etc.

Most of my doors are natural wood with a clear finish. Some are painted. I cleaned the painted doors with a soft nylon scrubbing sponge. If marks and nicks were present or the doors were dull, I simply repainted them. I scrubbed the natural wood

---

Doorknob dodging:

It took twenty years of professional painting for me to finally learn that loosening the two screws on the doorknob so I could paint around it sure beats trying to mask it or sash it with a brush.

---

with a good ammonia solution and a nylon pad. I cleaned with the grain of the wood and rinsed the cleaner off with a damp cloth. They were now clean, but a little dull. I made sure they were dry and with some extra-fine sandpaper, I again went over the door, lightly, with the grain. The sanding removed lint, dust and hair particles that got in the previous coat of finish. I took a cloth dampened with mineral spirits (paint thinner and tack cloths work, too) and wiped the doors to get off every speck of lint and dust. (By the way, I left the doors on while doing all this and put cardboard under them to protect the rug/floor.)

I applied a coat of low-gloss varnish (you could also use a polyurethane finish) to each door (even on the tops), rolling it on so it was evenly distributed, and then brushing with the grain to prevent runs and misses. Then I let them dry.

You won't believe the difference it will make in your doors' appearance and the ease of keeping them clean! It will take just a few hours and will help protect the doors from future abuse. Pick a day when the house is quiet—signs and warnings about keeping out of varnish aren't heeded. Do those doors on a dry summer day and they'll dry quickly (on a rainy day it can take 50 percent longer). As soon as your bedroom door is dry enough to close, take a rest. You deserve it for all the time and money you have saved.

Remember—where there's a wall, there's a way!

16.

If you have a dirty house and just a few minutes . . .

At my cleaning seminars and conventions, when I speak on time management, I always ask the audience (whose ages range from twenty-five to ninety-five):

"How many of you notice, as you grow older, that you find more time?"

Even in the largest groups, not one hand goes up; not even retired people report that they suddenly have "more time." My parents ran a large ranch almost alone, yet they still seemed to have time when they were younger to go fishing, visit neighbors, etc. After they retired, I couldn't believe how busy they were. I almost needed an appointment to see them. Now my own family is grown, too, but with more than a dozen grandkids and several businesses, I have to beg and pry and hustle to do half the things necessary to live a satisfied life. You know what I mean, it's happened to you. We just don't have the time to get our slice of life and still do justice to our home and its contents.

So I thought you might be interested in a professional strategy for cleaning the whole house ... in minutes. It's a way out for when you have "the house to clean": the whole house—living room, bedrooms, kids' rooms, kitchen and yes (shudder), even the garage—and there's no time for tooth-clenching or lip-quivering; the gunk has to go....

There are two possible approaches: either the whole house as a unit, or one room at a time. How about a compromise for maximum efficiency?

Trash and police

In these two operations, you do want to hit the whole place at once. Armed with a box or the biggest of all garbage containers, quickly scout the place and dump the trash and garbage—get rid of what's in the wastebaskets as well as what's just lying around (old newspapers, soft drink cans, petrified pizza crusts, etc.).

As for the clothes, cups, pillows, and all those "too-tired-to-put-back-where-they-belong" things—they're left in the nicest homes in the world by the most loving people. But they *are* left. To police the place, I carry a plastic laundry basket with me and toss in all the dropped socks and jackets, all the stray towels and tennis shoes. That way you can pick up the whole place really quickly, and when you get to the laundry room it only takes a couple of minutes to toss the dirty clothes in the hamper and quickly assemble everything else—dishes, books, magazines, mail, earrings, hats, duffel bags, tools, school papers, toys, etc.—together with its kind for later dispersal. Dump any questionable stuff into a box that you designate "Lost and Found."

If you do these two things first, you won't believe how much cleaning is already done when you hit the individual areas. You'll be amazed how fast you did all this—in maybe ten or fifteen minutes, especially if you do both jobs on the run.

Now the individual rooms: Which first?

Bedroom

Why? Psychologically, it's the easiest, and offers the most instant gratification. And it'll be pretty clean to start with now that the litter and clutter is gone. Only a few things remain. With all your equipment in your cleaning caddy and a lambswool duster in hand, start from the right and work to the left.

1. Making the bed. You should have made it when you got out, but if

you didn't, make two trips, one stop on each side. First go to the most restless sleeper's side, straighten out all the layers, and pull them into place (pull everything over about a foot farther than you need to on that side). Then go to the other side, straighten, and, when you pull the missing foot of cover back from the other side it will tighten the covers to perfection. Once you work up some speed, a bed should take between one and two minutes to make. If you follow my recommendation and use a comforter instead of bedspread you're looking at thirty seconds. Do the beds first so stuff won't fall in them as you dust.

2. Dusting. Start with the high dusting; get the cobwebs out of the corners. Don't take time to look and see if there are cobwebs; just take a second to hit those corners. Catch the wall lightly as you go by because dust hangs on the wall and, by keeping it down, you'll keep wall-washing to a minimum. Get the light fixtures, door frames, tops of the doors and drapes. As you move down off the high dusting hit the lamps on the dressers, the tops of mirrors and any furniture. Just dust around any doilies or dresser scarves. Then do the fronts and sides of the furniture and work from right to left around the room. (If you feel brave, step in the closet for a second and hit the dust on the shoulders of your hanging clothes.) Don't forget the front of the TV that's in every master bedroom in America. As you dust down the wall

172

to the floor make sure you remove any buildup from the bottoms of the furniture and the baseboards.

3. Now straighten the headboard, nightstand and dressing table.

4. With a spray bottle of glass cleaner and a cloth hit the mirrors, and then with neutral all-purpose cleaner do any handprints on the walls, door frames and dresser tops (they get pretty grungy from all those set-down coffee cups and pocket residue).

5. Now bring in the Eureka and do the vacuuming—start at the farthest corner of the room and work your way out. In quick routine cleaning like this, hit the traffic lanes and as far under the bed as you can reasonably reach. But keep that thing moving. As you back your way out of the room park the vacuum just outside the door. (And yes, clean the doorknob as you go.)

That was your bedroom, and you should have been able to do it in 7½ to 11 minutes, max. Now on to the guest room, or heaven forbid, the kids' room—but it does have to be done.

Kids' room

1. First remove any potentially damaging stuff (that might spill, grow mushrooms, or injure carpeting, furniture or innocent bystanders).

2. De-junk that thing that's old and worn and ugly and always in the way—they won't miss it.

3. As for litter, you trashed and dumped a lot on the initial run-through, so there'll be surprisingly little left. If you clean their room entirely you'll teach kids that

they're not responsible for their own messes, so sweep and pile the rest in the center and leave a note: "No McDonald's until all this is gone." Brutal, but effective.

4. Dust the available horizontal surfaces and spot-clean the black marks and handprints (the kids will *never* see *them*).

5. Leave the vacuuming for them, too. Vacuum handles fit any size hand, and what kid isn't just itching for a chance to drive something? If they can plug in a Nintendo, a vacuum is a cinch.

The time you spend in the kids' room will depend on how determined a delegator you are. If you get them to do what I've suggested above, you'll be out of there in 5 or 6 minutes. Otherwise, you'll probably spend 10-12 minutes in the junior jungle.

Halls and entryways

Halls are fast and easy; they're kind of the rapids of the home: little accumulates or stays there in the swift current.

1. Dusting is probably the biggest issue in a hall. All those bodies moving through distribute dust onto pictures, door frames and light fixtures. Hit the hallway running with your lambswool duster. The lighting in a hallway isn't always the greatest but you should be able to catch the cobwebs. Dust well. Get those corners, chandeliers, and the tops of wall-hangings and furniture. Don't forget the baseboard.

2. Spot-cleaning. Narrow halls (which means most of them) get fingerprints and bumps, grazes and leans.

Armed with your spray bottle of neutral all-purpose cleaner and cloth, touch them up. Get them as soon as you see them—wait for a month and you'll have a whole wall to wash. Don't forget the light switches.

3. Vacuum the entire hall, not just the traffic areas. Halls are kind of the doormat for the house, so they get it bad. And before you start vacuuming, sweep anything off the edges with a plain old broom.

You should be able to hustle through a hallway in no more than five minutes.

On the other hand, lots of housework originates in the area just inside and outside the door—the entryways to your house.

1. Hit the doors, ceiling, and railings with your lambswool duster.

2. Spot-clean any spills or marks on the walls (people are always going in and out of entryways with their hands full of everything from hero sandwiches to TVs).

3. Floors in entryways also get a beating from all the coming and going. If the entry has a hard floor (tile, ceramic, brick or wood), it probably needs mopping, so mop it at the same time you mop the kitchen. If it's a carpet or a hard floor that just needs sweeping, vacuum or dustmop now. Get up all that grit, gravel and other debris that will otherwise just get pulverized and tracked all over the house.

4. Vacuum your inside (and outside) floor mats (see chapter eight) well, and keep them vacuumed. They're your lifesavers.

Entryways are highly visible parts of a home, and a little extra time spent here—a total of 5-7 minutes—should keep them presentable.

Living room or family room

Avoid the temptation to switch on the TV and collapse a minute. Keep going! Remember the exercise you're getting, the calories you're burning, and all the praise you're going to get from the rest of the household when they notice how nice things look (fat chance, but dreaming always does a lot for our morale).

1. Straighten up everything first—furniture, pictures, books. It'll make you feel good.

2. Then dust everything. Always dust before you vacuum, so the clipped fingernails, bug bodies, and dead leaves will end up where the vacuum will get them. Work from the top down with your lambswool duster, and if there are blinds on the win-

NOW... Back to the U.S. Living Room Cleaning Open!

dows be sure to include them. Start with the top of the furniture, too, and work all the way down to the floor on each piece so you don't have to come back to do the low dusting. There's lots of dust within three feet of the floor, on the bottoms of the chairs and legs of the furniture. Work your way around the room this way and then finish off again with the baseboards.

3. Spot-clean the place (the carpet too, especially in the area of the TV and stereo). There are lots of food-to-hand and food-to-floor transfers here. (I call it "Orville Redenbacher residue.")

4. Spot-clean the windows and glass. (Notice I didn't have you clean the windows in the other rooms; best to do that with a squeegee as a whole-house project). But touch up any smudges here with your spray bottle of glass cleaner and a cloth.

5. Vacuum the traffic areas; remember, the edges and under and behind things don't really have to be done more often than once a month or so. Then set the vacuum outside of the room as a signal that the room is finished.

> What's the best way to clean ashtrays (if they aren't so far gone you'd better soak them in the sink)? Dump 'em, spray a couple shots of neutral all-purpose cleaner into them, and let them sit for a few minutes. Then come back and wipe them out with a dry cleaning cloth.

It shouldn't take more than ten to fifteen minutes to do a living room. If you have a lot of decorations it may take a little longer. But don't get caught up in knickknack renewal or you'll never get out of there.

Kitchen

I'd save the kitchen until last for several reasons. This is usually the depot for the rest of the house—where we bring things to be cleaned or emptied. The kitchen is the catchall, where we wash out vases and fill spray bottles, rinse mops and collect the garbage. Then, too, the kitchen is where we come for breaks and phone calls; if you clean it first, somebody (maybe even *you*!) is sure to come in there while you're cleaning the rest of the house and dirty it, which is demoralizing. If you get bogged down anywhere it's probably going to be the kitchen. Better to have that happen at the end of your cleaning than at the beginning.

When you do get here:

1. Dust everything from the top down. High dusting is critical in the kitchen because all the steam and vapors of cooking will turn dust into greasecake pretty quickly, and then it'll take a major wash job to get it off. If you keep it dusted this buildup will have less of a chance to develop. Still, it hardens pretty quickly in places such as the range hood and the tops of the cabinets, so for much of the kitchen a cloth dampened with dish detergent solution is unquestionably the best duster. The dish soap will give your wiper enough dissolving ability to remove the oil slick. Buff dry with a cleaning cloth right after you damp-wipe so you don't leave streaks or film.

> Damp-wiping is a two-step process: clean with a damp cloth, and buff and shine with a clean, dry cloth. This is especially important in kitchen-cleaning.

2. Hit the light fixtures and the tops of things—even above eye level—with a lambswool duster first and then the window ledges and moldings. Then with your damp cloth hit the handprints on the fridge and stove front, and the handle area of dishwashers, doors and drawers. Remember those smudge-collecting small appliances, being especially sure to polish these dry to remove any residue. If you come across

any hardened sticky spots, wet them down and let them sit a few minutes while you do something else—you should be able to come back and just whisk them away. This wash/wipe dusting is key to kitchen-cleaning. When you do it, save tables and counters for last.

3. Then straighten things in the kitchen area—the countertops, tools and decorations.

4. Do any dishes and pans that are left around, and wipe the tabletop, chair seats and counter. On countertops, start at the back and move canisters and small appliances out of the way. Wipe, then replace them as you go. Don't worry if any crumbs fall on the floor, because next. . . .

5. You do the floor. Sweep or dustmop carefully. On a light day that will be enough. If kids or company have

been around, just toss a shot of neutral all-purpose cleaner into a bucket of water and quickly damp-mop the floor (see page 100 for pro mopping technique). Any soap residue left will cause dullness, so if you have a super-shiny vinyl or ceramic tile floor, you might want to rinse with your mop, too, using a little vinegar solution (half a cup of white vinegar per gallon of water) to neutralize it.

6. While the floor dries, take out the garbage and wash the container.

All done!—in twenty to thirty minutes.

Once you get your system down, this whole-house overhaul can all be done in a couple hours. No, I'm not kidding. Soon you'll be racing the clock instead of watching it. A streamlined system like this may also eventually tempt some of the other household residents who haven't turned much of a hand to help in the past.

(If you live in a house rather than a condo or apartment, you'll want to go on to read the rest of this chapter.)

Stepping outside for a few minutes a week . . .

For my first twenty-five years in the professional cleaning business, we were taught (and believed) that the area right inside the door of a place created the first and overall impression of it, and thus we cleaned lobbies to death. About ten years ago a perceptive building manager pointed out that no, the parking lot and *exterior* entryway were actually the image makers. He was right. We all form a

preconception of the inside of a place by what we see and feel going in.

From then on we cleaned the area directly outside the door as earnestly as the area immediately inside—and with phenomenal results. This is only more true in a home—what do you think when you walk up a sidewalk or onto a porch that resembles an obstacle course of clutter? It sticks in your mind and poisons it even if the whole inside of the house is immaculate.

It only takes a few minutes a week to keep the outside nice enough to complement the inside. A little attention to exterior cleaning can also prevent lots of long-range problems inside. Let's take a quick trip around the outside now.

 ## Litter

Maybe it wasn't yours to begin with, but it is now. Litter around the front yard and the lawn is often the first declaration of dirt. Wrappers, cigarette butts, cans, wet envelopes and newspapers, animal drag-ins, dead possums—Mother Nature even chips in some in the form of fallen branches and rotting fruits.

Cure: Make it a practice to pick it up as soon as you see it, coming and going, and once or twice a month walk around the place with a little sack or box to police under the bushes and against the fence. If you do it right before you take the garbage to the curb you'll be dressed for it.

Driveway

We often have one vehicle per person, and they all bleed oil and transmission fluid, shed car interior fallout, and drip mud, snow and road cinders. This not only looks bad on the driveway, it can be tracked in and offend the house after it offends the eye.

Cure: Once the driveway is policed by hand or broom, an oil stain on a concrete driveway can be lifted the

Problem

STORAGE OUTDOORS. Is usually just a polite term for junk left outside and forgotten. It's big, ugly, easy to trip over or get cut on, and encourages termites, rats, and all their relatives.

SCREENS. Are often the real culprit when we look up and think: "Gosh, dirty windows!" An amazing amount of dust and dirt (not to mention bird doo and other things) can lodge in all those tiny openings.

DOORS. And the area right around them get hard use every single day—which means scuffs and scrapes as well as plenty of fingerprints and smudges.

PORCHES/STEPS. Are such handy places to set things, they end up in a dangerously cluttered condition. They also collect outdoor debris.

LITTER. Even if no one you know dropped it there, it makes the place look bad and encourages further littering.

WINDOWS. High ones are often dodged indefinitely because we don't feel like calling in the hook and ladder. And ground-level outside windows get mud-splattered, flyspecked, and cobwebby.

SIDEWALK/DRIVEWAY. A littered, stained walk or driveway gives a bad impression and worsens the track-in problem.

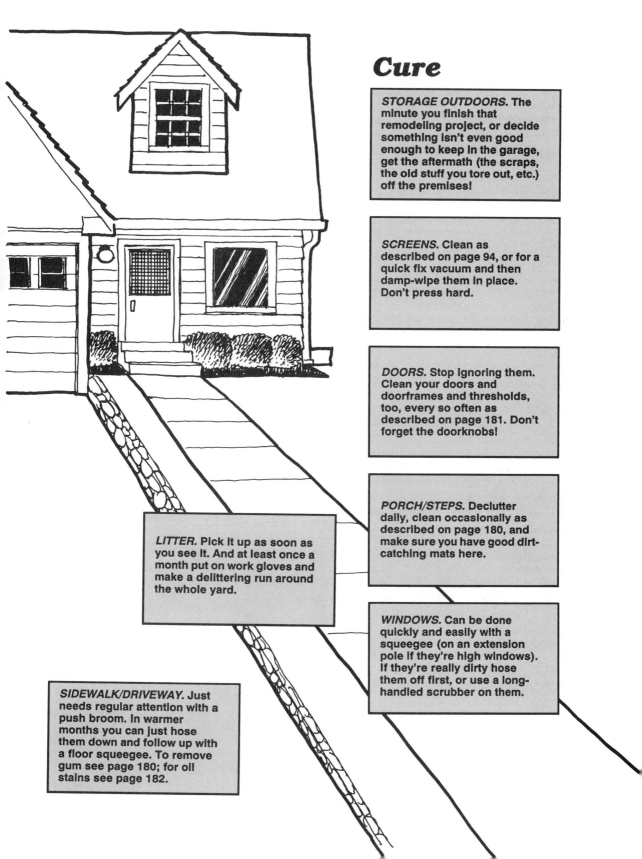

Cure

STORAGE OUTDOORS. The minute you finish that remodeling project, or decide something isn't even good enough to keep in the garage, get the aftermath (the scraps, the old stuff you tore out, etc.) off the premises!

SCREENS. Clean as described on page 94, or for a quick fix vacuum and then damp-wipe them in place. Don't press hard.

DOORS. Stop ignoring them. Clean your doors and doorframes and thresholds, too, every so often as described on page 181. Don't forget the doorknobs!

PORCH/STEPS. Declutter daily, clean occasionally as described on page 180, and make sure you have good dirt-catching mats here.

LITTER. Pick it up as soon as you see it. And at least once a month put on work gloves and make a delittering run around the whole yard.

WINDOWS. Can be done quickly and easily with a squeegee (on an extension pole if they're high windows). If they're really dirty hose them off first, or use a long-handled scrubber on them.

SIDEWALK/DRIVEWAY. Just needs regular attention with a push broom. In warmer months you can just hose them down and follow up with a floor squeegee. To remove gum see page 180; for oil stains see page 182.

same as one on a garage floor (see page 182). Hosing (during the above-freezing months) is a nice finale for the driveway.

● *Sidewalk*

This is the highway to the heart of your house, and all too often it's covered with mud, leaves, twigs, gravel, mashed acorns, leftover ice-melting chemicals, and of course a few flattened blobs of chewing gum. Is this how we want to introduce ourselves?

Cure: Get out a good, sturdy push broom (see Equipment Chart, chapter five) and use short strokes to sweep the debris off the sides. Or if it's only lightly littered, in the warmer months you can simply hose it. A clean, newly dried surface really impresses those walking across it. (That's one of the reasons people are so taken with Disneyland, as I discovered snooping about in the undercorridors with the maintenance people. They don't sweep every night, they hose things down.) Then take a floor squeegee and de-water the walk so the low areas won't have a chance to form scummy puddles as they dry. Policing the walk each day as you come and go takes only seconds and keeps sidewalks looking smart! (Pull those weeds in the cracks, too. If they keep coming back, pour in some salt water — not so much that it runs all over.)

Gum on sidewalks and paved parking areas isn't just ugly, it sticks to the bottom of your shoe on a hot day. Go out there when it's cold or at least cool, and you should be able to chip it right off with a chisel or a hoe. Be sure to pick up the pieces the minute they're free or you'll have a worse mess — they'll be tracked everywhere and get on everything. If it never gets chilly where you live, use a can of "gum freeze" from a janitorial-supply store. De-Solv-it or dry-cleaning fluid will take care of any remaining traces. Don't use solvents on asphalt!

As for moss, it not only gives the walk a five-o'clock shadow — when wet it's slicker than ice! Water alone won't remove it (it'll just make it grow), and bleach won't do it either. Mix a warm solution of neutral all-purpose cleaner and spread it generously on the spot. Let it sit awhile (but not until it evaporates), then scrub and loosen it with a stiff push broom, brush or hand floor scrubber. Then just flush it off with a hose (the solution won't hurt the lawn). If a bit remains, go after it again and get it now, while you have everything handy.

● *Porch*

This is often a permanent outdoor "junk room." Or if it's a prelude to the entrance we actually use, it gets more traffic and abuse than even the kitchen or bathroom, since it has both us and the elements to contend with.

Cure: Stop using the porch as a place to stash stuff you haven't decided what to do with. *Decide* — and either bring it in or get it out of there for good. Move out all the out-of-season outerwear, dry-rotted boots and mildewed tennis shoes. Make sure you have a good floor mat here, too (see chapter eight) — if you have an enclosed porch you have room for a good long one — and clean it often (just step out the door with the vacuum). Get rid of those cobwebs with a lambswool duster (on an extension handle if necessary). Regular sweeping of a porch is the number one way to keep dirt at a distance; swab it afterward occasionally with a solution of neutral all-purpose cleaner. Then scrub it lightly with a hand floor scrubber (see Equipment Chart, chapter five) and rinse. A fresh porch gives a good impression and prevents a lot of inside dirt.

● *Door area*

Doors and the area around them are about as concentrated an area for dirt collection as they come. We usually carry something with us as we come and go, and as we open and close the door—push, nudge, and lean against it—we usually transfer a little of it to the area, especially coming in from the garden or from fixing the car.

Cure: Most doors—painted or varnished wood, metal or plastic—can be cleaned the same way. Take a spray bottle of neutral all-purpose cleaner, a thick towel, a white nylon scrub sponge and a whisk broom, and visit all your outside doors, including the garage door.

1. Whisk and dust the entire door frame and doorway—the top and sides will have cobwebs, mashed bugs and static-clinging fuzz; the bottom (threshold) will have sand and debris in the crevices.

2. Spray the entire door (especially the area around the knob, and any spots) lightly with the neutral all-purpose cleaner, and while it "simmers" take your soft white nylon sponge and gently hit the black smudges or marks. Keep the surface good and wet while you scrub and don't scrub too hard—remember, the outside surface of the door oxidizes and if you scrub that off, the cleaned spots will be a different color.

3. Wipe the entire surface dry with a towel. Switch sides as it becomes soiled, so you don't transfer any dirt to already-clean areas.

4. The doorknob and area around it will be dirtier than it looks; hit it. Then check the doorbell, mailbox and little message area, if any. The windows and any light fixtures can be cleaned with a spray bottle of glass cleaner. You'll often find tape residue from decorations, messages, deliveries, etc., here—carefully use a little De-Solv-it to remove it chemically, rather than by scrubbing or scraping.

5. Storm doors: Get a lot of hard use and abuse, and most of them are made of two of the toughest materials to clean: aluminum and Plexiglas. Never take any aggressive cleaner or anything sharp to them. Clean them just like the other doors except be sure to dust or rinse any Plexiglas parts first to remove as much as possible of the dust and grit that can so easily scratch it. Unanodized aluminum, of course, will turn your cloth black everywhere you touch it, and you won't notice much difference in its appearance. Oh well, at least you'll *know* you have a clean door.

● *Windows*

The upper ones are only noticed from the inside, and they're not usually too bad anyway. But the lower windows are often splattered with bird droppings and mud from rain splashes, the sills and frames littered with dead bugs and paint chips. And the window wells are usually full of everything from lost caulk and broken glass to dog bones and deflated basketballs.

Cure: Clean the high windows like you do inside ones, with a squeegee (just add an extension handle). As for the lower ones, hose them off well first before you apply any cleaner with a window-washing wand. If they're really bad, use a long-handled scrubber (see Equipment Chart, chapter five) with a white nylon pad to clean them; rinse them well with the hose and squeegee them dry. Then put a bucket down in the window wells and (using a gloved hand) fill it up with all the awful stuff you find there.

● *Screens*

These slowly but surely get plugged up, dirty and damaged, and it ends up saying "sloppy."

Cure: If you don't have time to give them the whole treatment as described on page 94, sweep them lightly with a brush or broom, then damp-wipe them in place (don't push hard or your screens will soon sag!). Replace any that are ripped or bulged.

● *Outside storage*

The worst of outside cleaning is "stored" stuff, especially anything right up against the house or around the entrance or porch. All those broken bicycles, left-behind tools and containers, piles of rotting firewood, scraps and half-finished projects don't exactly project cleanliness and order.

Cure: Don't ever allow anything to be stored against or around the house. Get rid of it right now. It looks tacky, encourages pests, and injures people as well as siding. If it isn't worth storing in a garage, barn or shed, it probably isn't worth keeping. Pile it up by the back fence and cover it with a tarp if you must, but keep loose stuff away from the house—all of it!

Now I put away my cleaning tools, start my somersault of victory and then gasp. There's one spot of horror left—the garage.

● *Garage*

If the car(s) can even get in, it surely has junk fitted in all around it.

1. First and always, de-junk the garage. This is a regular ongoing process, not a once-a-year spring garage sale surge. You go to the garage for some reason almost every day, passing right by all this stuff. So take one or two things with you each trip and keep the junk controlled.

2. Pick up all the scattered tools and sports equipment and hang them up. If you've done this twenty-seven times this month already, it's time to take a break. Go down to K-Mart or somewhere and get some of those Rubbermaid shop organizers, and lick the problem once and for all.

3. Whisk (don't dust) off any horizontal surfaces such as tables, cabinets and shelves with one of those counter or foxtail brushes. You may find it hard to locate the horizontal surfaces—so de-junk more and do it anyway.

4. Treat the shop area the same as the kids' room. Trash the trash, remove anything deadly, and round up the rest. Then pile it neatly in the owner's territory.

5. Put all that broken stuff (the "I'm-going-to-fix-it-someday" junk) in a sturdy box and pray for its delivery.

6. Get out your push broom (if you have a garage you ought to have one!) and sweep the floor. (Sweep *around* the oil drips.)

7. As for the oil drips, sprinkle some sawdust or kitty litter on them, pour a little paint thinner on, and mix well. Then cover the spot or spots with some plastic wrap or a damp rag for a few hours. You've just created what we call a "poultice." It will suck up the oil and after it's done its dirty work you can sweep it away into the trash. If any stain remains it can usually be removed by scrubbing with a stiff brush and a solution of ordinary powdered laundry detergent and water.

17.

Painting without fainting

The construction company has just finished Betty Betterhouse's new home. Painting is all that's left to do before she can move in. The builder put a beautiful texture on the living room ceiling and some fine decorative masonry block work in the basement game room. Not wanting to mar the natural beauty of these surfaces, Betty asks that the painters not touch the living room ceiling, and has them apply just two light coats of paint to the masonry wall in the basement game room.

Betty moves in, and for two years she enjoys keeping the new home neat and clean. Gradually, she becomes frustrated with two areas in her house: the living room ceiling and the masonry wall. Some flyspecks, an erupting soft drink and a relocated pole lamp have left their marks on the pretty white textured ceiling. When Betty mixes some cleaning solution and tries to remove the blemishes, she is horrified at the results: When the liquid hits the ceiling, the texture dissolves and comes off! Although the texture had seemed to be as hard as concrete or plaster, it wasn't. The texture was composed of a water-soluble compound that, although it hardens, will soften again when it's wet. Betty touches up the marks with a little white shoe polish, but eventually she has only one alternative: to paint the ceiling.

One coat of an off-white latex paint covers the ceiling and it looks great, but its cleanability is still doubtful. One coat of paint is enough to prevent the texture from dissolving when it's washed, but streaks or lines will probably still occur because some moisture will penetrate the paint and react with the texture. As discussed in chapter 15, Betty really should give the ceiling two or more coats of paint for it to be cleanable in the future.

The cinderblock walls in the basement receive their share of the recreation room residue and need to be cleaned. When Betty tries to wash the painted blocks, she finds it almost impossible to get the dirt out of the pits and joints common in masonry construction. Betty should stop washing and apply a coat of block filler, followed by one or two coats of semigloss enamel. The block filler will fill the remaining pits and rough spots in the wall and the semigloss leaves a good, washable surface for the future.

Painting can be a powerful ally in your housecleaning efforts. I was a licensed paint contractor for several years and am convinced that a little painting wisdom can save a considerable amount of cleaning woes and hundreds of hours of cleaning time.

Although books of "slick quick" painting tips have been peddled for years, they haven't convinced many homemakers that the task of painting a home, inside or out, is easy and fun. Painting is generally considered a dreaded necessity; it can, however, be rewarding, physically and emotionally, if you go about it the right way.

Almost anyone can be a good painter. The basic cause of the home painter's discouragement and despair is that by the time you get fairly proficient in the task, it ends—and then it's three or four years before you pick up the paint tools and start the learning process all over again. If you'd keep it up for a few weeks longer, you'd conquer most of the problem areas and enjoy it. Don't think gimmicks, miracle tools, or "do-it-yourself magic gadgets" will make painting easy. Basic painting equipment—brushes, rollers and spray guns—can do it all, and in the long

Painting can reduce cleaning work up to 50 percent!

Fingerprints, marks, spatters, dirt ... all will easily clean off painted surfaces.

When it won't clean up, looks bad, needs protection, or you just don't feel good about it ...

PAINT IT!

run they're easier than the gimmicks, once you learn how to use them.

Summing up all painting wisdom in one volume is unimaginable; doing it in one chapter of a housecleaning book is impossible. So I resort to some brief instruction.

Prepare before you paint

"Efficient" painting begins before you paint: preparing yourself, your furnishings and the surface. The following suggestions will benefit all three of you. The mental anguish of mess and smell is what most people dread about painting. Minimize it!

1. Clean

If walls are very dusty, greasy or dirty, clean them prior to painting, using a good, strong ammonia solution that will quickly remove the dirt (don't worry about hurting the surface). Here is a place where the dry sponge can be a lifesaver. You can dry-sponge a flat-

or latex-painted bedroom down in minutes, then paint it. For other surfaces and problems, ask at your paint store—such service is part of the paint price. A rented pressure washer can have the exterior of a dirty house clean in a couple of hours.

2. Prepare

Use prepared spackle mix to patch holes. Pack the spackle tightly into the holes until it bulges (because it will shrink). Let it dry. After sanding it smooth, coat it with shellac to seal it. This will prevent dull spots in your paint job. As for nicks, bare wood, etc., always follow directions on the paint can. Use primer and *then* paint when surfaces require preconditioning—don't just use two coats of paint! A coat of primer is much better than a coat of paint as an undercoat.

3. Protect

Tromping through sheets of newspaper, half of them stuck to your feet with paint drops, while trying to untangle flimsy plastic dropcloths for your furniture will remove any doubts in your mind as to why Hitler was a painter and wallpaperer. Use old sheets to cover your furnishings and pick up a couple of ten-by-twelve- or twelve-by-fifteen-foot paint tarps—canvas or other heavy cloth—for floors. Hard paint droplets won't chip off cloth like they do off plastic. Cloths and tarps aren't expensive, will last for years, and you'll find many other uses for them.

4. Ventilate

For some reason most people think that heat is what's needed to dry things. Wrong. It's air circulation that does most of the drying. Cool air circulating freely will dry paint faster than a sealed house with the heat up to 80°.

Breathing paint fumes can be physically harmful as well as discouraging. Get plenty of air flow—it helps you *and* the paint!

Remember that pregnant women shouldn't *ever* paint, or even be around paint fumes.

Use the right paint

If you use a top-grade washable paint, you won't have to paint as often. Handprints, flyspecks, food, splashes, etc., penetrate into flat paint and often cannot be removed. Use enamel paint for more efficient cleaning, especially of surfaces that will be abused. I like satin enamel. Latex enamels are great; just make sure you prime the surface if you paint over old oil paint, or it will chip on you.

Buy well-known, high-quality brands. Good paint goes farther, covers better, and lasts longer than the bargain cheapies. The extra $5 spent on a gallon of paint is one of the best cleaning investments you'll ever make.

Select a reasonable color. Choosing the room color from a color chip has caused many a nervous collapse after the paint is on. Paint is always darker and brighter than you expected when you looked at the chip. When you get the shade and color you think you want, move a couple of shades lighter on the color chart. You'll probably be much happier with the results. Besides, lighter colors are more cheerful, reduce lighting costs, and simply look and feel cleaner.

Use as much of the same color throughout your home as possible. Too many homes look like an Easter basket because homemakers try to decorate their homes with paint. The color and style of modern furniture, drapes and carpet do a fine job of giving a home richness and taste. Using a single soft off-white shade on all the walls, ceilings and woodwork will allow your furnishings to flatter your home and will simplify your painting because it won't go out of style. (And all your touch-up paint is in one can.)

Buy professional paint equipment and take care of it

Most paint stores carry professional equipment. Selecting the right equipment isn't really difficult—just stay away from the $1.29 throwaway brushes and rollers. Good brushes and heavy-duty rollers will cover better, and apply faster and more evenly. Ask the dealer where the professional lines are and select a nylon bristle brush; nylon lasts and keeps its spring. An angled sash brush will do a lot for your aim on trim.

I use a thick roller cover on most jobs—⅜- to ½-inch pile—because it holds more paint and covers more thoroughly. (Most dealers, though, will tell you "thin for bare walls, thick for deep texture.") All rollers leave an orange-peel effect (which I like; if you don't you can lightly run a brush over it when you're finished and have a smoother, glossier job). Learn to use roller extension handles. They work beautifully with professional rollers and are much safer, more effective and less tiring than painting from a ladder. Using extension handles will be awkward at first, but they're faster than holding a roller frame in your hand. (They also get you back from your work so you can see what you're doing.)

A deeper roller pan or a bucket with screen will boost your efficiency and lessen the possibility of spills. Pick up a free five-gallon plastic bucket somewhere (the kind dry-walling compound, bulk peanut butter, etc., come in) and get a roller screen for it. They're quick, safe and easy to use. When you're at the paint store, be sure to get enough free paint sticks.

Don't forget to use your plank, ladder and box combination, too. They will make your painting task a lot easier.

Some tips on technique

● *Prevent drips*

Punching a hole with a nail in the inside lip gutter of the can will eliminate "can run."

When you first open the paint bucket, use an awl, punch or nail, and punch several holes inside the lid groove. All the excess paint that used to run down the side will run back into the bucket

and when the lid goes on, it will seal tightly without squirting paint all over the side or all over you.

● *Proper thinning may help your paint job*

Solvent evaporation causes many enamel paints to get "heavy" when

Buy good equipment

Buy a good grade of paint. Most of your work—and cost—is in the preparation for painting. The little more you spend on a good-quality paint will cover the surface faster and better, look better, and make all that hard work last much longer!

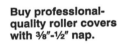

Invest in a professional roller frame with an extension handle.

Buy professional-quality roller covers with ⅜"-½" nap.

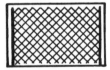

A roller screen and

a 5-gallon plastic bucket are an inexpensive, effective and easy combination to use.

Buy professional-quality brushes. Nylon bristles last and hold their "spring."

An angled sash brush will aid your trimming accuracy.

Get ample free paint sticks.

This is one place rags come in handy.

stored or while in use. Thin it down! Getting paint or varnish to a flowing consistency will create a brushed or rolled surface as smooth as silk. Use a recommended thinner (not gasoline or other substitutes) for oil-based or resinous paints; water for latex, of course! Go slowly—if you get it too thin, you can't thicken it. Letting paint run off a dipped stir stick is a good way to judge consistency. If enamel runs to a point two inches below the stick before it breaks into droplets, it's just right.

If your paint or varnish looks too thin as soon as you open the can, insufficient stirring is the most probable cause—the heavy pigments are likely to have settled on the bottom. Always have the paint store shake the can on their machine. It's much easier and safer—the lid could come off while you shake it.

People tend not to stir varnish enough. Because it's clear, it looks mixed and fools the user. Varnish "driers" settle out on the bottom, and if not stirred well, varnish will take forever to dry!

● Don't paint too heavily

When you do, the sharp, crisp trim edges and corners become so gobbed they make the house look cheap and sloppy (and you can hardly tell the trim from the wall). Any damage to the surface, which happens in even the best-kept homes, is deep and ugly and almost impossible to blend in when the surface is recoated.

● Prevent a dripping brush

Dip the bristles just halfway into the paint; then, holding the brush flat, wipe the back side and bottom of the brush across the bucket rim.

● Always drag the last stroke of the brush into the finished area

Don't pull it away. If you brush into the finished area, there won't be a brush mark.

● Roll properly

Even though you've rolled over a surface once and it appears covered, it isn't. Cross over it three or more times for a good-looking, well-distributed paint job. The first roller pass appears adequate, but small "pinholes" or air holes are there that won't show until the paint is dry. Always roll in an up-and-down pattern.

Trimming the fuzzy edges of the roller will help minimize roller lines.

● Paint in this order:

When painting a room, trim around the ceiling and woodwork first, so that the paint you roll on later will lap over the trimmed edges and they won't show (use the paint can as a "trim bucket" so you can avoid the inconvenience of dipping a brush into a roller pan). Roller-paint walls next. Dip the roller in the paint, roll off the excess on the screen, then apply it to the wall, always going up on the first stroke so paint won't puddle down. Paint woodwork last, preferably with a semigloss enamel. Always do the baseboards last, because your brush (and paint) will pick up all kinds of hair and lint from the carpet or floor.

Cleanup

The most dreaded part of painting won't be a chore at all if you always scrape the paint out of the roller before you try to wash or clean it out.

Roller cleanup

A roller can hold up to a cup of paint. Before cleaning, always scrape a roller with the groove in the handle of the paint stick.

When you're finished cleaning it, always take the roller off the frame and let it dry.

Use the curve in the handle of the paint stick or the side of a putty knife for this messy job. Some rollers can hold about a cup of paint, and leaving it in results in a waste of paint, solvent and cleaning time. If you don't scrape it, you can wash it, squeeze it, and never seem to get anywhere—paint will come out of rollers forever. If you've scraped it properly, you can clean a roller in minutes with a small amount of thinner or water.

Once the roller is scraped dry, place it in an empty pan or bucket with a few cups of thinner, squeezing and massaging with your hands to loosen the remaining paint. Repeat until the solvent comes out clean, then spin the roller vigorously on a pole or post (or your arm, if you're desperate). Centrifugal force will throw the moisture effectively out of the nap. Rollers and brushes used in latex paints are most easily cleaned under a stream of running water, either in the sink or outside with a hose.

Get all the paint you can out of a brush before cleaning by wiping it on the inside edge of the bucket or by painting it dry. Dip it in the solvent and swish it around to release (dissolve) the paint on the bristles. Again, a quick spin between your palms will accomplish more than ten minutes of sloshing. When the brush doesn't cloud the thinner, it's clean. A couple of tablespoons of vegetable oil on the brush will preserve and soften it for its next use, even if that's a long way off. When finished, seal the brush in aluminum foil or plastic wrap; the oil can be wiped off with a rag when you use it again for enamel, but it should be washed with soap and water prior to use with latex.

Always keep leftover paint for touch-up. Seal it well, and label it. Small glass jars with tight-fitting lids make fine touch-up containers.

Brush cleanup

Pour paint thinner or water in a bucket and let the brush soak a bit.

Agitate up, down, around. Repeat if traces of paint remain in the solvent.

Then spin the brush dry. Repeat.

Wallpaper removal

In my first fifteen years of cleaning contracting, I did an enormous amount of wallpaper removal. You might like to know in a few minutes what it took me fifteen years to learn.

If you can avoid removing wallpaper, make every effort to do so. But if you can't, don't waste your time and money getting steamers, magic wallpaper paste dissolvers, torture boards with nails in them, and other gimmickry. I stewed and sweated with all of them for hundreds of hours, thinking something must be wrong with me. (Little did I know that everyone who uses these has the same results and the same paranoia about their efforts.) With all of their "magic," and five helpers, the lady of the house and I would end up with putty chisels or knives, picking, gouging and scraping off scraps of wallpaper.

The best thing to do is to get a bucket of warm water and a big sponge. Set up your plank so that you can get at the entire surface you want removed. Then wet down one end of the area as heavily as possible (just so it doesn't run down the wall too much). Cover the entire area, then go back and start over again, again and again. It really isn't much work, it's just boring. But keep wetting it. After about thirty minutes of wetting, check a

place or two. If it's quite loose, pull the paper off; if not, keep wetting. Don't get anxious. If you wet it enough, the stuff will come off in a big sheet. Then wipe the soggy glue off the wall so it will be in good shape.

If wallpaper has ten coats of paint over it, you have four logical options: panel the wall, move, make it eleven coats of paint, or cover the wall with some sort of sheet rock texture compound. If both wallpaper and paint are still firmly attached to the wall—not peeling or "bubbling" off—this last is probably the best option if you want to combine good looks with ease.

If you don't want to be practical, however—if you really love that house, you really want the wallpaper off, and you're willing to suffer—that's when you get the boards with the nails in them. You need to scratch through those ten layers of paint to be able to wet down the paste on the wallpaper beneath them, because the whole trick is to get water underneath the paint. You might even want to add some paste dissolver to the water you use. But basically, after beating through that paint with the boards and nails, you keep wetting down the wall, and wetting down the wall, and wetting down the wall, and then you get scrapers and putty knives and start pulling pieces of it loose. There's no neat or pleasant way to do it, but it *can* be done.

18.

Why not be a professional housecleaner?

Can you picture yourself next Monday morning? It's 9:00. All your housework is done. Your home is organized, and you're leaving it to go clean four other homes . . . for $10 or $20 an hour? No, it isn't a fantasy or a joke.

One of the biggest economic and social realities of the '90s is the two-career family. The effects of an extra job on family and marital relationships can be problematic. But that doesn't eliminate many families' growing need for a second income. Homemakers with

or without children have flocked to the job market in an attempt to meet ever-mounting inflation. To secure employment, many have found it necessary to purchase extra transportation, accept close to minimum-wage jobs, hire expensive child-care services, and spend a lot of money on a business wardrobe. Actual benefits from most homemakers' second jobs would be questionable if both direct and indirect costs were calculated.

Why go through the expense of all that overhead to gain a tiny percent of income when you can double your profit for half the emotional and physical price you're paying? Why not start your own professional housecleaning business? It's not only possible, but it will offer you some great personal and family advantages:

1. Excellent income: $10 to $20 per hour for your time.

2. Tax deductions and depreciation breaks.

3. The potential for family involvement.

4. The ability to work on your own schedule, part time or full time.

5. Rewarding social and educational experiences.

6. Regular physical exercise.

7. Equipment to do all your own housecleaning.

8. The opportunity to pick your own working associates.

9. More control over your time and environment.

Why get a job that makes it impossible to spend any time with your spouse or friends? Why have children you can't enjoy? Why fight traffic and parking and rigid schedules every day? Why answer to "bosses"? Why tolerate excessive deductions from

your check? Why clear just a small amount of money for forty hours of hard work? On your own terms and at your own energy level, in your own selected environment, you could make the same money in half the hours and feel better physically and emotionally.

The market for housework is wide open. There isn't a household in America that doesn't need housework done—and many will hire it. Think of all the two-career families that desperately need help keeping the house clean. The maid business is booming!

Many struggling homemakers can't cope with their own housework, so that leaves the majority of your neighborhood or town needing help. You can provide it! There are lots of cleaning companies, but good professional housecleaning companies are hard to find.

If you are a woman, you have the advantage over a male in landing a professional housecleaning job. Homemakers are extremely particular as to whom they turn loose in their houses to clean, and you, another homemaker, will more easily win their trust.

Though the image of being a "cleaner" and the hard work involved are big concerns to most potential scrubbing entrepreneurs, I assure you that handling the "image" is fun. And hard work will make you twice the person you are now!

The predominant fear most people have about trying their own business is, "Can I get customers?" This will never be a problem if you do high-quality work for an honest price. Even when I first started out, my success rate in getting the jobs that I bid was nine out of ten.

If you just follow the directions in this book, you'll know more about housecleaning than anyone you'll ever work for. Every job will multiply your experience. You'll find that with your skills you can consistently average $8 to $12 per hour. Sometimes you'll get

as high as $25 per hour on special jobs.

Regular everyday housework-type services (sweeping, vacuuming, dusting, etc.) are always in demand. But almost anyone can do that kind of housework, at about the same rate of speed, and this holds down the worth of such jobs. Try to specialize in the areas where the average homemaker struggles: floors, walls, window-washing, rugs, etc. Competence in these areas will lead you to other, even more lucrative, jobs.

Getting started

The idea of getting started seems to cause even the most talented to shake in their boots. I know you can do it, and once you start, you'll look back, after the first three jobs, and laugh at yourself for being nervous about it. Visions of arming yourself with a mop bucket and dust cloth and parading up and down the streets beating on doors for business are out. You want to go to work, not jail! The following are some good ways to get started. (And don't be afraid to call people in the business—in other towns—for advice. They'll help you.)

1. Get a name and a slogan
Just think—a chance to name your own company! Avoid personal names like Mabel's Cleaning, Betty's Broom Service, Jones Cleaners. Instead, use names like Century, Belair (like car names)—except relate it to homes. Such names have a ring of authority, and will inspire confidence. (Would you rather be termite-proofed by TermiteMaster or Joe the Bug Stomper?) Just be sure you don't use someone else's name.

2. Print cards or leaflets
Always use a picture or visual symbol on your "advertising" literature of any

kind. A bit of creativity, some rub-on lettering, some help from an artist, or a little free help from the printer will give you an inexpensive but effective tool to attract business. Avoid tacky "clip art" decorations. Be fresh and original. Your materials should be professional-looking and eye-catching.

Shop around for a good local printer and print at least several hundred for the best cost breaks.

House Cleaning / Janitorial Service / Painting / Rugs & Upholstery

3. Check into rules and regulations

Make a call to state, federal and local tax offices and the telephone company and explain to them the scale on which you intend to operate. If you're just going to do an occasional job, with no employees, they'll probably say "no problem." But if you're going to operate on a large scale, hire a couple of neighbors, have a vehicle, etc., it's best to inform the agencies involved. The Yellow Pages, or your local Small Business Administration, will direct you to the right place to find rules and regulations. Explain your intention, and regulatory agencies will generally send you everything you should know, free. They are fair, friendly, and will tell you exactly what's needed to operate a business. Don't get buffaloed by this part. It's easy, and the cost to you generally is little or nothing. "Acting dumb" to see what might happen seldom pays.

Check with your insurance company. The personal liability coverages you have now may also cover you and your little business, but check it out. Insurance companies don't cover workers or workmanship, only liability. If you fall through a window or rip a couch while washing the ceiling, you're covered under the liability section. However, if you break the window or rip the couch while working on it, *you* are responsible. Arm yourself with the necessary insurance, but don't get caught up in morbid fears of what might happen.

You'll have a few bad experiences, but be careful and conscientious, and your victims will have great compassion.

4. Advertise

A business card pinned up in a laundromat or on a supermarket bulletin board

House Cleaning / Janitorial Service / Painting / Rugs & Upholstery

Spring Clean-up Specials

Let Varsity bring spring to you.

- *Window Washing*
- *Floor Stripping*
- *Wall Washing*
- *Carpet Shampooing*
- *One-Time Clean-ups*
- *Insurance Estimates*
- *Painting*

Don A. Aslett, Owner **(208) 232-8598**
311 S. 5th
P.O. Box 1682
Pocatello, ID 83204

Reminder: Use Varsity for your summer painting needs!

may have some success but usually won't get you the kind of people you want to work for. If they can't afford a washing machine, they generally won't be able to afford you.

Classified ads in the newspaper are always good. Dropping cards off at local businesses gets both owners and clients. But the best advertising for housecleaning is unquestionably the personal referral. People who have their homes cleaned professionally love to brag about it, and if you do a good job, you'll never be able to handle the work that will flow in. A card or two left at a house or a business you clean will quickly find its way into the hands of friends, and you'll find your way into another assignment. If your work is good (even if it's a little expensive), your business will boom and prosper.

5. Start small, and test it out
You'll be surprised what happens. One thing it will do is make your own housework easier and simpler.

6. Some of the best sources for work
(and reliable payment) are:

- Local personal residence cleaning
- Smoke-loss cleaning jobs for insurance companies
- Small medical or professional offices
- Construction cleanup, such as in new housing developments

7. Some accounts to avoid:

- People moving out and away
- Shopping malls and supermarkets (there's often no clear-cut authority to make decisions or payment)
- "Maid" work for finicky folks

8. Hire cautiously
Wrapped up in the thrill and vanity of becoming a "big boss," you may discover a tendency to promise every ambitious or down-and-out friend a job. Be careful. You could end up working for *them*. Once your friends, relatives, or other job-needing associates go on a job with you, you may feel obligated to keep them on every job, even if they turn out to be worthless. You could end up spending your time assigning, supervising and cleaning up after them. Go slow. Start with yourself and a reliable helper, and work up from there.

9. Get your own equipment
You wouldn't be very impressed if a high-class restaurant asked you to bring your own dishes, or if a surgeon asked you to furnish the scalpel. There is power and mystery in "professional equipment and supplies." They are dependable and deductible, as well as usable in your own home.

Don't go over your head on expensive specialty items if your business doesn't justify it. The Equipment Chart in chapter five should give you a good start. Put your name and emblem on all your equipment, for security and advertisement. You don't need a great deal of equipment, and you can store it in the garage and transport it in your car. If your business expands and you need a bigger vehicle, get a van. You don't need a $20,000 fur-lined one. A van three to ten years old is fine because you won't be driving it that much— maybe a couple of miles, and then it's parked for hours while you clean a house. There's no sense carrying the insurance, interest and overhead on an expensive new vehicle, because you'll probably only put 5,000 or fewer miles a year on it, as most of your work will be close to you. Paint your van white or a bright color and letter it; it will be great advertising. Don't let your family use it to go fishing or haul firewood or hot-rod around in. Have a few simple shelves built into it, and install curtains if there are any windows. The curtains will serve two purposes: they make the van look more homey, and they reduce temptation to thieves.

10. Involve the family

These days there aren't enough paper routes or grocery store bagging jobs to go around. Once you get clients who love and trust you, they'll need other services such as painting, grass-cutting and yard work. This is a natural for your children while you clean house. Imagine your spouse cleaning the fireplace or toilet bowl under your strict supervision. (It will probably never happen, but it's a great thought!)

11. Fill your work list and time schedule

Having a small housecleaning business isn't going to give you an ulcer. The fact that you book your own clients leaves you the master. You have the freedom to work just a couple of hours a week — or eighty, if you have the energy. Everyone's family and social obligations are as unique as his or her physical stamina and emotional needs. If your children are in school, you'll have three hours in the morning and three in the afternoon. You could work all week or once a week. Many businesses like their cleaning done from 4:00 to 6:00 a.m.; for a nervous-energy type like me, that's a good time. You're the captain of your own ship; you decide when, where and how. If you can't conform enough to meet a client's particular wishes, then don't; they can get someone else. The reason you got into the business was to run it your way, not to let it run you.

12. Learn to bid your work

Don't work by the hour! Everybody in the world thinks a "cleaning lady" or a "janitor" should get a few bucks an hour. If you quoted $5 an hour to wash someone's windows she'd gasp unbelievingly at your nerve, even if you told her it would only take three hours ($15). However, if you said, as you wrote the price on your card and handed it to the homemaker, "I have looked at your windows carefully and feel that, considering labor, materials and equipment, I can do them for $30," she would nod gratefully. Most customers find that a set price is more acceptable than a per-hour rate. Plus it's a relaxed situation — they know what it's going to cost.

The most-asked question in the industry is, "How do I know how much to bid?" That's easy: Figure how long it will take you and multiply by what you want to make an hour. The better and faster you become, the more you should charge. After a few months, you'll know your actual production time and will be able to estimate closely. You'll over- or underestimate a few times (you might have to work free a few times) — and you'll learn from it. But once you get good, your confidence will "wax" strong, and you'll get almost every job you bid. The following table of average professional costs will give you some guidance in getting started.

Remember, this table is only a guide. You'll be able to plug your own figures in after a little experience. Who you work for, as well as the quality of home and furnishings you work on, will make a lot of difference in the amount of cleaning time required. Much depends on the total area, size of rooms, type of paint on the walls (enamel or flat), density of furnishings, who furnishes the equipment, whether you or they get the area ready, the level of previous maintenance, how far you have to travel, etc. You'll have a few losses, but that will stimulate your desire to be more accurate, and you'll get good!

Always bid work. This is the basic formula for success in your own busi-

Bid Estimate Guide

(These are ball-park averages—your area, location, the state of the economy, and the desperation of the client or the prospective cleaner can affect these prices in either direction.)

Walls and ceilings *Cleaning*	per sq. ft.	small room	medium room	large room
Hall	3–4¢	$ 9	$12	$14
Den	3–4¢	13	18	22
Recreation room	3¢	20	27	32
Living room	5¢	20	28	38
Dining room	5¢	14	18	20
Bedroom	5¢	12	17	23
Entrance	5¢	7	10	15
Bathroom	5¢	7	10	14
Kitchen	5–6¢	16	27	37
Stair landing	6¢	14	16	22
Utility room	6¢	12	14	16

Hard-surfaced floors	lightly soiled	average	filthy
Clean	3¢ (per sq. ft.)	5¢ (per sq. ft.)	7¢ (per sq. ft.)
Clean and wax	8¢ (per sq. ft.)	10¢ (per sq. ft.)	12¢ (per sq. ft.)
Strip and wax	10¢ (per sq. ft.)	12¢ (per sq. ft.)	14¢ (per sq. ft.)

Carpets			
Vacuum and spot clean	1¢ (per sq. ft.)	2¢ (per sq. ft.)	3¢ (per sq. ft.)
Surface clean (spin bonnet)	4¢ (per sq. ft.)	5¢ (per sq. ft.)	9¢ (per sq. ft.)
Shampoo and extract	9¢ (per sq. ft.)	12¢ (per sq. ft.)	14¢ (per sq. ft.)

Windows (per side)			
Small, accessible	4¢ (per sq. ft.)	5¢ (per sq. ft.)	6¢ (per sq. ft.)
Large, accessible	3¢ (per sq. ft.)	4¢ (per sq. ft.)	4¢ (per sq. ft.)
Small, inaccessible	5¢ (per sq. ft.)	6¢ (per sq. ft.)	7¢ (per sq. ft.)
Large, inaccessible	4¢ (per sq. ft.)	5¢ (per sq. ft.)	5¢ (per sq. ft.)

Upholstery			
Small chair	$ 3 (each)	$ 4 (each)	$ 7.50 (each)
Large chair	10 (each)	12 (each)	15.00 (each)
Small couch	20 (each)	25 (each)	35.00 (each)
Large couch	30 (each)	40 (each)	50.00 (each)

Furniture *Clean and polish*			
Small end table	$1.00 (each)	$1.50 (each)	$ 2.00 (each)
Average TV	2.00 (each)	2.50 (each)	3.00 (each)
Piano	4.00 (each)	4.75 (each)	5.25 (each)
Desks, dressers	3.50 (each)	4.00 (each)	5.00 (each)

Contract cleaning	small office	med office	large office
	7–10¢ per sq. ft. per month	6–7¢ per sq. ft. per month	5–6¢ per sq. ft. per month

Targeted hourly production rate	light cleaning	med cleaning	heavy cleaning
	3,000 sq. ft.	2,800 sq. ft.	2,000 sq. ft.

(When estimating square footage, consider only the areas you will actually clean.)
Other business operation costs:
    Vehicle—charge 25¢ a mile
    Overhead—add 5% to your total bid to cover phone, advertising, etc.
    Daily vacuuming, dusting, watering plants—add $8.50 per hour to the contract amount.

ness. On a bid job, you can earn twice as much money by the hour if you work twice as hard.

But unless the customer demands it, or the job is very small, never give a bid price at the time you go to look at a job. Leave the customer convinced that you're the best-qualified person for the job and that she'll miss out if she doesn't have you do the work. (Brag on yourself a little.) Return home, prepare the bid, and mail it to the customer. Handing the customer a bid and then standing and waiting for a decision creates an unpleasant atmosphere. Especially with large expenditures at stake, the customer likes to study the bid and think it over before making a commitment. A commitment given in haste or under pressure often develops into a bad customer relationship and affects the job and the promptness with which the bill is paid.

The proper conversation while the job is being estimated can make a big difference. If you can see that money is a problem at the moment, and if you know that her credit is good, let a prospective customer know that you're agreeable to arranging suitable terms. (Compensate for this in the bid.) Remember, jobs you consider small or common may be great and expensive decisions for some customers. Take your time, examine the whole job, and add your personal touch to the negotiations. Don't be an estimator who deals only with square footage and not with people. The personal touch can be one of the biggest factors in whether or not you get the job.

Helpful techniques in preparing a bid

When preparing a bid, itemize and describe clearly the service you will provide. Picture words and specifics are much more effective than the bare minimum of information. For example,

here are two ways a job could be described in a bid to paint a floor:

Example A
Painting porch floor, one coat gray enamel: $45.00

Example B
Preparation of complete rear porch floor area including light sanding, renailing protruding nails, removing all dust and foreign material, and applying one coat of Benjamin Moore Floor and Deck Enamel in Dover Gray color. Total cost: $44.50

Almost anyone would accept the second bid rather than the first because it appears to offer more for the money. "Preparation" is simply getting the area ready, and both bids include that. But Example B *tells* the customer about it. "Light sanding" means removing paint blisters or scaly areas, and "renailing protruding nails" may take three or four minutes. "Removing all dust and foreign material" just means sweeping the floor. Example A didn't even bother to tell the customer that the floor would be swept. "Applying" is a professional word; "painting" is Tom Sawyer stuff. Professional-sounding words in your bid will help sell the job.

For large or long-term jobs, submit your bid with a one-page standard contract agreement form. Most office-supply stores have them; your name can be stamped or printed on the blank form. Once a relationship of trust is established with a regular customer, a contract may not be necessary on every job.

Tips of the trade

Here are some of my "Key Management Secrets for Successful Residential Cleaning." These are the small things that help get a job done—and help keep a customer for life.

1. Don't lend or rent out your equipment. Few people know how to care for professional equipment, and a lost or damaged part can cost you a month's profit.

2. When bidding a job, project the idea: "We are professionals who can and will take care of your problems."

3. Be careful about bidding or giving prices by phone. Type of paint, condition, location, accessibility, and the personality of the client can all create a bidding problem if you don't look over a job in person.

4. Show up at the house dressed for the occasion. A clean uniform always makes a good impression.

5. Carry crisp business cards, a new dry sponge, a clean notepad. Everybody likes to be the first one.

6. Tell the customer what will clean and what won't. Don't say "if" or "maybe."

7. Point out any damage or problem subtly, but don't criticize sloppy painting or construction—chances are they or their grandpa did it.

8. With urine stains and smells—dogs, kids or other—advise the customer about permanent damage.

9. Look for more work as you go along. Mention it in a helpful way, without applying pressure. They'll appreciate it and gain confidence in you.

10. Always know beforehand who has the keys, how you'll get in and lock up, and who is authorized to be there.

11. Will there be water? Light? Heat? Don't make any assumptions about utilities—it can cost you all the profit.

12. Volunteer to repair things (touch up nicks, refinish doors, etc.) if you can do so profitably. If they hired you to clean, it's certain they'll need other chores done around the house.

13. Even if the job you're doing is inside, ask about exterior cleanup.

14. Problem items: Some appliances can take longer to clean than a $30 room, yet charges of more than $5 will stagger the customer. Kitchen floors can be much the same problem. Be careful.

15. If you send a crew, always designate one person as "the boss" so the owner only needs to communicate with that person. If about every hour "the boss" makes quick rounds, nodding and grunting a few corrections and/or praises, the homeowner will feel greatly relieved that someone is in command and that he or she will not have to inspect. "The boss" should also sell future jobs while there.

16. Even though the job is done, always list in detail the operations performed; this makes customers feel good and helps get future jobs.

17. Always do some extras at no charge; after you've finished the job, casually point them out. If the owner finds a speck or two after you're gone, he or she will be less likely to call.

18. Always lock the house if you leave and no one is there.

19. Use professional forms for equipment, material and operations.

20. Never, *never* arrive late.

One of the best and most complete books available on starting and running your own cleaning business is *Cleaning Up for a Living*, which I wrote with one of the sharpest minds in the business, Mark Browning. Both this book and a complete cleaning business startup kit (including models for all the forms and contracts you need) are available from The Cleaning Center, P.O. Box 39-H, Pocatello, Idaho 83204.

19.

Your reward: There *is* life after housework

Well, that's it. We've covered enough aspects of housework to provide a fresher, more realistic view of the subject. And until a robot is developed that can be programmed to do your housework for you, you'll find the methods and equipment outlined in the foregoing eighteen chapters to be the next best thing for getting the most work done in the least amount of time.

Don't come unglued if you discover that even after applying all the best methods of housecleaning and home management, you sometimes experience the mundane realities of the profession. Every job has them, and housework is no exception. So brace yourself, and take it with a smile, for you too are vulnerable to slipping vacuum belts, flyspecked windows, plugged drains, sticky floors, ring around the collar, muddy boots, tidal waves of dirty laundry, and five dozen cookies to bake for the Halloween party (on two hours' notice).

But you've made tremendous progress! You've learned how to clean house faster and better. You've also seen the error of the notion that everything to do with cleaning and housework is dull, unglamorous and unrewarding.

I've been exposed to the same image you have of "the cleaner," and am still confronted with it every day. When I started my business while going to college, I received newspaper

write-ups and a lot of publicity, and everyone admired my cleaning activities — as long as they were leading to something else. When I finished my schooling and still remained a cleaner, my social prestige diminished greatly. Several little incidents brought this to my attention.

One time I was doing a special job in a bank, cleaning the vault floors with a buffer. Customers were drifting in and out of the lobby, casting pitying glances, as they usually do, at the "janitor." At the time I had five children and was deeply involved in community affairs — I was a Scout leader and was active in my church, I attended concerts and art shows, and I thought I was riding the tide of social prestige along with the rest of upstanding society. One of the bank's customers was irritably dragging her loud and disobedient child along when suddenly, in disgust, she grabbed the little fellow, shook him violently, and, gesturing toward me, said, "Behave, you little snot, or you'll end up just like him!"

As the years have gone by, I've found that woman's opinion of cleaning people is nearly universal. Whenever I mingle socially and my community work or other accomplishments are described, some newcomer will always ask, "Well, what does he do for a living?" A hesitation and silence follows every time, because nobody wants to say, "He's a cleaning man."

People who meet me on the street and remember me from the early days because of the publicity my housecleaning business received will inevitably ask, "Well, how are you, Don? What are you doing now? Are you still a. . . ." They always hesitate because they can't bring themselves to say "housecleaner."

While she was at college, my daughter Laura skied at the nearby resorts whenever she and her friends got the chance. Since she had the car that could haul the most skis and students, it was generally used as a taxi. After everyone was loaded in and they were off to the mountain, someone in all the chatter would always comment, "This is sure a nice car. What does your dad do for a living?" And Laura always answered cheerfully, "He's a janitor." The interior of the car would go silent for approximately three minutes, no one knowing what to say. Finally, in a politely patronizing voice, someone would say, "That's nice."

One of my managers, right after he was listed in *Who's Who in Technology Today in the U.S.A.*, was registering his wife at the hospital to have a baby. When the clerk asked him his occupation, he answered confidently, "Janitor." She looked up at him and said shyly, "Oh, come now. You don't really want me to put that down, do you?"

I could relate dozens of such stories, all hinging on the questionable status of being a "cleaning person." The image that society associates with cleaning—both in business and in the home—is totally incorrect.

I assure you, voting in a Senate chamber is no more important than cleaning a bed chamber! A glittering five-star restaurant has no more vital things take place in it than your ordinary, everyday kitchen. The home is the most sacred and exciting place on the face of the earth. For anyone to pronounce that caring for a home is a hardship, a drag and a bore is only to admit a lack of imagination. Those who clean and care for a house, whether on a full-time basis or in addition to another career, can get great satisfaction from it.

Remember, though, that a house is to live in, not live for. Cleanliness is very important, but it should never become all-important. There is merit in being meticulous, in adding that extra touch of excellence to your efforts, but there is also room for caution here: Our zeal to achieve superior results can become slavish devotion to meaningless detail.

Homes are more than showcases and status symbols. Your home is the background against which your life is lived, your retreat from the world's buffetings. Why direct all your efforts toward impressing society? There's great fun and satisfaction in giving yourself to your surroundings, and in making your home a pleasing reflection of your personality and interests.

People will enjoy coming to your house, not because of its impressive trappings and expensive adornments, but because so much of *you* is there.

Personal freedom is life's real reward. Housework is an important and worthy endeavor, but the less of your life it requires, the more will be available for other pursuits that add dimension and joy and meaning to living. Housework may have become your responsibility, but it is not your destiny. Your real role in the home goes far beyond housework.

Pulpit, pedestal or poetry cannot enrich the lives of others like a clean, happy, well-organized home life can. Humankind needs examples of order and confidence, and both of these virtues can be superbly exemplified in the home.

Children, and grown-ups too, need order in their lives. A feeling of contentment, comfort and well-being grows out of neatness and order, not clutter and chaos. Self-esteem and achievement germinate in a quality environment, and no environment is more influential than the home. Our home atmosphere has a great influence on all of us—it can affect lives far more than any movie star, president, or professor. The spirit of our home can touch and change not only all those who enter and all who live there, but our own close personal relationships. It can make us irresistible as people — someone not just to be needed, but loved and appreciated.

The home is the power lever of the world, and *you* control it.

Why do we mind the time spent cleaning?

The whole thrust of humankind is to do, build or create something that will last forever—be it a family, a reputation, a building, a poem or a pyramid. We want something that will last, maybe for thousands or tens of thousands of years, to testify to our lives of hard work and inspiration....

And then there is housework—especially cleaning. We spend many (including some of the best) hours of our life making something beautiful and presentable—a glossy floor or sparkling windows, a dust-free curio cabinet or lint-free living room rug—then a few hours or a few days and little appreciation later it's gone, and we're right back where we began. We size it all up, the thirty or forty tasks that we do over and over each day, and think, "I should look forward to doing *this*?"

Yes, and here's why: When it seems you've been unjustly stuck with cleaning up behind someone or something, think past that dirty pad—launch pad, I mean. There's always cleanup after launching any worthwhile project. As a giant life-enhancing cargo is launched into space to impact the world with scientific excitement and information, we hear and read about this great accomplishment, yet it rarely occurs to us that it left a dirty launchpad behind. Yes, getting that payload raised and up and out left the place blackened, sooted, smoked, scratched and scummy, just like getting a family launched into life. Great meals, great buildings, great novels, bumper crops and crown jewels all create some dust and mess getting the job done. Cleaning it up is not only worthwhile, it's actually part and parcel of the end result. Cleaning affects the quality of life much more than parties, socials, entertainments, vacations, etc., and look at all the effort

and money we pour into them. So just think as you clean up, "This is not the aftermath, but the launch.... I'm preparing for the lift-off of great things."

When you think of the impact, the accomplishments of the "clean" you've created in your life, when you focus on the end result, cleaning feels good and necessary and even noble.

Not for women only . . .

Managing the home usually ends up being a woman's responsibility, not necessarily because she is a woman, but because no one else can or will do it as well. Some men think they can, but they can't.

If mechanics were all that was involved in homemaking, men might be as good at it as women are. But when it comes to bringing out the charm of a room, or adding the beauty and special warmth that make a clean home more than just a clean house . . . well, that transcends the realm of applied science or mechanics, and I'll admit without reservation — that usually takes a woman!

It's not surprising that men were for so long the ones out in the world plowing the fields, sailing the ships, operating the machines, and haggling in the business world. With brawn and a little brains, men can be taught to handle those things.

But the home is where we need the artists — the greatest concentration of intellect and sensitivity, creativity and devotion. It's the home front that needs the natural diplomats and the real multifaceted managers.

It is a delight and a marvel to see what a woman can do with a house. I'm continually in awe of a woman's ability to make things inviting with cheerful decorating ideas, imaginative color schemes, plants and flowers, and

Maybe some day cleaning will be part of male fantasy.

all the special little touches that have such a pleasant and positive influence upon our moods and senses.

In teaching, marriage counseling, and employing thousands of people, I have found that women are special! On speaking assignments, for example, I've faced every size and type of audience imaginable, but every time I face an audience of women, I feel a great deal of warmth and compassion. It is real and it radiates from women in a way that it doesn't from men. Many a philosopher and psychologist has tried to convince me that women are as mean, evil, scheming, and lazy as men, but I'm positive the philosophers and psychologists are wrong. I grew up in a good home, and my sister, mother, aunts, and grandmothers were all beautiful, positive people. I was eighteen before I ever heard a woman swear. The longer I live, the more apt I am to place a woman on a pedestal.

If you are not experiencing exhilaration from your role as a homemaker, it may be because your family has so much emotional and physical clutter that they can't reach each other to give love and appreciation. There is no greater goal or achievement on the face of the earth than the opportunity

to love and in turn be loved. Thrashing around in the clutter of a home too often thwarts the opportunity to achieve this. Skilled, efficient house care will take fewer hours, fewer supplies, fewer repairs, will prevent tension, and will give us more room and a greater capacity to grow into new friendships and experiences. First things first. *Living* is life . . . and we want to have as much of it as possible after housework!

You can save about 75 percent of the time, tools and money you spend on cleaning if you use the methods and materials the professionals do— and if you face the ultimate problem of housework:

Ninety percent of housework is caused by men and children and...

ninety percent of the work is done by women.

If they're old enough to *mess* up, they're old enough to *clean* up. Remember that your resources include your family's ability to pick up after themselves and otherwise help out.

What you used to see as the thankless chores of housework might well be some of your greatest teaching moments. Remember the potential lesson to be taught the next time you (1) spend four hours preparing a lovely family dinner and end up with only a three-foot stack of dirty dishes; (2) spend sixteen hours sewing a satin drill team costume and are rewarded with a whimper about the hemline; (3) proudly present a fat, tidy row of freshly ironed white shirts and he says, "Where's my blue one?"; (4) are on duty around the clock nursing the family through a siege of the flu, yet when it's your turn to collapse into a sickbed, there's not a soul around to nurse you; (5) know the kids are home by the trail of coats and books left in their wake or by the jam and peanut butter and empty glasses covering the counter.

Remember, if you don't teach them, who will?

It's not a woman's job to clean, but tradition takes time to change. Millions of readers have gotten quite a chuckle from chapter four's observations on getting help from husbands and children, and this is probably still the case in the majority of homes across the country—but it's a slowly shrinking majority. There are ever more enlightened men out there who've always liked things clean but wanted an efficient way to accomplish it without making it a full-time job—they've found life after housework and are giving it to their offspring and mates. I give a standing ovation to the rising minority of homes where everyone takes care of him- or herself and is not dependent on Mom to pick up and take care of everything. Cleaning isn't women's work, it's the work of those who created the need for it, and I promise you I won't rest until that truth is taught to all and practiced by most. One day, if you hang in there, you will start hearing "our washer," "our fridge," "our sink," and "my vacuum," instead of the feminine labeling of all cleaning tools so popular for so long now. Help me out; give cleaning books (or a copy of *Who Says It's A Woman's Job to Clean?*) to the groom, the athlete, the son, the engineer, the father. It's slow, but you watch: It will work. I see a change coming.

THERE IS LIFE AFTER HOUSEWORK!

Index

About the Author

Don Aslett isn't just convinced that there is life after housework: He champions the belief that there is life everywhere every minute, and that everyone has a sacred obligation to take full advantage of it. Since his birth in a small town in southern Idaho, Don has pursued every channel of opportunity available to him. Teachers wrote on his grade-school report cards, "He intensely takes over and never runs out of energy." At age fifteen his parents taught and then assigned him to operate eighty acres of the family farm; he still found time to participate enthusiastically in high-school athletics, school government, and church and community projects. Don left the farm for college knowing how to work for the other guy, but found it unchallenging—and so launched his own career in cleaning, organizing a group of college students into a professional housecleaning and building maintenance company called Varsity Contractors.

But Don's first love, writing, was never dormant. Throughout the years of building a family and a business, he amassed volumes of notes on a unique variety of subject matter. In 1979, at the request of thousands of homemakers who wanted his housecleaning seminar information in writing, he wrote *Is There Life After Housework?*; the first edition alone sold half a million copies in the United States and England and was translated into German, Dutch, French, Swedish and Hebrew. In 1982, Don followed with *Do I Dust or Vacuum First?*, and in 1984, *Clutter's Last Stand*. In the years since, "America's Number One Cleaning Expert" has authored eight more bestselling books on cleaning and decluttering, from *Who Says It's a Woman's Job to Clean* to *Make Your House Do the Housework* to *The Stainbuster's Bible*.

Today, Don is chairman of the board of Varsity Contractors, a multimillion-dollar enterprise that now operates in fourteen states, and the owner of a maintenance consulting company. Don is a popular youth speaker and leader, devoting much of his time to family, church and scouting. He and his wife Barbara are building the world's first maintenance-free house in Kauai, Hawaii, but they still spend much of the year at the Idaho mountain ranch on which they raised their six children and numerous foster children—who now visit regularly with *their* children.

Acknowledgments

Like housework, a book is not just one person's doing. The author throws all his ideas and energy into it, but a fine finished volume like this is the work of a team of people.

I'd like you to meet them, so that if you bump into them in Yellowstone Park or the Smithsonian, you'll recognize a few others who have helped to make housework easier. . . .

The number one helper was *Gladys Allen*, a highly organized mother of many as well as a De-Junking engineer and entertainer. She beat out most of the male chauvinism that still lurked in my soul.

Next, attorney *John Preston Creer* forced me to sit down for a year and put my thoughts on paper.

Ernest Garrett first slashed the preaching and ego out of the draft.

Clark Carlile, my college speech teacher (and a successful publisher himself), forbade me ever to lose my humor and my "enthusiastic" style of expressing myself—he said it would go a long way toward making a book people might actually want to read.

Mark Lloyd Browning, one of the finest technical minds in the country and a regional manager and vice-president of my cleaning company, kept a keen eye on the "chemistry" in these pages and keeps me from killing any more canaries with ammonia. And *Jim Doles*, who provided similar assistance on this Tenth Anniversary Edition.

Carol Cartaino, the all-time best editor in the world. (Gadfrey, would I hate to clean her house!) And her editorial tennis partners, *Anita Buck* and *Tobi Haynes*.

Budge Wallis, *Bill Brohaugh*, and all the rest of the determined WDB team.

Judith Holmes Clarke, who first made me understand the importance of good visuals, and whose sprightly illustrations brought the first edition of this book to life.

David Lock, who brought his special impish touch to the illustrations of the British edition and gave us all inspiration for the next edition on these shores.

Craig LaGory, book designer and illustrator par excellence—who finally got a chance to do for *Life After Housework* what he did for *Clutter's Last Stand*. He kept coming up with good ideas and he kept his cool always, even when we said: "Her eyes are still too close together," or "The rags don't look raggedy enough yet". . . .

And of course my deepest thanks to you, the tens of thousands of you who have written and called and threatened to get the information you wanted. Anything we didn't get in this time, you may have to pray for. . . .